AFRICAN THEOLOGY EN ROUTE

AFRICAN THEOLOGY EN ROUTE

Papers from the Pan-African Conference
of Third World Theologians,
December 17–23, 1977, Accra, Ghana

Edited by
Kofi Appiah-Kubi
and
Sergio Torres

ORBIS BOOKS
Maryknoll, New York 10545

Third Printing, September 1983

The text type for this book is 10 on 12 Garamond No. 3. It was set by Hugo Taylor on AKI typesetting equipment and phototypeset on a Mergenthaler V-I-P.

Library of Congress Cataloging in Publication Data

Pan African Conference of Third World Theologians, Accra, 1977.
  African theology en route.

  Includes bibliographical references.
  1. Theology, Doctrinal—Africa—History—Congresses.
I. Appiah-Kubi, Kofi. Torres, Sergio. III. Title.
BT30.A4P36 1977   276   78-10604
ISBN 0-88344-010-5

Contents

PART THREE
LIBERATION CURRENTS

EPLIOGUE

Preface

Kofi Appiah-Kubi (Ghana)

"How can I sing the Lord's song in a strange land," in a strange language, in a strange thought, in a strange ideology? (cf. Ps. 137:4) For more than a decade now the cry of the psalmist has been the cry of many African Christians. We demand to serve the Lord in our own terms and without being turned into Euro-American or Semitic bastards before we do so. That the Gospel has come to remain in Africa cannot be denied, but now our theological reflections must be addressed to the real contextual African situations. Our question must not be what Karl Barth, Karl Rahner, or any other Karl has to say, but rather what God would have us do in our living concrete condition. For too long African Christian theologians and scholars have been preoccupied with what missionary A or theologian B or scholar C has told us about God and the Lord Jesus Christ.

The struggle of African theologians, scholars, and other Christians in ventures such as this consultation is to find a theology that speaks to our people where we are, to enable us to answer the critical question of our Lord Jesus Christ: "Who do you (African Christians) say that I am?" Our attempt is to rescue theology from the shelves of the universities and the sanctuaries of the churches and to make it a living, dynamic, active, and creative reality in our societies.

In our theological task our orienting principle should be the poorest of the poor in our communities. The challenging question posed by millions of poor people to present-day Christianity, and therefore to theology, is: Where is the "abundant life?"—for they see nothing but abject poverty, hunger, disease, ignorance, oppression, discrimination, torture, rejection, and dehumanization all around them. If our theology is to have any message of hope for the majority of our population, it must learn to be the soul of the soulless and the voice of the voiceless.

Our theology should be dynamic, ready to change and address itself to all situations in time and space. It should be liberating, freeing us from all chains, including social, racial, economic, cultural, and even confessional domination. Above all it should be healing and reassuring. It should free itself from empty arrogance and absolutism and allow the Holy Spirit to direct its path toward a total fulfillment.

To be able to read the signs of our times, African theology should tap the resources of our entire community, in arts, literature, sculpture, and all human and academic disciplines, especially the social sciences. It should be a theology of the people, by the people, and for the people. The task is too precious, urgent, and important to be left only in the hands of church functionaries or theologians; thus the involvement of men and women of all walks and stations of life is called for. It should be office theology, farm theology, market theology, street theology, household theology, etc.

The following articles are an attempt, simply the tip of an iceberg, at the enormous task facing African theology. These selections are a result of the Pan-African Conference of Third World Theologians held at the Ghana Institute of Management and Public Administration (G.I.M.P.A.), Green Hill, Accra, Ghana, from December 17 to 23, 1977.

The articles, though varied in style and content, commend themselves to be read in the spirit of unity in diversity, for irrespective of our geographical, social, cultural, confessional, and even linguistic boundaries, we see the black world as one. It is this oneness that justifies the need for dialogue and explains a common concern for all our people. Our solidarity will undoubtedly urge us on, strengthening us in our common struggle with and for the total liberation of poor and oppressed peoples the world over. Our vision is that one day the poorest of the poor can rise up and affirm to the whole world: "Now we no longer believe because of what you told us; we have heard him ourselves and we know that he really is the Savior of the world" (John 4:42).

It remains for me to say a word of gratitude to all those who helped our dream become reality in a very small way through this conference. We are grateful to the numerous agencies and individuals that supported us financially, emotionally, and spiritually. In particular we want to mention the Rev. C. S. Powell of the African Committee of the Division of Overseas Ministries of NCCCUSA, Emilio Castro and José Chipenda of the World Council of Churches, Rev. François Houtart, Sister Margaret Coakley, and Dr. Wilhelm Wille. We thank the members of the Support Committees in the U.S., Canada, and Europe, and the various church communities scattered around the world who through prayer and practical participation urged us on when our strength failed us. We are indebted to the churches and Christians in Ghana and especially the director and staff of G.I.M.P.A. for their wonderful hospitality.

Our thanks go to the participants and contributors who traveled the great distances during the Christmas season to make the conference a success. To Bishop P. K. Sarpong of the Catholic Diocese of Kumasi for sharing his diocesan facilities and pesonnel, in particular Fr. J. Amoako-Adusei, who acted as treasurer for the Organizing Commitee as well as for the conference, goes our special appreciation. To the local organizing committee and the staff, especially to the able and dedicated secretary, Victor J. Asumin, we say, "Well done." Our gratitude also goes to Sister Virginia Fabella, M. M., for her help in the conference and in preparing the materials for this book, as well as to John Eagleson of Orbis Books for his expert advice and assistance. Above all let me give thanks to the Lord who has helped us realize that the things that unite us are greater than those that divide us.

AFRICAN THEOLOGY EN ROUTE

1

Opening Address

Sergio Torres (Chile)

Let me start with a prayer of gratitude to God Almighty, who has convened us here today to praise his mercy and to sing his love.

We have come from all over the world to begin the second stage of the Ecumenical Dialogue of Third World Theologians, which we initiated last year in Dar es Salaam.[1]

We come to learn and to share, to engage in dialogue with our brothers and sisters of Africa, to express our admiration for the struggles in which they have been and still are involved, and to make our contribution to the discovery of a theology that will be relevant to the poor and oppressed peoples of the world.

I speak on behalf of the Executive Committee of the Association of Third World Theologians to remind all of us of some of the conclusions of our first meeting in Dar es Salaam, where we set some directions for the theological task in the Third World.

I cannot pretend to talk about African theology. African theology has to be developed by Africans and for Africans. For five centuries, others, primarily white people, have pretended to talk in the name of Africans. However, I want to introduce this week of study, prayer, confessions of faith, and hard work by sharing some of the convictions of a fellow Christian, a Christian who shares the concerns and the hope of our brothers and sisters of Africa.

THEOLOGY AS IDEOLOGY

Today we have to assess the results of past actions as well as detect the "signs of the times" (see Luke 12:54–56). It has been a real surprise and a painful process to discover that the theology that we people of the Third

3

World have received from the missionaries was not a universal theology, but a European theology, a white theology, a male theology.

A few theologians and other Christians in the Third World have made this discovery in the last ten or fifteen years. It is true, however, that the majority of the churches in the Third World still live with a European or North American model of theology, worship, and organization. Our task is to help clarify and unmask the ideological use of theology. This is what we want in our program of Dialogue of Third World Theologians. We want to share our experiences and enrich each other in the growth of a more relevant way of theologizing.

In trying to understand the causes of the failure of European theology, we discover something very important. In the words of the Dar es Salaam statement:

Theology is not neutral. In a sense all theology is committed, conditioned notably by the social-cultural context in which it is developed. The Christian theological task in our countries is to be self-critical of the theologians' conditioning by the value system of their environment.[2]

European theology, from the Reformation to the theology of hope on the Protestant side, and from the Council of Trent to Vatican II on the Catholic side, has been a response to certain concrete historical situations. I say a response to *certain* situations, because the churches and theology were very much linked to the dominant class of Europe and did not speak on behalf of the poor and the oppressed. The theologians did not denounce slavery; they did not speak out against the exploitation of the working class by the bourgeoisie during the Industrial Revolution, and they were accomplices in the international system of exploitation under colonialism, neocolonialism, and imperialism.

With a few exceptions, the theologies of the times did not address the situation of the poor. The themes of the theological discussion about God, Jesus Christ, and salvation were abstract concepts divorced from the historical Jesus, who identified with the poor of his time. On this point, Catholics and Protestants were the same. Thus, European theology, with a few exceptions, played an important role of ideological legitimization of an economic mode of production that has caused many injustices both in Europe as well as abroad in the Third World. If the dominant white theology of Europe did not speak on behalf of the poor and the oppressed class, neither did it speak on behalf of the people of color.

Whether Rome, Wittenberg or Geneva prevailed, whether justification before God occurred through works or through faith, . . . for the red, the yellow and the black all this was irrelevant. It did not change their condition. For the white confessors of the faith, regardless of their particular Christian line, the people of colour were all destined for bondage; "oneness in Christ" might pertain to heaven, but certainly not to this earth.[3]

CRITERIA FOR THIRD WORLD THEOLOGY

If we do not want to repeat the mistakes of the past, we have to look at present realities, because it is in this framework that we have to do our task of theologizing. Our theology in the Third World has to be relevant to the poor and the victims of all oppression whether of race or sex or class. I want to describe some of our basic assumptions in our effort toward a theology in the peripheral countries of the Third World.

1. *The God of the poor:* The history of the salvation written in the Bible is a long account of the interventions of God in favor of the poor and the oppressed. This is the essential point of view in our theological task. It is the criterion for legitimization of any attempt to talk about God, Christ, salvation, and the church. A theology that does not act on behalf of the poor and the oppressed is not Christian theology. It stems from a different faith. It is not ours. Ours is a theology for the poor countries and for the poor in those countries.

2. *A new epistemological approach:* The traditional way of knowing considers the truth as the conformity of the mind to a given object, a part of Greek influence in the western philosophical tradition. Such a concept of truth only conforms to and legitimizes the world as it now exists.

But there is another way of knowing the truth—a dialectical one. In this case, the world is not a static object that the human mind confronts and attempts to understand; rather, the world is an unfinished project being built. Knowledge is not the conformity of the mind to the given, but an immersion in this process of transformation and construction of a new world.

This new epistemology has to be applied to the revealed truth of Christianity. Theological truth is not only the conformity of the mind to revelation as it is contained in Scripture; it is also the discernment of present evil in the world and in human hearts, judged by the message of the Gospel and the discovery of the movement of redemptive and liberating history. Divine truth is redemptive, but the norm of theological truth comes from its role in the ongoing process of world-building. Our theology in the Third World must apply this epistemological approach in its research and endeavors.

3. *Praxis, faith, and theological reflection:* The starting point of theology is faith, faith not just as an intellectual concept or acceptance of the message of the Gospel, but as an encounter with the Lord, as love and commitment for others. To have faith means to follow Jesus, to be obedient to the authority of the Word of God by making it alive in serving our sisters and brothers.

Social analysis interprets love and translates commitment into a context of practice or praxis. Personal praxis is participation in the process of transformation of society. God is leading the world toward "the new heaven and the new earth." Through praxis, people enter into their historical destinies. Praxis means action combined with theory; action shapes theory, which then redirects action, and so on—all situated within a global perspective. As people engage in praxis, both they and their world change.

It is necessary, therefore, to relate Christian theory with historical movement—to interlock faith with praxis. Interpreted in the light of Christian faith, praxis acquires a deep meaning, for it is perceived as the locus where the promise of the salvation of Jesus is fulfilled and where Christian faith and fidelity are verified.

4. A different ecumenism: All Christians acknowledge the Scriptures as the norm of the church's faith and practice. We agree that in the Old Testament and in Jesus Christ God has made himself manifest in a definitive and unconditional way, and we hold that the written record of this sacred history gives the church access to these divine events as the source of its wisdom.

At one time the disagreement among the theologians on the normative function of the Bible defined the confessional differences between Catholics and Protestants. Today it seems that the disagreements cut across these ecclesiastical boundaries.

A theology in the Third World believes that the old ecclesiastical and doctrinal disputes that have divided the church for so long are not relevant anymore. There is a change in the focus of theology and a change in the methodology of theology. In the past, the questions in traditional theology were raised from within ecclesiastical institutions. Today, while not abandoning that perspective, Christians and theologians want to understand the meaning of the Word of God present as judgment and grace in history, both personal and social, for this generation.

While the organized efforts of ecumenism are still valid, we prefer in this meeting to explore the will of God for our poor countries, to work together and not to emphasize our differences. This assembly tonight is a fitting example as well as a sign of hope for a new kind of ecumenism. Our unity is in praxis as service for the poor.

5. Worship of God and service of neighbor: I would like to note a doubt that sometimes is raised among us. Some question this perspective as too much focused on this world. They say that we sometimes forget that salvation comes from God and that our efforts for justice go against the biblical imperative. We must answer this question from the perspective of the Third World. Our concern for the hungry, naked, and imprisoned (see Matt. 25) is now the concern for structural change, for a new economic order. There is a radical unity between the love of God and concern for people (see John 3:17).

We are not talking about a synthesis of faith and moralism. We know and confess that the fulfillment of salvation history lies beyond the present horizon of our existence. But we also know that the revelation of God's salvation does not take place outside the context of our earthly situation. In our world, life is heavily burdened with evil. This puts faith in tension and struggle. But God tells us that he will one day triumph powerfully over the forces of darkness.

RESTRUCTURING THE SOCIAL ORDER

When I was in Germany recently somebody told me this story: During a theological lecture, a student asked his professor why theologians in the past did not react against the slave trade. The response was "They did not know that the trade was going on." We can say with Paul, "They are inexcusable" (cf. Rom. 2:1). We cannot accept such an explanation; it is impossible to be the contemporary of such an infamous trade and be ignorant of it.

Likewise Christians will blame the theologians of today if we fail to recognize the "signs of the times." We consider that the "signs of the times" for our continents are strongly related to the gap between the rich countries and the poor countries. We do not want to ignore the "slave trade" of our own day, namely, the structural injustices of the economic and political order.

A political hope for the poor and peripheral countries in the Third World is called the New International Economic Order.[4] It is the effort of many peoples, organizations, and countries that think that a complete reconstruction of the economic world is needed. The countries of the First World oppose these efforts. The poor countries have been trying in different ways to gain some concessions. So far, the poor countries are losing this battle.

Recently the North-South discussions about the gap between the rich and the poor countries were discontinued. Moreover, the poor countries have been disappointed with the efforts on the governmental level and have come to believe that it is the organized efforts of the poor themselves that will effect real change in the structures. The enemies of the New International Economic Order are not only the countries of the First World but also the wealthy classes within the Third World. All this cannot be a matter of indifference for the theologians and other Christians who are trying to talk on behalf of the poor and oppressed in the Third World.

I think that God is calling the churches of the rich capitalist world to play a different role. I am afraid that they are not listening to this call. They have too many organizations and structures to support. However, I think that there still is time and hope for change. We believe that God is merciful and his love lasts forever. Some Christians of the rich world have started timid efforts to denounce the injustices of the present structural order, to call for support of the New International Economic Order, and to become a prophetic minority inside their countries, clamoring for justice, repentance, and conversion. Unfortunately, as a whole the churches support the present economic system and live from it.

I consider the representation of black North Americans here in this conference a symbol of hope. Although some blacks in the U.S.A. are simply looking for a better place inside the system and are unconcerned about blacks in the ghetto and the poor in the Third World, I see a new international consciousness in the black community in the U.S.A. It is to be hoped that the minority groups in the U.S.A., the workers of the industrialized countries, and migrant workers everywhere will extend their vision beyond the borders of their own countries.

But God is calling us who are gathered here, too. Let us be very careful to avoid any kind of selfishness and pharisaism. Good and evil are not divided according to North and South. Let us remember forever what John says: "If somebody thinks that he is not a sinner, he is a liar." To belong to the developing countries does not mean that we are saved or that we are sinless. We also have to repent and look for mercy and forgiveness.

The new elite of the independent countries of the Third World have been "westernized." They have learned and treasured the values of western civilization. Many of them want political independence and the transfer of power, but they want to keep western values. This is an important decision and a crucial crossroads that is before us: how to reconcile the legitimate values of civilization that belong to humankind at this stage with the traditional values of nonwestern civilization.

We belong to the educated class of our countries and easily adopt its style. We live physically in the Third World, but our houses, our books, our way of life, are British, French, American. How many of us actually live with the poor and share their experience? How many of us work with the workers and peasants as companions in the struggle?

All this program of dialogue among theologians of the Third World could be useless, hypocritical, and counterproductive if we talked on behalf of the poor but did not share their conditions as Jesus himself did. But poverty itself is not an ideal. As Gutiérrez has established, our poverty has to be a cry of protest against the laws of oppression and poverty.

The efforts for a New International Economic Order and the personal commitment to the struggle and conversion in our daily lives are the framework of a theology in the Third World.

CONCLUSION

As I said before, I don't dare to talk about African theology but I do talk, and strongly at that, about the need for a theology in the Third World that will shape our churches and our lives and will be a sign of hope for the people of our countries.

As executive secretary of the Ecumenical Association of Third World Theologians, I speak on behalf of the Executive Committee; I want to thank the African Organizing Committee for this promising theological conference. I know that they have worked hard to make it possible.

I salute the African participants, the Asians, the Latin Americans, and the blacks coming from the U.S.A. and the Caribbean.

I welcome the presence of friends from the First World representing their churches, denominations, and organizations. Through them I thank all the people and institutions that have contributed financially to this conference. They belong to that minority that is trying to respond to the call to conversion and we appreciate their solidarity with us.

That is my vision. I see Christians of the First World and of the Third World, working together to overcome forces of oppression and aiming at a New International Economic Order, a new prophetic commitment, and a new theological reflection.

After we have read the "signs of the times" and engaged in the struggle for change and development, then we can reflect, evaluate, internalize the Bible as normative, and develop our theology. It doesn't matter if some First World theologians say that our theology is only a passing fad.

I salute the people of Ghana. Twenty years ago, Ghana was the first country in Africa to be independent. Whatever the final judgment on the government of President Kwame Nkrumah, there is no doubt that he was a brilliant representative of Pan-Africanism; because of him the name of Ghana was the pride of people all over the world. William E. B. Du Bois is another person I want to remember. An adopted son of Ghana, he was the father of Pan-Africanism.

I thank God for his love and his mercy. I confess Jesus as my Savior and my Lord, and I ask the inspiration and blessing of the Spirit for this Conference.

"To him be the power and the glory."

NOTES

1. All the position papers as well as the final statement have been published: Sergio Torres and Virginia Fabella, M.M., eds., *The Emergent Gospel: Theology from the Underside of History* (Maryknoll, New York: Orbis Books, 1977).

2. Ibid., p. 270.

3. Helmut Gollwitzer, "Why Black Theology?" *Union Seminary Quarterly Review* 31, no. 1 (Fall 1975): 41.

4. The "Declaration on the Establishment of a New International Economic Order" and the "Programme of Action," General Assembly Resolution 3201 (S-VI) and 3202 (S-VI) may be found in United Nations Institute of Training and Research (UNITAR). *The New International Economic Order: Selected Documents, 1945–1975,* 2 vols. (New York, 1977).

PART ONE

NEW PERSPECTIVES

We believe that African theology must be understood in the context of African life and culture and the creative attempt of African peoples to shape a new future that is different from the colonial past and the neo-colonial present. The African situation requires a new theological methodology that is different from the approaches of the dominant theologies of the West. African theology must reject, therefore, the prefabricated ideas of North Atlantic theology by defining itself according to the struggles of the people in their resistance against the structures of domination. Our task as theologians is to create a theology that arises from and is accountable to African people.

—*Final Communiqué, Pan-African Conference of Third World Theologians*

2

Church Presence in Africa: A Historical Analysis of the Evangelization Process

Ogbu U. Kalu (Nigeria)

LOCATING THE PROBLEM

History moves on two planes. At one level is the dominant western canon of *what happened,* history as *res gestae.* In the nineteenth century when historiography was slowly emerging into a scientific mold, Ranke and others assiduously pursued the collection of data with which to reconstruct *what happened* in the past. The most significant achievement of this trend was to enthrone archival research as an essential element of the historian's enterprise. Some argued that history is a science because the systematic reconstruction of what happened in the past eschews value judgments. They have been proven wrong, for careful focus on what happened still involves selection of data and still betrays the ideology of the historian. It is increasingly becoming obvious that historiography is basically ideology, that, in spite of a certain degree of scientific methodology, history has been constantly used to shape the future and to underprop preconceived goals.

An obvious proof of this assertion is the genre of historiography that we can call "missionary history." Missionary history was and still is being written by missionaries and their protégés who have swallowed missionary ideology hook, line, and sinker. Missionary history is propagandist and unanalytical. It is designed to boost morale and yield human and material resources for continued propagation of the Gospel from Greenland's icy mountains to the dark corners of Africa where witch doctors allegedly hold people in fearful sway.

Naturally, missionary history has focused on how the Gospel came to different areas, the daring men who brought it, and the difficulties and successes in the enterprise. At the turn of the century, such accounts bore fearful titles that revealed the perspective of such historiography. Eva Stuart's two volumes on the Qua Iboe Mission were a panegyric of the missionaries (*Aflame for God; The Quest for Souls in Kwa Iboe Country*).[1] At a later period she surveyed the progress of the Gospel among the cannibals of the Yoruban country. Jacob W. Richards, as late as 1957, entitled his book *Cannibals Were My Friends*. This helped to make him a daring hero at home and elicit financial support. F. D. Walker struck the chord of popular imagination in his *Romance of the Black River* and capitalized on the hypnotic lure of Africa in *Call of the Dark Continent*. Many such titles formed the staple diet of those whose interests were aroused in stirring Exeter Hall-type revivalist meetings.

It was this literary genre that helped produce the enthnocentrism that virtually ruined the achievements of the missionary enterprise. Moreover, this kind of historiography overemphasized the role of missionary agents and ignored the socio-economic and political background of the host communities.

The second level of historiography probes beneath mere events. It constitutes a more perceptive approach. The history of Christianity in Africa is not only what missionaries did or did not do but also what Africans thought about what was going on and how they responded. A creative historical analysis of the presence of Christianity in Africa must be carried out on this second plane. It should analyze the inner dynamics of the evangelization process, perceiving that process as an *encounter* between viable cosmologies and cultures. This method rejects European Christianity as the starting point of African church history. On the contrary, Africa and its cultures constitute the starting point. There should be no attempt to romanticize either tradition; it is assumed that in the fiery encounter with European Christianity the dead wood in both traditions will be *exposed*. This is an activist historiography rejecting the European luxury of scholarship for its own sake. It is knowledge become commitment.

This perspective involves a reappraisal of the dominant methodology in the study of African church history. Analysis of the presence of Christianity is actually a study of religious change. The factors involved in religious change in Africa are many, and the numerous methodologies that have been utilized demonstrate their complexity.[2] According to John Peel, most studies can be characterized by one of two broad emphases: the policies of the missionary societies (the prime agents of change), and the character of the African societies (the arena of change). He argues that historians have tended to emphasize the former and social scientists the latter. Historians were led to such emphasis because of the availability of missionary documents and archives.[3] But missionary propaganda neither operated in a social vacuum nor failed to modify the social context; therefore, it must be studied with interdisciplinary tools. Though statistical fads and bloodless, wooden models have led historians to be cautious toward sociological methods, it is becoming obvious that church historians will have to use methods from other disciplines to engage in local historical studies in order to usefully analyze religious change.

AN ALIVE UNIVERSE: THE AFRICANS' WORLD

R. S. Rattray in his empathetic study of Ashanti religion and culture portrayed Ashanti cosmology as an alive universe, meaning that, notwithstanding missionary attitudes, they had a viable cosmology that maintained an effective social order.[4] Admittedly many such cosmologies exist in Africa, but a basic structure undergirds all of them.

Africans perceive their universe in cyclical terms. Existence and time move in repeated and endless cycles. The cyclical mold is perhaps derived from the flow of the agricultural and festival seasons. Human beings, who are at the center of this universe, move from birth through various roles in the human world to death. But death does not constitute a terminus. In fact, from the period of old age, people begin to consort with those in the spirit world until they are called to join them.

The spirit world itself is a mirror of the human world both in topography and social organization. The dead continue to be active in family affairs. The only difference is the form of this participation. They are invisible and possess spiritual powers that they can use on behalf of their human families for good or evil, depending on the type of relationship that exists between the living and dead branches of the family. For instance, if the dead are not given due and proper burials, their existence in the spirit world would be unhappy and they would probably return as evil spirits for vengeance. If death is handled with proper ritual correctness, the dead reincarnate and go through the cycle endlessly.

Africans have a three-dimensional conception of space. The Supreme God and the major divinities of the communities inhabit the sky; patron gods or nature spirits live on earth with the prominent Earth Mother; the ancestral spirits live in the world beneath, the spirit world. Their abode under the earth is most clearly indicated by the ritual gesture of libation or in the planting of a pot at the head of a grave.

Evil spirits move around the human world. The evil spirits are those who (*a*) did not live good lives on earth, (*b*) died "bad deaths," for instance, from plagues, inexplicable diseases, or accidents, (*c*) had their corpses mutilated, (*d*) did not have proper burials, or (*e*) are generic evil spirits, like the prototype Devil, or infant spirits who visit the earth for agreed brief periods thereby torturing their parents. The presence of evil spirits makes life in the human world extremely precarious.

Worship is an elaborate series of manipulative rituals designed to harness the resources of the good deities in order to ward off the machinations of the evil spirits and to control space-time events. It is becoming much clearer from various studies that, notwithstanding the attributes of the Supreme Being, communities appeal to the lower divinities and spirits: patron spirits, nature deities, and ancestors. Individuals resort to divination, magic, witchcraft, veneration of ancestors, and the aid of the extended family circle. There is extensive room for appropriating more gods if they *prove effective* in controlling space-time events.

The ethical implications of such a cosmology are immense. There is a tendency to explain causality by appeal to inscrutable gods and forces rather than to empirical factors. Emphasis is placed on rituals and customs to the neglect of experimentation and change. It is felt that social and moral orders are preserved and well-being ensured by scrupulous attention to customs and taboos. The paradox then emerges that though human beings are central in the cosmology and human life is held sacred, human life is easily sacrificed to appease the gods. Human sacrifice becomes understandable and slavery and other caste categories bother no consciences. Sensitivity to psychological problems like insanity and schizophrenia is lacking. Unusual phenomena like twin births, earthquakes, and diseases such as epilepsy are easily attributed to the gods and approached with awe. A bustle of propitiatory activities assuage the alleged anger of the gods.

The dynamics of traditional social organization in Africa emerge from this cosmology. Economic and political orders are imbued with sacredness, thus blocking agricultural experimentation. The Earth Goddess sanctions economic regulations. Men are too weak to tame the forces of nature. Sex and wealth differentiations and vast segments of the socialization process operate through secret societies. Social entertainment is primarily in the celebration of the gods as guests in the human world: new yam festivals, masquerades, outings of secret societies. The masquerades that grace most dances and festive occasions represent the gods and ancestors. In the Yoruba Egugun Festival, the dead visit to warn the living about the dysfunctional immoralities in the human world.

Almost as a protective insulation, the community becomes very important. There is a deliberate effort to whittle down individualism so as to exult the community. The age grade system, the secret societies, and a host of social mechanisms are designed to tear individuals away from themselves and even their lineage to affirm and sustain the community. The community, in turn, affirms and sustains them. Identity, sense of well-being, and conception of success are dependent on being in tune with one's community. There is little of the ennui and anonymity that characterize modern, industrial urban existence. Communalism operates on the triad footings of the family, the clan (or extended family), and the total community. The well-being of the community is guaranteed by the founding ancestor. The importance attached to the patron spirits of a community, to the all-seeing, protective family, and to the communal ancestors breeds a tendency toward a narrow and closed conception of one's spatial scale or bounds.

In traditional African societies, the cosmology is tightly constructed because of the precariousness of life. Paradoxically the very element of precariousness forces communities to seek more avenues for acquiring spiritual forces and mechanisms for combatting evil forces, thereby creating openings for religious change.

MISSIONARY IDEOLOGY

The bane in the study of the evangelical process in Africa has been the inadequate understanding of the dynamics of the home base. In fact, the attitudes and policies of missionaries in Africa can best be explained by the situation at home. Recruitment problems, for instance, led to an influx of artisans into the missionary ranks. Training programs had to shift from a scholarly emphasis to utilitarian, make-shift alternatives. Funding continued to be uncertain except among the highly-organized Roman Catholics. This meant poorly-educated staff whose grasp of biblical theology was mediocre; the criterion for candidacy increasingly turned to spiritual commitment.

Missionaries came not only with various European and American cultural values but with an identifiable ideology characteristic of their age. Beyerhaus and Lefever have attempted to show that missionary goals and aims differed;[5] individuals and confessional groups developed varying goals and strategies. However, at the start of the enterprise, there was a fairly homogeneous ideology. Though the Portuguese pretended to be looking for a mythical kingdom of Prester John and were inspired by the scientific advances of the Renaissance, their main aim was economic and their view of Africans was racist. Reasons for the nineteenth-century revival of the missionary enterprise include scientific discoveries, voyages of exploration, new and aggressive mercantalist economic theories, scientific theories of racism, and competition for plantation colonies, as well as humanitarianism, anti-slavery movements, resettlement of liberated slaves, and the desire to convert souls allegedly headed for perdition.

Christians had the schizoid problem of asserting the biblical image of the human being and yet absorbing the racist theories that suffused their intellectual and social milieu.[6] The writings of prominent evangelicals, the sermons and speeches in the revival meetings and recruitment drives, the fund-raising techniques,[7] and training curricula are replete with documentary evidence of such theories.

Fred W. Dodds, the most aggressive and successful Primitive Methodist missionary to Eastern Nigeria at the turn of the century, painted a lurid picture of his mission field for *The Primitive Methodist Leader* in 1917:

In February 1915 for the third time I arrived at Bende to attempt anew the dredging and purifying of that ugly jungle pool of heathenism, with its ooze-life of shocking cruelty, reptilian passions and sprouting evil, spreading itself broad in the shadows amidst the most fruitful land on earth. . . . Thus Christianity views her domain-to-be, lifting herself high above the secret springs of paganism's turgid streams below.[8]

Admittedly Dodds was playing to his audience. The Secretary of the Society, A. T. Guttery, often badgered the field workers for articles and photographs to be used in the *Herald* and the *Leader*. These articles had to be sensational enough to capture the imaginations of donors and fundraisers.

Missionaries came with the same ideologies that underpropped the imperialist expansion of Europe in the nineteenth century. Young men read G. A. Henty's novels and the descriptions of voyages of discovery like Swan's *Letters* and Livingstone's accounts, including the famous *Dr. Livingstone's Cambridge Lectures,* where he intoned: "I go back to Africa to make an open path for commerce and Christianity." Forrester's *A Passage to India* has captured the underlying ideology more vividly than many arid treatises on imperialism. Above all, missionaries came with an amazing degree of confidence in the supremacy of Christianity and European social and economic order. They came with the certainty that they were obeying the Great Command to go into all the world, baptizing and making disciples of all nations. Such a sense of certainty often produced hard-headed insensitivity toward indigenous cultures. It has been shown elsewhere that while the colonialists and missionaries agreed on the objective of spreading civilization, colonial officers were more sympathetic toward the indigenous cultures.[9]

We must note, however, that missionary attitudes toward African cultures changed as exigencies of the field forced constant reappraisals. Ranger has delineated such change of attitude in the Anglican enterprise in the Masasi district of southern Tanzania. After the Maji Maji rising of 1905, the University Mission to Central Africa (UMCA) realized that it had to come to terms with *Jandos,* the initiation rituals of the people. A creative attitude toward it produced other successful forms of adaptation that became proverbial in missionary circles of the time.[10]

Certainly, the strongest characteristic of the missionary enterprise was the constant reappraisal of policies and strategies. Conferences were held to share the experiences of various denominations operating in different countries. After the Edinburgh Conference of 1910, communication channels were formalized and an attitude highly critical of current strategies emerged. Such strategies included intensive pulpit ministry, court alliance, door-to-door canvassing, industrial and freed slaves homes, Christian villages, trading companies, schools, hospitals, and other social welfare agencies, Bible translations, use of vernacular, and native agents. Hardly any of our contemporary issues in mission (indigenization, selfhood and aid, involvement in issues of social justice, and even moratorium) were not raised and debated. Modern missiology often seems like a mere accumulation of papers rehearsing old solutions. Christianity has survived in Africa because of this self-criticism, constant search for relevance, and a modicum of *metanoia*.[11]

THE BATTLE OF THE GODS

The conflict with African cultures occurred precisely because missionaries came with a different worldview. Robin Horton has sketched out areas of continuity between African traditional thought and western science.[12] But there are crucial differences. For instance, the western idea of time is conceived linearly as a continuum. This creates a powerful and dynamic conception of the future that is pregnant with possibilities for change, experimentation, and a new life. Hope becomes the essence of life; the forces of nature and fear are combatted with the idea of progress. At one level, the psychology of dominance in the western world was a product of this worldview.

Thus in cross-cultural mission, there was not only *interest conflict* but also *value conflict*.[13] Often scholars have focused on issues (like polygamy, taking of titles, marriage ceremony, etc.) without relating the conflict over these issues to the overarching problem of conflicting cosmology and conflict over core values.

The impact of the Christian worldview on Africans cannot be exaggerated. Years ago, when Christopher Hill, Master of Balliol, Oxford, studied the Civil War in England, he took a strange perspective by emphasizing "the intellectual origins of the civil war." His basic contention was that ideas had power that coalesced other variables and catalyzed change. In spite of the difficulties in trying to explain change by appeal to a single cause, it is obvious that Christianity in Africa contributed immensely to changes in worldview. To cure ailments with injection was to attack the system of rituals, divination, and priestly functionaries and their explanation of reality. Ajayi has shown how in Nigeria Christianity bred an elite group whose political and economic ideas were radically transformed by education. The same is true for the whole Third World.

The most vulnerable area of traditional life battered by Christianity was social organization. A provincial resident in Eastern Nigeria aptly summed up the missionary enterprise in 1919:

The influence of the Churches is increasing to such extent that parish cohesion and organization is fast becoming at least as strong as indigenous cohesion.[14]

The missionaries realized that "heathenish and pagan" religions were inextricably woven into other cultural ingredients; therefore, all were to be destroyed before a new Christian religion could be radicated. Their analysis was accurate. As John Pobee put it, "All evangelism is in some sense subversion" involving a change of loyalties from blood ancestors among whom Jesus historically and physically is not.[15] In this perspective it makes sense that missionaries raged against the traditional marriage system, kinship loyalties, rites of passage, social clubs (especially secret societies), traditional medicine, oracles, and the series of festivals that celebrated the agricultural cycle. The Christian community was a new community ranged against the traditional background, a "River Between," as the novelist Ngugi would put it. Denominational rivalry, which is recently getting some attention from historians, exacerbated the social divisions.[16]

African response to Christianity took varied forms. Some, like the irrepressible King William Dappa Pepple of Bonny, took an agnostic pose:

He thought the serpent ought to have been destroyed. He thought people must have been fools to attempt to build a tower to reach heaven. "You say God was plenty vext at man for doing worse things, and then you tell me he go kill his son to please himself: What fool palaver that be."[17]

Others literally accepted what they heard, especially frightened by the eschatological emphasis that was the homiletical staple of the early missionaries. Two elements of the African world—the instrumentalist approach to religion and the vivid awareness of demonic forces—made excessive demands on the traditional religion. The failure of the gods in crises opened the cosmology to the acceptance of new gods. Christianity triumphed when the gods of the fathers could no longer protect. The Africans, with their precarious vision of a human world besieged by evil forces, sought more potent protectors.[18]

Unfortunately for Christianity, such triumphs were ephemeral. In certain places, inhospitable climate, poor communication, lack of protection from gun boats, hostile or frightened chieftains, and mere adherence to traditional religion militated against evangelism. Most of the early missionary enterprises collapsed as whites huddled to the coast abandoning the interior. Only the expansion of European governments scrambling for spheres of influence and the impressive power of new medicines saved the enterprise. (Perhaps one should also include the mysterious agency of the Holy Spirit.)

Moreover, African believers started a conscious pursuit of contextualized Christianity under a native pastorate[19] or within Independent churches. The alternatives were either schism or Africans bishops.

Africans joined battle on three fronts. Custodians of tradition attempted to protect the traditional culture that bound the community together; nationalism aided this effort. On another front, the educated elite sought power within the church. A third group founded their own independent churches. The result is that traditional values have persisted and Christianity in Africa has achieved a local flavor.

Christianity has spread enormously in Africa, but the resultant church is basically weak. Christianity must be traditionalized in African culture so that the dead wood in both will be destroyed and a new form can emerge.

NOTES

1. See also E. W. Smith, *The Blessed Missionaries* (Cape Town: Oxford University Press, 1950). The genre of missionary historiography still needs an irenic and analytical study.

2. See O. U. Kalu, "Gods in Retreat: Models of Religious Change in Africa," *Nigerian Journal of Humanities* (University of Benin) 1, no. 1 (1977).

3. John Peel, "Religious Change in Yorubaland," *Africa* 37, no. 3 (1967): 292–306. See also J. F. A. Ajayi, *Christian Missions in Nigeria* (Evanston, Ill.: Northwestern University Press, 1965); F. L. Bartels, *Roots of Ghana Methodism* (Cambridge, Eng.: University Press, 1965); Roland Oliver, *The Missionary Factor in East Africa* (London, New York: Longmans, Green, 1952); E. A. Ayandele, *The Missionary Impact on Modern Nigeria* (New York: Humanities Press, 1967).

4. See Theodore H. von Laue, "Anthropology and Power: R. S. Rattray Among the Ashanti," *African Affairs* 75, no. 298 (January 1976): 33–54.

5. P. Beyerhaus and H. Lefever, *The Responsible Church and the Foreign Mission* (London: World Dominion Press, 1964); J. E. Branner, "Roland Allen: Pioneer in a Spirit-Centered Theology of Mission," *Missiology* 5, no. 2 (April 1975): 175–84.

6. P. D. Curtin, "Scientific Racism and the British Theory of Empire," *Journal of the Historical Society of Nigeria* 2, no. 1 (December 1960): 48.

7. O. U. Kalu, "Children in the Missionary Enterprise of the 19th Century," *The Calabar Historical Journal* 2, no. 1 (1977).

8. F. W. Dodds, "Two Years with the Ibo, 1915–1917," *The Primitive Methodist Leader,* 1917, p. 524 (available at the Methodist Missionary Society Archives, London).

9. O. U. Kalu, "Missionaries, Colonial Government and Secret Societies in South-Eastern Igboland, 1920–50," *Journal of the Historical Society of Nigeria,* forthcoming, December, 1978.

10. T. Ranger, "Missionary Adaptation of African Religious Institutions: The Masasi Case," in Ranger and Kimambo, *The Historical Study of African Religion* (London: Heinemann, 1972).

11. See O.U. Kalu "The Future of Missions in Africa," paper read to International Round Table, Princeton, April 1974.

12. Robin Horton, "African Traditional Thought and Western Science," in M.F.D. Young, ed., *Knowledge and Control* (London: Macmillan, 1971), pp. 208–26.

13. Gerald E. Bates, "Missions and Cross-Cultural Conflict," *Missiology* 5, no. 2 (April 1977): 195–202.

14. National Archives, Enugu, File 42/19 OW DIST. 9/5/6.

15. J. S. Pobee, "The Church and Community," *African and Asian Contributions to Contemporary Theology* (Consultation, Bossey, June 8–14, 1976).

16. F. K. Ekechi, *Rivalry and Scramble in the Missionary Enterprise* (London: Frank Cass, 1971).

17. J. Smyth, *Trade and Travels in the Gulph of Guinea* (London, 1851), pp. 89–95.

18. See O. U. Kalu, "The Precarious Vision: The African's Perception of His World," in *Readings in African Humanities,* forthcoming.

19. Hollis Lynch, "The Native Pastorate Controversy," *Journal of African History* 12 (1960).

3

The History of Theology in Africa: From Polemics to Critical Irenics

Ngindu Mushete (Zaire)

"African theology" is an enormous subject that obviously cannot be treated in any detailed way in a few short pages. Moreover, at the present time African societies are growing more and more complex in their development. Any quick survey of their major structures could easily be regarded as superficial.

Granting, then, that there is need for a more detailed analysis of works in progress and results already achieved, I would like to consider briefly three currents that typify theology in Africa today. They are missionary theology, so-called African theology, and "black theology" as exemplified in South Africa.

MISSIONARY THEOLOGY

What is the aim and goal of mission work? To this question one can give three general answers, which have become the theses of various schools of thought. For one school, the aim of mission work is the *conversion of the infidel*. For a second school it is the *establishing or implanting of the church*. For a third school it is *giving birth to a native church and helping it to grow properly;*

This is a summary version of a lecture given to the Catholic Theology Faculty of Kinshasa on April 25, 1977. It is based primarily on firsthand knowledge of the sources. I also owe a debt of gratitude to three other briefer but suggestive essays: L. Hurbon, "La théologie missionaire en procès," in *Parole et Mission,* 1970, no. 53, pp. 513–25; Edouard W. Fashole-Luke, "The Quest for African Christian Theologies," in the *Scottish Journal of Theology,* 1972, no. 29, pp. 159–75; and *Manifeste des théologiens du Tiers-Monde* (Paris: Edition du Centre Lebret, 1976).

this means helping it to assume its proper role and responsibility in communion with Christ and all other local churches.

Theology Centered Around the Salvation of Souls or the Conversion of the Infidel

Developed and defended in particular by the missiological school of Münster, this kind of theology polarized missionary reflection for several centuries, right up to the start of the twentieth century. For a long time it has embodied the proper and specific goal of missionary activity. The proponents of this theology, such as T. Ohm and K. Muller, reject the theory of implanting the church. According to them, this theory has no foundation in the thought of St. Paul: "The so-called theory of implantation finds no confirmation in St. Paul, though he is wholly and completely a missionary. . . . He has no thought whatsoever of making the establishment of a church the proper, specific, theological goal of his apostolic activity."[1] For these theologians "the essential role of missions is to heal, convert, and Christianize people." The essential task of the missionary "is to proclaim the Gospel, to be the herald of Christ's good news."[2] Solidly grounded on the adage, *extra ecclesiam (romanam) nulla salus,* theology centered on the salvation of infidels logically led its partisans to wholly disqualify the cultural and religious traditions of African peoples.

The theoreticians of this theology were imbued with an excessive zeal to defend the oneness of Christianity and to distinguish it from what was commonly but improperly called "paganism." They thus tended to forget that the saving God is omnipresent, that there exists a universal revelation above and beyond the bounds of any "special" revelation (i.e., the Judeo-Christian one),[3] and that salvation can be obtained through non-ecclesiastical channels as diverse as the various ideals and humanisms nurtured by human beings.[4]

Another disadvantage of this theology deserves mention. Fashioned on the basis of a dualistic anthropology, this particular theology ran the dangerous risk of disregarding the concrete, historical dimension of the integral salvation brought by Christ. It thus lent credence to the Marxist thesis that religion is the opium of the people, as I have tried to show elsewhere.[5]

The Theology of Church Implantation

Starting in the 1920s, some European theologians elaborated and imported into Africa a mission theology centered around the establishment of the church in a given country.

Whereas the aforementioned theology of conversion saw the souls of black people living in darkness and the shadow of death, the theology of implantation was solidly ecclesiastical and even ecclesiocentric in its orientation. On the clean slate, or the slate wiped clean, of people without culture or civilization, missionaries were to establish the church as it had been known historically in the West. Its personnel, its methods, and its works were to be copies of the western church. As H. Maurier puts it:

Missionaries have in effect labored to implant the Roman Catholic church in countries in which it did not exist and which no longer belonged to it. Missionaries have not usually taken conscious note of the fact that they are agents of Christian *Romanitas* in nonwestern countries. They say, for example, that they want to save souls, to spread the true faith, or to preach the Gospel message. All that is true, of course, but they do this by implanting the Roman church, its doctrine, its liturgy, its discipline, its organization, and its outlook. They do all this without consciously adverting to it. It is taken for granted that the Roman Catholic church is the only true church of Jesus Christ and the only bearer of salvation.[6]

This brand of theology, initiated by P. Charles, S. J., views the implantation of the church as the goal of missionary effort. With varying shades of emphasis, many adhere to this theology today: e.g., J. Bruls and J. Frisque, and their periodical *Eglise Vivante,* from Louvain; P. Masson, also of Louvain; the Swiss J. Beckman and W. Bühlmann, with their *Revue Nouvelle de Science Missionaire;* P. Seumois in Rome; and A. Mulders and E. Loffeld of Holland.

Their criticism of the theology of conversion is that its proponents assign a goal to mission activity that is really the general goal and aim of the church. The church must preach the Gospel and convert sinners always and everywhere, whether those sinners be baptized or not. In the eyes of those who favor implantation, mission work must establish the church where it does not yet exist visibly. It must give stable and perduring organization to the various means of salvation: i.e., the clergy, the laity, religious, communities, and Christian forms in general.

When it comes to evaluating the results of mission work, we find two opposing positions. The optimistic evaluation is represented by someone like Msgr. Delacroix, one of the more recent historians of mission work:

In the first few centuries the spread of the church . . . was confined to the borders of the Roman Empire. The missionary expeditions of the Middle Ages barely managed to get beyond the Mediterranean world; those that did go further had no real future. The missionaries of the fifteenth and sixteenth century established the church in three sectors of the American hemisphere. . . . Today mission work has succeeded in spreading the message of the cross everywhere: not only to countries that had been temporarily closed to it (e.g., China, Korea, and Japan) but also to the unexplored northern and southern reaches of the Americas and to the recently discovered regions of Africa, Indonesia, Australia, and Oceania. With the exception of such regions as Afghanistan and Tibet, we can say that present-day missionary work has established the church in even the most remote corners of the earth.[7]

The facts themselves are undeniable, so there is solid ground for Delacroix's view. Others, accepting the same facts, arrive at a very different evaluation. For example, Hans Küng has this to say:

Following the example of Paul, the church became Greek with the Greek world and barbarian with the European barbarian world. However, it has not become Arabic with the Arabs, black with the blacks, Indian with the Indians, or Chinese with the Chinese. Viewed as a whole, the church of Jesus Christ has remained a European-American affair.[8]

A non-Christian author goes even further: "It is hardly debatable that despite the awesome and incessant efforts of the church, which have been supported by a large public in Europe and America, Christianity has gone down to resounding defeat in Asia."[9] I would only point out that the theology of church implantation has given rise to paralytic Christian communities. Mere copies of the European model, they have shown no initiative, creativity, or originality. They pray with borrowed words, think by proxy, and operate by way of Rome, Paris, London, and other European capitals.

Vatican II and the Theology of the Local Church

Vatican II also offered an answer to the question cited above: What is the nature and end of mission work?[10] Without providing a systematic theory, Vatican II did offer elements of an answer. Those elements were taken over from the two schools of Louvain and Münster, though these would seem to contradict each other.

The conciliar decree *Ad Gentes* employs the traditional terms and formulas: e.g., Christian witness, propagation of the faith, preaching, the assembly of the people of God, establishment of the church, and so forth. It avoids taking a rigid, one-sided stance (see *Ad Gentes,* chap. II).

However, the central affirmation of Vatican II has to do with the true and authentic catholicity of the church. The Council solemnly declares that *the church is one and diverse.* It is not diverse for want of being something better; it is diverse by virtue of its very nature. As *Lumen Gentium* points out, the church is built up as a community of many local churches:

Moreover, within the Church particular Churches hold a rightful place. These Churches retain their own traditions without in any way lessening the primacy of the Chair of Peter. This Chair presides over the whole assembly of charity and protects legitimate differences, while at the same time it sees that such differences do not hinder unity but rather contribute toward it. Finally, between all the parts of the Church there remains a bond of close communion with respect to spiritual riches, apostolic workers, and temporal resources. For the members of the People of God are called to share these goods, and to each of the Churches the words of the Apostle apply: "According to the gift that each has received, administer it to one another as good stewards of the manifold grace of God" (1 Pt 4:10) (*Lumen Gentium,* 13).

AFRICAN THEOLOGY

Unlike the theologies mentioned above, "African" theology attempts to take due account of the Africans to whom the faith is addressed. It takes note of Africa's culture, religion, and civilization. It advocates the right of African Christians to ponder Christianity and its truth in their own terms. In a work of major historical importance, *Des prêtres noirs s'interrogent* (1956), the authors had this to say in their Foreword:

The African priest must say what he thinks about the church in his own country in order to advance the kingdom of God. We do not claim that the black priest has never gotten a hearing, but amid the tumult of voices talking about missions his voice has often been tiny and easily muted even though he would seem to be the most qualified to speak.

For the sake of clarity and ease of presentation, I shall distinguish two stages in the development of this African theology. One might be called the theology of adaptation, which centers around stepping stones in the development of African Christianity. The other might be called a more critical African theology.

The Theology of Adaptation

Only two basic approaches are open insofar as evangelization is concerned. One approach maintains that we are dealing with an encounter between the church as it evolved historically in the West and the peoples of Africa. The task, then, is to adapt the practices of the western church as much as possible to the socio-cultural life of the African peoples. The second approach looks at the members of the African community who have heard and accepted the Christian message and who are now trying to proclaim and live it out in their own cultural milieu. Gradually this milieu is purified and superseded through a life of faith exercised with full freedom. This paves the way for a new and perhaps unforeseen incarnation of the Gospel message.

The latter approach is in line with the doctrine of Vatican II. In Europe it has effected the incarnation of the Gospel message in western cultures. The former approach has been that of many bishops and priests in Africa. It is the approach of adaptation.

Proponents of the theology of adaptation envision a church and a Christianity that is African *in color and visage.* Indeed that is the title of a book by one of the chief forces behind African theology. In his book entitled *Un visage africain du christianisme,*[11] Abbot Mulago has this to say:

The herald of the gospel must not be simply a transmitting agent between the Roman Catholic church and the people who are to be won to Christ. One can Christianize a people only when one begins by trying to understand them, unless of course one is content with a superficial brand of Christianity. And of course one must go further than that. Having penetrated the outlook, culture, and philosophy of the people to be *conquered,* one must engrave the Christian message on the soul of the proselyte. Only this approach will offer enduring results.[12]

Mulago goes on to say: "The word 'adapt' may shock certain ears. We need only point out, however, that it means presenting dogma in a form that is accessible to the people" (see the encyclical *Humani Generis, A.A.S.,* 32, 1950, pp. 567–78).

Proponents of this stepping-stone theology are numerous today.[13] They include such figures as P. Tempels,[14] V. Mulago, [15] M. F. Lufuluabo,[16] D. Nothomb,[17] and A. Kagame.[18]

The chief merit of these theologians has been to remind us, in season and out of season, of the need to incarnate the Gospel message in other cultures besides the European one. The theology of adaptation has also had a real influence on the "Africanization" of esslesiastical personnel, catechesis, and the liturgy, to mention just a few of the more salient areas.

Granting all that, however, we must conclude that its scientific theology, in the strict sense of the term, has been rather meager. The point deserves discussion in detail. To put it briefly here, the major defect of this theology of adaptation has been its *concordism.* It tends to equate Christian revelation with the systems of thought in which it has found historical expression. How deeply can we really penetrate into religious truth if we set up a comparison between certain elements of African culture isolated from their overall context on the one hand and Christianity viewed as a closed system of absolute truths on the other hand? As Hurbon has pointed out clearly:

The adaptation to native cultural values of which there is so much talk is often nothing more than a process of nativizing the Roman church. The latter maintains its prior positions intact, justifying this by references to its prior history which was often utilized precisely for such justification. It is the last court of appeal, the definitive and defining one for all other positions.[19]

Critical African Theology

To avoid the dangers of such concordism a significant group of theologians have been working to construct a dynamic and critical-minded African theology over the past fifteen years. The group includes native Africans and other theologians working in Africa. Instead of looking for sound African values that might be Christianized, these theologians seek to tackle theological problems at their very roots and thus lend their presence to forward-looking theological research.

Among them we find two major preoccupations. First, they seek to establish closer contact with the major sources of revelation: the Bible and tradition. Second, they want to open up wholly to the African milieu and its problems. Let us consider these two facets in greater detail.

First of all, the desire for renewed contact with the word of God proclaimed and pondered by the church has brought us several valuable works in the realm of fundamental, historical, and biblical theology. Confining ourselves to Zaire and acknowledging the incompleteness of our list, we might mention the various works of Bishop Tshibangu on theological methodology,[20] the patient work of Abbot Ntedika on Christian origins,[21] and the exegetical monographs of Abbots Atal[22] and Monsengwo.[23]

This desire to return to the sources naturally has led to a passionate debate on "African theology." It seems to me that one fact has not received enough attention as yet. Thanks to their undoubtedly fruitful studies of history and exegesis, African theologians have become vividly aware of the living, historical character of theology. They have come to realize that all theology is culturally and socially positioned.[24] It could not have been otherwise. There are points of contact and intermingling between the word of God and human society, between theological elaboration and social analysis; and it is better to be aware of them than to ignore them or feign ignorance.[25]

Here is not the place to describe the origin and growth of the debate over African theology. That has been done by more than one person already.[26] I shall only point out that various African theologians are well aware of the social and cultural factors conditioning theological discourse. They regret the cultural imperialism of some of their western colleagues. The latter, feeling no self-doubts whatsoever, give undue preference to European culture, feeling that it is the locus and highpoint of human universality.

The notion of a universal theology, like that of a universal philosophy, is a myth. It has no foundation in revelation, faith, or history. As Charles Wackenhein puts it:

Nothing is more normal than a multiplicity of theological approaches. Diversifying factors are related to differences in cultures, conceptual categories, and even individual temperaments. Whoever the author of a given piece or passage in the New Testament may be, we can detect the diversity of theological treatments in that work. This diversity in Christian thought was greatly accentuated from the second century on, when the proclamation of the gospel reached differing cultural milieus.[27]

Bishop Tshibangu offers this comment:

Since the beginning of Christianity two characteristic theological currents have developed. One is what is called western theology, the other is what is called eastern theology. These two theologies are relatively opposed to each other. This was the occasion, if not one of the causes, of the schism produced between East and West, as Vatican II itself acknowledged.[28]

Let us take cognizance of this fact and remember it. Against the proponents of some universally valid theology, Africans assert the right and the necessity of a specifically African theology. Such a theology would not necessarily be based on Greek philosophy and its confreres. It would accept and value the cultural and religious experience of the African peoples, and it would attempt to reply to the questions raised by African society and its contemporary development.

This explains the second characteristic of African theology mentioned above: i.e., its openness to the world. While remaining faithful to the essentials of Christian revelation, some theologians are trying to offer a truly African answer to the new questions raised by the present-day situation in Africa.

This is evident in the attention given to the theology of the local church, the theology of the laity, the theology of non-Christian religions, various Christian expressions of African origin (e.g., *jamaa*), and the different pastoral and theological periodicals now being published (*AFER, Au Coeur de l'Afrique, Cahiers des Religions Africaines, Revue Africaine de Théologie,* etc.). It is also evident in the success of the theological study weeks and seminars held in Kinshasa. Each year pastors and theologians gather to discuss some vital question affecting the African churches.

The same openness to the world can be seen in more technical works by theologians. They clearly want to overcome the standing temptation of concordism, and they are also appealing more openly to the human sciences. Today and in the future such an appeal is both proper and necessary.[29]

Merely by way of example I would cite the thesis of Abbot Nyom on the virtue of religion in day-to-day life. In a new vein and with a new emphasis he scrutinizes the oft discussed themes of the sacred, prayer, and the oneness of the person as they are viewed by the Bantu.[30] Then there are the works of J. S. Mbiti on religious philosophy (*African Religion and Philosophy,* London, 1969) and African theology (*Concepts of God in Africa,* London, 1970; *New Testament Eschatology in an African Background: A Study of the Encounter Between New Testament Theology and African Traditional Concepts,* Oxford, 1971). The book by Rev. Mpongo (*Pour une anthropologie chrétienne du mariage au Congo*[31]) contains excellent insights on the prospects for an African marriage liturgy. And the recent work by Abbot Nyeme examines Tetela morality and its concept of moral fault.[32]

We would not do justice to these efforts if we said that they represented merely an "Africanization" of forms. But if we examine the research of African theologians, we will find other works that explore matters even more deeply. There is the work of Abbot O. Bimwenyi, for example.[33] He attempts to offer a comprehensive and explicative[34] African theology. In it African culture is not merely described. It is integrated into a broader conceptual whole that allows for a critical re-examination of the basic data of Judeo-Christian revelation (see *Ad Gentes,* 22).

BLACK THEOLOGY IN SOUTH AFRICA

This theology is a movement both in thought and in action. It offers a critical examination of racism viewed as a structural phenomenon of global extent that is historically bound up with the expansion of European capitalism. It has also been inspired by the social situation of oppression and segregation that has afflicted blacks in the United States and South Africa.[35]

The term "black theology" derives from North America and appeared in South Africa around 1970. Its first promoters were A. Cleage and, even more important, James H. Cone.[36] In the American context one of its purposes was to meet the challenge of the Muslims, who claimed that Christianity was functionally incompatible with the yearnings of black Americans for dignity, justice, and equality.

In Africa the first public discussion of "black theology" took place in March 1971. The participants met to discuss James Cone's *Black Theology and Black Liberation.*[37] Since then we can distinguish four major viewpoints or approaches in the black theology of South Africa.[38]

Black Theology

At first this trend was represented by a white theologian, Basil Moore, the leader of the University Christian Movement (U.C.M.).[39] It basically agrees with the views of black theology in the United States as proposed by James Cone. Taken up by such African theologians as Manas Buthelezi, it forges a strong link between black *consciousness-raising* on race, politics, economics, and culture and *black theology.* It emphasizes the importance of a black African theology that will totally free blacks from any African theology that is merely cultural in expression. According to Manas Buthelezi, the latter merely looks to the past and seeks to justify the present situation of black people.[40]

African Theology

This trend has been vigorously espoused by Douglas Makhatimi, a friend and colleague of Manas Buthelezi. Grounded on biblical faith, it seeks to express itself in the mental and verbal categories of the philosophy of black people. Here the distinction between white and black is not just sociological. It is primarily cultural and philosophical. That is why it deliberately moves away from the various European theologies that have inspired James Cone, e.g., the theologies of Moltmann and Tillich.[41]

African Religions

A third current is based on African religions. It raises questions about the novelty and univocalness of Christianity. Some who uphold this view claim that they can discern a basic agreement between African religions and the Judeo-Christian religion. Okot O'Bitek, of the University of Nairobi, goes even further and maintains the necessity of a straight return to traditional African religions. He views them as superior to Christianity.[42]

Independent Churches

The fourth and last current starts off from various independent African churches. It sees them as the privileged locale for black theology. Victor Mayatula of the Bantu Bethlehem Christian Apostolic Church of South Africa is one of those who has strongly emphasized the link between black theology and independent African churches. Both, he maintains, seek to elaborate a discourse of liberation from a colonial situation.

Quite aside from the severely negative aspects of black theology, it does seem to be an authentic theological development. It is clearly a situational theology that seeks to raise the consciousness of Africans by analyzing their socio-cultural experience in the light of Judeo-Christian revelation.

CONCLUSION

So we come to the end of this presentation of theological research in Africa, which is both too long and too short. One clear fact has obviously escaped western humanity for a long time. It is that there is not *one* world but *many,* not *one* history but *many,* not *one* theology but *many,* not *one* space or milieu but *many* that are different and perhaps even antagonistic.

The fact is that each group of people and each human community conceives and organizes its historical life, not according to some universal, immutable model but according to its own situation in space and time. Perception of the world and of values always depends on the *place* where it is done. Insofar as human beings live in different places, they conceive and live out their human relations, culture, and religion in different ways. We must take cognizance of that fact and remember it.

I hope that our meeting here in Accra will help us Africans to progress in our quest for an authentic African theology.

—Translated by John Drury

NOTES

1. K. Muller, "Das Missionsziel des Paulus," in *Zeitschrift für Missionswissenschaft und Religionswissenschaft,* 1957, pp. 99–100; cited by T. Ohm, *Faites des disciples de toutes les nations* (Paris: Editions Saint-Paul, 1964), 1:23.

2. T. Ohm, ibid., p. 272. H. Maurier, "La mission demain à la lumière de la mission hier," in *Eglise et Mission* (Brussels), no. 205 (1977): 41.

3. Emilio Castro, the Director of the C.W.M.E., said this to Figueira: "This is the new factor in the missionary situation and in the ecumenical-theological reflection: Christ is at home everywhere in the world."

4. J. Dournes, *Dieu aime les paiens* (Paris: Aubier, 1963); idem, *L'offrande des peuples* (Paris: Cerf, 1967). Also of interest is J. Kerkhofs, "Vers d'autres formes d' une assistance des croyants sur le plan international," in *Eglise et Mission,* no. 202 (June 1976): 5–12.

5. See my article, "Christianisme et authenticité en Afrique noire. Le cas du Zaire," in *Le Monde Moderne* (Paris), no. 12 (1976): 41–59.

6. H. Maurier, "La mission demain," in *Eglise et Mission,* no. 205, p. 35.

7. Msgr. S. Delacroix, *Histoire universelle des missions catholiques* (Paris: Grund, 1957), vol. III (*Les missions contemporaines: 1800–1957*), pp. 12–13.

8. Hans Küng, *Concile et retour à l'unité* (Paris: Cerf, 1961), pp. 14–15.

9. K. M. Panikkar, *L'Asie et la domination occidentale* (Paris, 1956), p. 400; in Eng. see *Asia and Western Dominance* (New York: Day, 1954).

10. See Edouard Loffeld, *Le problème cardinal de la missiologie et des missions catholiques* (Rhenen: Editions "Spiritus," 1956).

11. Published in Paris in 1965 by Ed. Présence Africaine.

12. A. Mulago, *Un visage africain du christianisme,* p. 23.

13. By "stepping-stones" we mean certain beliefs, rites, symbols, gestures, and institutions of traditional African society that seem compatible with the data of Christian faith.

14. See especially his book, *Nôtre rencontre* (Leopoldville-Limete: Ed. du Centre d'Etudes Pastorales), vol. 1, 1962, p. 207; vol. 2, in manuscript, 1962, p. 133. Also see A. J. Smet, "Le Père Tempels et son oeuvre," in *Revue Africaine de Théologie* (Kinshasa) 1, no. 1 (1977): 77–128.

15. Besides his already cited work, see "Le christianisme face aux aspirations de l'ame bantu," in *Antennes* (Louvain), 1962, pp. 473–86; "Symbolisme dans les religions traditionnelles africaines et sacramentalisme," *Revue de Clergé Africain* 27 (1972): 467–502. This periodical will henceforth be cited as *RCA*.

16. See "Valeurs bantoues à christianiser," in *Eglise Vivante,* no. 15 (1963): 357–64; *Orientation préchrétienne de la conception bantoue de l'être* (Leopoldville, 1964); "Valeurs des religions africaines selon la Bible et selon Vatican II," in *RCA* 24 (1967): 318–41; "Mentalité religieuse africaine et christianisme," ibid., 22 (1967): 318–40; *Mariage coutumier et mariage chrétien indissoluble* (Leopoldville, 1968).

17. See especially his book *Un humanisme africain. Valeurs et pierres d'attente,* preface by A. Kagame (Brussels: Ed. Lumen Vitae, 1965).

18. See, for example: *La philosophie bantu-rwandaise de l'être* (Brussels, 1956); "Le sacré paien, le sacré chrétien," in *Aspects de la culture noire. Recherches et débats du Centre Catholique des Intellectuels Français* (Paris, 1958), pp. 126–45; "Conscience chrétienne et conscience africaine," in *Cum Paraclito,* special issue.

19. L. Hurbon, *Dieu dans le vaudou haitien* (Paris: Payot, 1972), p. 33. Also see Ntedika Konde, "La Théologie au service des Eglises d'Afrique," in *Revue Africaine de Théologie* 1, no. 1:30.

20. T. Tshibangu, *Théologie positive et théologie spéculative, position traditionelle et nouvelle problématique* (Louvain: L'Université; Paris: Béatrice-Nauwelaerts, 1965). My work is in the same line. See my article "Connaissance de foi et raison historique chez Lucien Laberthonnière," in *Revue d'Histoire Ecclésiastique* 69, no. 1 (1974):68–92; and my forthcoming book *Le problème de la connaissance religieuse d'après L. Laberthonnière.*

21. See especially his book *L'évocation de l'au-delà dans la prière pour les morts. Etude de patristique et de liturgie latines, IVe–VIIIe S.* (Louvain: Editions Nauwelaerts; Paris: Béatrice-Nauwelaerts, 1971).

22. D. Atal, *Structure et signification des cinq premiers versets de l'hymne johannique au Logos* (Louvain-Paris, 1972).

23. L. Monsengwo Pasinya, *La notion de nomos dans le Pentateuque grec* (Rome, 1973).

24. See my article, "Unité et pluralité de la théologie," in *RCA* 22 (1957):593–615.

25. For failure to recognize this fact the Catholic church suffered the violent crisis of modernism at the turn of this century. It was a serious crisis and we are just beginning to gauge its consequences. See E. Poulat, *Histoire, dogme et critique dans la crise moderniste* (Tournai: Casterman, 1962); idem, *Catholicisme, démocratie et socialisme* (Tournai: Casterman, 1977). Also see A. Gesche, "Dieu et société," in *Revue Théologique de Louvain* 7, fasc. 3 (1976): 274–95.

26. The Catholic Theology Faculty of Kinshasa has for some years now held the fore in the discussion of African theology. Some of the major writings indicative of various positions are: T. Tshibangu and A. Vanneste, "Débat sur la théologie africaine," in *RCA* 15 (1960): 333–52; B. Studer, "Encore la théologie africaine," in *RCA* 16 (1961):105–29; L. Elders, "Christianisme et cultures," in *Nouvelle Revue de Science Missionaire* 18 (1962):1–21; R. Antoine, "Christianity and Cultures," in *The Clergy Monthly* 26 (1962):116–26; *Colloque sur la théologie africaine,* Fourth Theology Meeting in Kinshasa, July 22–27, published under the title *Renouveau de l'Eglise et nouvelles Eglises* (Kinshasa, 1969); T. Nyamiti, *African Theology: Its Nature, Problems and Methods* (Kampala, Uganda: Gaba, 1971); idem, *The Scope of African Theology* (Kampala, 1973). For an overall view of the question see T. Tshibangu, *Le propos d'une théologie africaine* (Kinshasa, 1974).

27. C. Wackenheim, *Christianisme sans idéologie africaine* (Paris, 1974), pp. 71–72.

28. Tshibangu, *Le propos d'une théologie africaine,* p. 5. On the legitimacy and necessity of theological pluralism see the interesting fifteen propositions of the International Theology Commission. They were adopted in the plenary session of October 1972; see *La Documentation Catholique* 70 (1973):459–61. Also see M. Decerteau, "Y-a-t-il un langage de l'unité," in *Concilium* 51 (1970):77–89.

29. See, for example, G. Tavard, *La théologie parmi les sciences humaines,* Coll. Le point théologique, 15 (Paris: Beauschesne, 1975).

30. "Le sacré et l'unité de l'homme chez les Bantu du Sud-Cameroun. Perspectives morales et pastorales concernant la vertu de religion dans les conditions de vie des Basa," Catholic Theology Faculty of Lille, doctoral dissertation, 1964, 2 vols., mimeographed.

31. Published in 1968 in Kinshasa-Limete, Zaire.

32. Nyeme Tese, *Munga. Ethique en un milieu africain. Gentilisme et christianisme* (Rome, 1975).

33. O. Bimwenyi, "Le Dieu de nos ancêtres," in *Cahiers des Religions Africaines* (RCA) 2, no. 4 (1970):137–51; "Pertinence et originalité du langage religieux. Mémoire de licence en théologie," Catholic University of Louvain, mimeographed, 1973; "Discours théologique négro-africain. Problème de fondement," doctoral treatise in theology, Catholic University of Louvain-La-Neuve, mimeographed, 1977.

34. See the concepts of "comprehension" and "explication" according to L. Goldmann, *Pour une sociologie du roman* (Paris: Gallimard, 1964), p. 353f.

35. On the historical context of black theology see, for example: O. Klineberg, *Characteristics of the American Negro* (New York: Harper, 1944); G. Myrdal, *An American Dilemma: The Negro Problem and Modern Democracy,* vol. 1 (New York: Harper, 1944); E. Digby Baltzell, *The Protestant Establishment: Aristocracy and Castes in America* (New York: Vintage, 1966).

36. See James H. Cone, *Black Theology and Black Power* (New York: Seabury, 1969); idem, *A Black Theology of Liberation* (Philadelphia: Lippincott, 1970). Also see Rubem Alves, *A Theology of Human Hope* (Washington, D.C.: Corpus, 1969). On the impact of American black theology on Africa see Henry Mottu, "Noirs d'Amérique et opprimés du Tiers Monde à la recherche

d'une Théologie de la libération," in *Bulletin du Centre Protestant d'Études*, 1972, no. 1.

37. The text is reprinted in M. Mothabi, *Essays on Black Theology*, Johannesburg, U.C.M.; new edition entitled *Black Theology: The South African Voice* (London: Hurst, 1973).

38. My remarks are inspired largely by David J. Bosch (University of South Africa in Pretoria), "Currents and Cross-currents in South African Black Theology," in *Journal of Religion in Africa* (Leiden), 1974, pp. 1–22. Also see H. Bucher, "Black Theology in South Africa," in *Nouvelle Revue de Science Missionaire* 29 (1973):191–99; reprinted in *African Ecclesiastical Review* 15 (1973):329–39.

39. A movement of multiracial character. Disbanded in 1972 because of its radical options, today it represents the stance of the Organization of Black South-African Students.

40. This judgment is clearly too summary in form. See what I said above about the context, problems, intentions, and methods of African theology.

41. See, for example, W. Eteki-Mboumoua, "Africa's Cultural Revolution," in *South African Outlook*, October 1969.

42. See Okot O'Bitek, *African Religion in Western Scholarship* (Nairobi, n.d.).

4

Self-Reliance of the African Church: A Catholic Perspective

P. A. Kalilombe (Malawi)

INTRODUCTION

In May 1974 the Third Assembly of the All Africa Conference of Churches, meeting in Lusaka, Zambia, dared the young churches of Africa to call a "moratorium" on overseas aid in personnel and finance; there was an immediate reaction not only in Africa itself but all over the Christian world.[1] Passionate voices were heard either approving or criticizing this call.[2] The moratorium debate has indeed become the forum for a thoroughgoing reassessment of the theology and practice of "missions" in the Christian churches. A cluster of topics related to the missionary enterprise has had to be tackled afresh. What is the true nature and objective of missionary work? What impact does the aid in personnel, expertise, and material resources offered by the older churches of Europe and America have on the young churches in the mission territories? If these younger churches are to grow into mature, self-reliant communities, what should be the relationships between the older churches and the younger ones? These and similar questions are being asked, in one form or another, by the churches in Africa today. The passionate interest that has been aroused by the moratorium debate is a proof that the questions at stake are really fundamental and decisive; a proof too, perhaps, that their serious discussion has been long overdue. The basic point is evidently the urgency for the churches in the missions to throw away the crippling ties of dependence on overseas aid and the need for them seriously to adopt ways and means of becoming self-reliant ecclesial communities.

The intention of this paper is not to attempt once again a detailed justification of the need for such self-reliance. Over the past few years such demonstrations have been only too abundant. In the realm of ideas and intentions we have gone about as far as we can go. One even begins to experience a sort of lassitude as the same arguments are rehashed over and over again with growing stridence, just as a coward who does not dare to act keeps shouting threats of big deeds and bravado. The great merit of the AACC's call for moratorium lies in that it goes beyond the mere restating of the need for self-reliance and proceeds to lay down practical lines of action.

Here we would like to take up the challenge at that practical level insofar as it confronts the Roman Catholic church in Africa. After examining the way the Catholic church has attempted to tackle the questions raised by the moratorium call, it will be possible to undertake an assessment of the effectiveness of such attempts, and then to suggest alternative ways of facing those same problems.

FACING THE PROBLEM

At the time when the call for moratorium was stirring up much discussion in Protestant church circles, there was a feeling that the Catholic church did not seem to be worried by the questions at stake. Perhaps this feeling was created by the fact that the African hierarchy, in their capacity as leaders of the Catholic church in Africa, had not yet taken the pains to publish any dramatic and official statement on self-reliance comparable to the one made by the AACC. There was even the impression that the church was deliberately ignoring or evading the issue.

But this was a false impression. In fact the Catholic church was following the whole debate with acute interest. The AACC May 1974 meeting itself had been attended by several Catholic observers, and the proceedings and conclusions were covered by influential journals, like the *African Ecclesiastical Review (AFER)*.[3] In his annual report of November 1975, the Secretary-General of the Pontifical Works, the Roman department directly responsible for aid to Catholic mission churches all over the world, made an extensive allusion to the whole moratorium issue.[4] This is ample proof that the Holy See itself had been following closely the trends of thinking on this whole question of self-reliance.

All along, the church has been tackling these same problems but perhaps from angles that are slightly different from the basic optics of the AACC moratorium statement. Given the special way that the Catholic church has traditionally understood missionary work, and given too the concrete history of Catholic missions and the typical methods that have been evolved in the course of this long history, it was normal for the church to situate the problem of selfhood for the young churches in a quite different context, and consequently to go about solving it in a different way. As we shall see, it was only in October 1974, some months after the Lusaka meeting of the AACC, that the African Catholic hierarchy finally got down to comparing notes with their non-Catholic counterparts. But long before that the Catholics had been attempting to face the issues in their own way.

"AFRICANIZING THE CHURCH," OR THE TACTIC OF "ADAPTATION"

Already in 1956, when a group of Catholic priests studying in the Pontifical Universities of Rome published the book *Les prêtres noirs s'interrogent* ("Black Priests Are Questioning Themselves"), it was clear that the phase of radical questioning about the selfhood of the church in the missions was well under way.[5] But at that time the watchword was "adaptation." Reflecting on past missionary attitudes and practices, these priests advocated a change of heart. They called for a stop to seeing missionary work as an indiscriminate condemnation of the way of life of the evangelized peoples and an imposition on them of western culture in the name of Christianity.

"Adaptation" meant that evangelization should take the people's way of life seriously. Christianity was to espouse the forms of the local culture. The valid elements of the people's way of life, as it results from the old and the new, must replace the imported forms under which Christianity has been preached. This adaptation was to be made in all aspects of church life: catechesis, liturgy, art, theology, church discipline, and so on.

This demand for adaptation has been going on all these years. It received a definite impetus from the Second Vatican Council (1962–1965). Behind it lies the desire for a real selfhood of the church in the mission lands. Many concrete efforts have been made to implement it, mainly in the area of liturgy: the use of local tunes, vestments, art forms, ritual, etc.

Curiously enough this whole movement has not found much favor with large sections of the faithful in the mission lands for the benefit of whom it was meant in the first place. There even is a measure of growing opposition to it, especially among African bishops, priests and religious, and not a few of the educated local people.[6] It is sometimes said that this is due to the fact that such people have been unduly "westernized," and have lost touch with their own culture, thus tending to become conservative and "more Roman than Rome itself." While that may be a partial explanation, it fails, I think, to pinpoint the real cause of this astonishing disenchantment.

Paradoxically one cause is the zeal with which some expatriate missionaries have embarked on this adaptation. To begin with, one can hardly blame the local people for questioning the sincerity and good intentions of people who, as a group, have shown for years a consistent contempt for and misunderstanding of this same local culture. Why all of a sudden this strange about-turn? Why this rush to pre-empt a movement that should normally be initiated and conducted by the local people, in their own way, and at their own pace? Even where sincerity and good intention are evident, participation by expatriates has resulted in a number of unacceptable products and *faux pas*. It has often been accompanied by ill-timing, impatience, and undue imposition— especially the unconscious but extremely repulsive presumption of "knowing better than the natives," knowing what is best for them, or assuming the duty of thinking, feeling, and deciding for them.

This last point brings us to the root of the whole matter. Adaptation as currently practiced has become largely odious because it negates the very aim of the movement: selfhood, self-determination, self-reliance of the local church. What people are objecting to is not so much the changes in themselves. What puts people off is that such adaptations should again be imposed from outside just as they have always been. No real degree of selfhood is achieved if it is still the expatriate who tells the local church when and how to adapt! There is no selfhood if the local church's performance, be it liturgy, or art, or theology, still needs the condescending approval and ratification of the expatriate and is constantly subjected to judgment by the expatriate's own standards. This is no real Africanization, but merely another, more subtle, form of domination. And so this tactic of adaptation has not yet produced convincing results in the area of selfhood. Perhaps it was, after all, dealing with mere symptoms and consequences of dependence, instead of attacking the real roots of that dependence.

"MORE LOCAL VOCATIONS"—THE KEY TO SELF-RELIANCE?

Parallel to the movement for "adaptation," another development has been gaining ground in the Catholic mission territories: an all-out drive for the "localization" or "indigenization" of church leadership. The earnestness of this drive in recent years is a measure of the importance that the Catholic church attaches to this "localization" as a strategy for attaining church maturity and self-reliance, the way such maturity has been envisaged traditionally.

Starting with the mid-fifties a rapid change of guard has been taking place, whereby more and more Africans have been ordained bishops and have replaced missionary expatriate ordinaries. An idea of this rapidity can be gained by looking, for instance, at statistics for the Eastern Africa countries of Kenya, Malawi, Tanzania, Uganda, and Zambia.[7] In 1961 the total number of ordinaries at the head of ecclesiastical territories in these countries was forty-seven. Of these, thirty-nine were expatriates, and only eight were Africans. Fifteen years later the picture has completely changed. In 1976 there were sixty-seven ordinaries in all, and a full fifty of them were Africans, as against seventeen expatriates: a 525 percent increase in African ordinaries, as compared with a 56 percent decrease of expatriates. In most other countries of Africa the trend is much the same.

It is clear that this indigenization of church leadership is a bid to render the church in Africa self-governing or, more appropriately, self-ministering. As a matter of fact the drive for more African bishops is just one part of a wider project: the localization of church personnel, that is, the increase of African church leaders who can eventually replace the overseas missionaries. By "church personnel" here we mean those leaders in the church who, because of ordination or special religious consecration, are expected to be at the disposal and service of the church organization full-time and completely: priests and religious (sisters, brothers, and members of other religious orders of men and women). The term "vocations in the church" refers to these people. In the traditional setup of the Catholic church as an organized institution these members are indeed the hub of church life and activity. On them rests the main burden of organizing, controlling, and executing both those spiritual and sacramental services around which ecclesiastical life gravitates, as well as the various organisms of educational, health, and social ministration that are normally associated with the church's presence and insertion in society.

From the earliest stages of Catholic evangelization in Africa tremendous efforts have been made to recruit and form ever larger numbers of local priests, brothers, sisters, and religious. It must be admitted that, given the formidable odds, in many mission territories these efforts have been astonishingly rewarding. To take again, as an example, the five countries of Eastern Africa in the fifteen years between 1961 and 1976, this is what we find. Whereas in 1961 there were only 577 African priests but 2,294 expatriate ones, in 1976 the situation was visibly changing: 1,303 African priests as against 2,515 expatriates. This is a 126 percent increase for the local priests, and only a 10 percent increase for the expatriates. The case of African sisterhoods is even more impressive. In 1961 the African sisters numbered 2,389 while expatriates were 2,027. In 1976 the statistics give 5,012 African sisters and 2,766 expatriates.[8] In this case of Eastern Africa the future seems to inspire optimism because in general the number of candidates for priesthood and religious life has kept growing.

This success in local vocations is of vital importance as far as the Catholic church is concerned, because traditionally the growth of the local church and the progress toward self-reliance have been measured primarily in terms of such "vocations." There has always been a deep-seated, albeit tacit, assumption that the Catholic church in Africa will have gone a long way toward maturity when the totality, or at least the majority, of its priests, brothers, sisters, and religious will be local people rather than expatriates. All other desirable effects in the way of selfhood of the local church will follow once this strategic aim has been achieved. At the risk of sounding irreverent, one might summarize this assumption as: Seek ye first local vocations, and the rest will be added unto you!

But is the validity of such an assumption borne out by facts? In other words, can it be demonstrated that as more and more local people take over from expatriates, the local church is becoming correspondingly more self-reliant—more self-ministering and more self-supporting? Is the local church becoming more adapted to the conditions of the local people? Is it answering better their needs and problems?

"CARBON-COPY" SELF-RELIANCE?

We shall have the chance, later on, to examine statistics and facts capable of helping us to answer these questions in more detail. But for our present purposes all we need is a general picture of the situation, which is so evident it does not require such detailed proofs. In spite of this rapid Africanization of church leaders and personnel, there does not seem to be any noticeable diminution of dependence on aid coming from outside. On the contrary.

This is clear in the domain of material resources, such as money needed for the upkeep of pastoral workers or religious members, or for running the different services in the church. A reasonably decent upkeep of an average African bishop with his local clergy and religious means an impressive annual budget for food, clothing, board and lodging, medical expenses, maintenance and repair of houses, salaries of workers, hospitality, and so on, not to mention "pocket-money" for various personal needs which include help to a whole line of relatives and friends. For the accomplishment of their pastoral and church commitments they will need another budget for churches, seminaries, schools, health and social institutions, salaries of catechists and other employees, office equipment, transport (cars, motorcycles, repairs, insurance, fuel). In the past, when expatriates were the majority, the resources needed were not the responsibility of the local church. They came as a matter of course from overseas. But when the local people take over, how much of these resources can reasonably come from the contributions of local Christians who are mostly poor folk barely managing to subsist at a material level inferior by far to that of their ecclesiastical leaders and personnel? Let us face facts: the more the "local vocations" increase the greater becomes the need for outside material help. African church leaders end up becoming chronic and professional beggars of outside help, because the churches they are expected to care for are such that they cannot subsist on local resources alone.

And what about the problem of personnel? As local vocations grow, does the need for outside helpers diminish proportionately so that there is hope that the local church will eventually become self-ministering? In theory, perhaps yes. But in practice matters are not as simple. The growth of vocations is a sign of the growth of the local church itself. Now, as the church grows, the needs of this church keep growing and becoming more complex. They require a larger number of people to meet them and a wider variety of expertise. There are needs stemming from the growing of the church body itself: pastoral care, sacramentalization of the faithful, ordinary parish work. But there are also needs for expansion of the church into new geographical and human areas, or for meeting new problems (e.g., urbanization, refugees, migrant labor, ecumenism).

As local vocations become more numerous, they either get absorbed into the already existing positions, or are assigned to new jobs. Often enough however, the growth of the church creates the need for specialists, and it is not always possible to find them among the local people. And so there is still the need to call for outside help. In any case, one still has to discover a church that feels it has all the personnel it needs!

My own conviction is that, unless the structure and form of the local churches change, there will never come a time when the traditional local vocations will be enough to meet fully the requirements of those churches. And why is this? First, because these so-called "local vocations" have very little to do with the real key to self-reliance. It is not priests or religious that can make a church self-reliant; it is the laity, because they are *the* church, the majority among the People of God, and therefore the only force that can decisively influence the life of the church as a whole. Any church is worth what its laity is. If this majority adopts ways and means of rendering the local church self-ministering and self-supporting, only then can you talk about the church being on its way to real selfhood. On the contrary, the "vocations" are simply a small minority, a special elite, in the ecclesial body. Their role is to serve the rest of the church. Multiplying them does not automatically modify the real state of the church.

The second reason is this: the "local vocations," as they exist today, are the most obvious and best manifestation of what actually prevents the local churches from being self-reliant. The final obstacle to selfhood is that the local churches in the mission lands have usually been nothing more than imitations or "carbon-copies" of the older churches of Europe and America. The way these mission churches exist and operate is not primarily determined by the local situation: the culture of the people, their needs, their problems, their possibilities, or their outlook. No, it is first and foremost pre-determined by customs, prescriptions, and standards coming from elsewhere, and only secondarily from the exigencies of the locality. "The church" in the missions is usually a foreign reality, an imported organization. And the local vocations are the best example of this foreignness.

Let us be clear here. We are talking about the concrete forms of the church's existence in a given locality and among a concrete people. We are not speaking about those general and basic norms and requirements in faith, cult, and ecclesial life and work that make up the foundation of the unity of the church everywhere and at all times. These are, and should, remain invariable. But when they are given concrete expression, it is the conditions of time, place, culture, needs, and possibilities that determine what form exactly they are going to take. By and large, the concrete forms that the church has taken in Africa have not been determined mainly by the actual conditions of African realities, but by those of overseas countries and cultures. We in Africa are simply trying to copy these forms without stopping to ask ourselves whether the forms are tailored to suit the actual life of the majority of members in the church.

Take for example the organizational structure of the church. Admittedly there have to be such things as dioceses and parishes, with adequate instruments to make them effective church structures. But does that mean their size, the church buildings and equipment, the system of bureaucracy, and the various organizations and their mode of operation should try to imitate those of Europe? Our churches do indeed require bishops, priests, and religious. But is it necessary that their style and standard of life, even down to their dress, should be a copy of those of Europe and America? If the churches abroad find it relevant and possible to run big schools and hospitals and other such sophisticated institutions in competition with the state, are we obliged in Africa to do likewise? We forget that in those other lands those forms are possible because they are supposed to answer local needs and because the Christians in those churches can afford them. But our people here do not necessarily need exactly the same things, nor can they afford them. If we persist in wanting to have these things as our friends overseas, then we have to accept remaining forever dependent on the aid from those churches abroad who alone can implement and finance them.

When you look carefully at the whole problem, you find that the main cause of all this imitation is a serious misunderstanding and confusion. We have tended, especially in the Catholic church, to confuse *unity* with *uniformity*. We are rightly preoccupied with being one with the rest of the church in the world, and we rightly take pride in knowing that the church that we have in Africa is the same as that spread all over the universe, the same as the one that has existed throughout the centuries since the time of Our Lord and the Apostles. But we somehow get the funny idea that such a unity has to be expressed and preserved by means of uniformity in accidental details. We imagine there is a sort of palpable pre-existing model or "master" out there which, in all its details, is the norm and standard of the church of Christ. So we strive to reproduce in our situation this imaginary model. We feel that our churches would be false, inferior, or substandard if they did not reproduce as much as possible the concrete details of that model. But we fail to realize that this imaginary "master" is nothing else but our image of the churches from abroad: a combination of accidental elements resulting from the particular experiences of the church in Europe and America. There is nothing really Catholic, universal, or perennial about it.

THE PRESENCE OF MISSIONARIES SERIOUSLY QUESTIONED

We have attempted to show how the Catholic church went about, in its own way, enabling the local churches in the mission territories of Africa to become more independent and self-reliant. Strategies such as "adaptation," Africanizing of church leadership, and promotion of local vocations were attempted. Although these attempts went some way toward solving the problems, they did not provide completely satisfactory results. The questioning continued and became more acute due to other factors that complicated the situation even further.

The most significant of these factors was the decolonization process going on all over Africa, especially beginning with the mid-fifties. Country after country became politically independent from the former colonizing powers and embarked on the difficult task of growing into autonomous self-determining nations. For many people there was an obvious parallelism between colonization and missionary work. They felt that, just as the former colonizers were handing over responsibility to the local people, in the churches too the missionaries should rapidly transfer power to the local members of their churches. This was indeed happening in most places.

But there was a feeling that in several instances the process was too slow: there was an inadmissible lag in the churches behind the political process of independence. People made ominous remarks about the churches being the last bastion of colonialism. In some newly-independent nations, like Guinea, Zaire, Algeria, or Uganda, patience seemed to run out. Missionaries were asked to leave either en masse or in large numbers. In other countries where there were internal struggles (Nigeria and Sudan) or where anticolonial fighting was still in progress (the Portuguese colonies), it became increasingly unsafe for foreign missionaries to carry on with their normal work. Many chose to leave or were forced to do so.

Even in those countries where the situation was not as dramatic, it has been increasingly difficult for foreign missionaries to stay on or for new ones to come in. There have been frequent deportations on all sorts of grounds, and in many new nations the influx of outside church personnel is subjected to a severe screening process that is often discouraging by its sheer slowness and the burdensome restrictions. These conditions demonstrate the provisional and temporary character of the missionaries' role in these nations. Their presence is no longer taken for granted, and they start to wonder whether they are really wanted.

An additional problem has cropped up in the Catholic church itself: the crisis of missionary vocations. In actual fact the crisis in priestly and religious vocations has become generalized in the whole world for the past fifteen years. But the missionary organizations that used to supply the young churches annually with new workers have been particularly hit. Where formerly they could send scores of new missionaries, today they are lucky if they can manage to fill in the gaps caused by deaths, repatriation, or abandoning of priestly or religious life. In many ecclesiastical territories of Africa, it is no longer a question of expanding missionary operations, but rather an attempt merely to keep things going through the device of ever thinning out the remaining personnel. This causes problems for the local churches, while among the missionaries there are more and more cases of overwork, fatigue, and nervous breakdown. Local vocations, even in the luckiest countries, are no real solution either. To start with, many countries of Africa have very few local vocations and have been relying totally on missionary workers. But even where local vocations are prosperous, these can barely fill up the gaps created by the shortage of missionaries.

WHAT IS THE FUTURE OF THE LOCAL CHURCHES?

The local churches in Africa, especially their bishops, have not failed to take notice of these developments. The general reaction is one of alarm and desperation. As the situation stands today, if outside help in missionary workers and in material resources stopped suddenly, it is difficult to see how the young churches could continue to exist and to function adequately. Nobody denies that the time has come for the churches to strive toward self-reliance. But how? In desperation the local churches are trying to buy time by attempting to keep things going as before. Bishops continue appealing to the churches abroad for as many missionaries as they can spare. They try to reason with their own governments in a bid to retain the few missionaries still around. Appeals for funds from overseas continue too. There seems to reign a kind of strange "hope against hope" that the good old times will still continue for a while.

But the missionaries themselves are becoming more and more restless and wish to know what the future has in store for them. For most of them the difficulties of the moment are "signs of the times" calling for a courageous rethinking of the role of the missionary in the young churches today. It is evident that things will never be the same again. But what is God asking of them in the remaining time? Is their continuing presence not a hindrance to the young churches in their coming of age? Should they accept to simply hang around instead of deliberately "phasing out" in order to help the young churches to start standing on their own feet?

For a long time it was not apparent that the church leaders in Africa were seriously addressing themselves to these questions. When the AACC in May 1974 officially formulated their answer to similar questions by proposing the moratorium, most Catholic missionaries manifested the wish that their own leaders would finally express their answer too. The chance for this came in October of that same year when a representative group of the African hierarchy was in Rome taking part in the Bishops' Synod on "Evangelization in the Modern World."

THE CATHOLIC BISHOPS' ANSWER
TO THE CALL FOR MORATORIUM

The first formulation of the bishops' answer is to be found in the *Report on Experiences of the Church in the Work of Evangelization in Africa,* particularly in chapter 4 ("Young Churches") and chapter 6 ("Special Concerns of Evangelization in Africa," especially no. 7: "Partnership between the Older and Younger Churches").[9] This report had been prepared for presentation to the Synod by Bishop James Sangu of Mbeya (Tanzania) by putting together various reports received from episcopal conferences all over Africa. Without explicitly saying so, this document provided elements of answers to the questions that the call for moratorium had confronted.

The African hierarchy, however, thought that it was not enough to address the important question of self-reliance in this rather passing manner. So they sat down to work out what they wanted to be a complete and ex professo exposition of their thinking. This resulted in a special document: the *Statement of the Bishops of Africa: Coresponsible Evangelization,* which was released at the end of the Synod. It is a comprehensive answer not only to the questions put by the missionaries, but also to the "Call for Moratorium" that the AACC had launched earlier in the year. Although these documents do not attempt to answer the questions point by point, their message is clear. It may help, however, to group together its main lines.[10]

In the first place, it is clear that the Catholic bishops are in total agreement with their Protestant colleagues of the AACC about *the aim* of the moratorium: it is absolutely urgent for the churches in Africa today to strive toward self-reliance.

The aim of evangelization in Africa is and must be the establishment of a self-supporting Church both in personnel and material support (*Report,* p. 4).

But the bishops disagree with the Lusaka declaration concerning *the means* to attaining this self-reliance. Specifically, they do not think that declaring a moratorium on foreign personnel and material aid is a realistic way to achieve the desired aim:

There are some who insist that for the Young Church of Africa to become quickly self-ministering, self-propagating and self-supporting it is imperative that expatriate missionaries should leave since their presence in Africa constitutes a hindrance to the growth of the Church in Africa. This is a narrow and misleading viewpoint (*Report,* p. 5).

To begin with, the declaration of such a moratorium does not even seem necessary today. The number of missionaries is diminishing rapidly of its own accord. Due to the vocation crisis and to the growing difficulties for expatriates to enter African countries, there is already what *Mission Trends* calls a forced moratorium.[11] At this stage there is no danger whatsoever that we shall be swamped by missionaries! So we do not need to make a special effort to diminish their number.

In the opinion of the African bishops, the same holds true for overseas material aid. Whatever may have been the case in the past, today it is becoming more and more difficult to obtain even the bare minimum of funds needed to keep things going. Mission appeals in the overseas churches are becoming less and less productive. The annual grants from Rome, which for most dioceses in Africa are the only regular source of help, are diminishing when they should be increasing, given the worldwide inflation whose effects are much more severe in Africa. There is surely not the slightest possibility that we shall be swimming in money in the foreseeable future. Why then should it be necessary to declare a special moratorium on something that is diminishing anyway?

But more than that, the bishops felt that, at this decisive stage in the history of our young churches, renouncing the available outside help in personnel and finance, far from helping our churches to reach self-reliance, will simply defeat that very purpose. It will just help to kill the churches. At this stage, self-reliance is not yet a reality; it is simply a project. To achieve it there is need for a period of transition during which it will be necessary to lay solid foundations for such self-reliance. This means that we shall have to dismantle the former systems that used to create our dependence and set up new ones capable of generating local resources. For instance, if you want some day to become self-ministering, then you should now multiply and equip adequately the institutions capable of producing the ministers you need. If our communities are to learn to be self-supporting, they will have to be trained and guided. All this laying of foundations calls for all the possible personnel and resources we can avail ourselves of. At this stage therefore, outside help is not a hindrance, but precisely a welcome asset. A wise policy here is not to reject it, but to learn to use it strategically.

DIFFERENT ECCLESIOLOGIES?

At the meetings in Rome during which the *Statement* was hammered out, there was a particular view widespread among the bishops. It was felt generally that in the last analysis the difference of approach to the problem of self-reliance, separating the AACC advocates of moratorium from the African Catholic bishops opposed to it, was based on differences in the respective underlying ecclesiologies.

The moratorium position was said to reflect the traditional Protestant slant which emphasizes the autonomy of each ecclesial community and puts a premium on the "local-ness" of each church, even when organisms of communion and collaboration among these churches operate on wider levels (national levels, AACC, WCC). In the Protestant tradition, these wider organisms do indeed express in a visible way the unity of churches in faith and obedience to the common Lord. But they are not a call to, or an expression of, a strict constitutional and binding structure necessitating links of organic interdependence or juridical subordination. They are simply a fraternal but free association of otherwise self-contained and independent churches or groups of churches. Such an ecclesiology lays store by each local church's self-determination, its internal capacity to be self-reliant, and its freedom from undue outside pressures. The ever-looming danger is indeed that when pushed to extremes, these tendencies may result in each church being caught up in isolation, individualism, and lack of effective openness to other communities. Some bishops thought that the general orientation of the call for moratorium, and some overtones in its statements, were largely tributary to such an ecclesiology.

For its part, the Catholic church tends to stress the universality of the church and to value above all the relations of interdependence and exchange that should link the different communities of the worldwide church. Hence the ideas of "co-responsibility," "communion," and "partnership" that punctuate the two documents:

The idea and ideal of Partnership (brotherhood, Christian Family, co-responsibility, fellowship, Community Sharing, give-and-receive relationship) was actively present from the very beginning of the Church. . . . The manner in which partnership operates will depend on many variables such as the cultures, traditions and the needs and abilities and potentials of the partners. The practice of partnership will build and enhance the idea of real belonging to the Church, to the Family of Christ, to the People of God where the members of the Old Churches and the Young Churches are equal partners in promoting the welfare of the Church and bear the responsibility as equals (*Report,* p. 11).

Faced with such a situation, the time has come for us to insist on the master-ideas of *communion* in faith, hope and love and *co-responsibility* between Churches in order to find together real solutions to the above problems (*Statement,* p. 19).

Collegiality, co-responsibility, ecclesial communion are synonyms for the same basic reality that we are members of the same family; each one, and all together, are responsible for the Church of God spread over the whole world. Nobody is a stranger in the house of God. This is something all must realize, especially all those who undertake the work of evangelization (ibid., p. 21).

OUTSIDE HELP THAT RESPECTS
THE SELFHOOD OF THE LOCAL CHURCH

This insistence on "co-responsibility" was in fact meant to be an answer to the question that many missionaries had been asking: "Are we still needed?" The bishops are saying that outside help is still welcome, but on certain very clear conditions: missionaries from outside are coming to help and not to dominate, to cooperate and not to dictate. They come to put themselves at the disposal of the local church, under the leadership and initiative of the local leaders.

This cooperation will have to take on new forms. Missionaries coming from abroad will take into account the aspirations of the young Churches for more autonomy and responsibility. They will be available for and participate in the searchings of the young communities under the direction of the local hierarchy (ibid.).

It is important to make explicit what may not be so obvious here. This declaration is based on the conviction that it is impossible for the local church to be authentically autonomous and self-determining even while receiving the help of outside personnel. All that is needed is a change of spirit in both the local church and the missionary from abroad. The local church has to assume real responsibility and initiative, while the expatriate collaborator learns not to dictate but only to serve. The statement assumes that this change of spirit is feasible.

We notice the same conviction as regards financial help from outside. Here too the underlying conviction is that it is possible for the local church to practice financial self-determination even when it gets help from abroad. The giving churches from overseas must not use their donations as a means of imposing themselves on the young churches who receive their gifts. After all, their giving does not entitle them to any feeling of superiority over the churches to whom they give: what they are offering to these churches is not their own exclusive possession, but the common treasure given by God for the benefit of the whole church. They were merely stewards of it, obliged in conscience to share with their sister churches when these stand in need. Like the servant in the Gospel, when they have acquitted themselves of their duty of sharing, they can only say: "We are unworthy servants; we only did what we had to do" (Luke 17:10). This change of spirit goes farther. The conviction must grow that the material goods are not the only, or indeed the most important, treasures that must be shared among the churches. There are other treasures (like living faith, rich ecclesial experiences, fervent fraternal love, prophecy, justice, hospitality, etc.) which God may have lavished on those churches that are perhaps materially poor, and which may be lacking in the affluent churches. This makes it possible for all churches to be at once givers and receivers. And so the bishops declare:

The young churches in their pursuit of financial autonomy call upon their flocks to be more self-supporting, and, at the same time, call upon their elder sister churches for help in a spirit of sharing and communion. Financial help coming from outside must be integrated into projects planned and to be worked out by the local churches, instead of being decided upon unilaterally and handed over too mathematically. He who gives enriches himself. . . . A new approach to ecclesiastical goods needs to be worked out in the interest of better evangelization. Temporal goods are at the services of the Church for the salvation of the world. There is no place for saying that the rich give and the poor receive. There is only diversity of ministries and services (ibid., p. 21).

DIFFERENT ECCLESIOLOGIES
OR SIMPLY DIFFERENT STRATEGIES?

These points made by the African hierarchy are very important for an understanding of the way self-reliance is being actually pursued by many local churches in Africa. The statement itself does not seem to have caused in the churches the same commotion as did the moratorium call. This is probably because the position taken by the bishops has very little about it that is really new or radical. On the contrary, it is agreeably reassuring to both parties: to the missionaries and the overseas churches, for now they know that they and their help are still needed and welcome; to the local churches too, since they can now look forward to continuing outside help while enjoying the satisfaction of being autonomous and self-determining: a wonderful feat indeed of having your cake and eating it too!

Let us first of all dispel some misunderstandings and half-truths. If the bishops have dissociated themselves from the moratorium call it is not simply because they are Catholics. On this point there is nothing really confessional.

Quite a number of non-Catholic bodies and individuals have in fact reacted to the call for moratorium in the same way as the Catholic bishops, and in almost identical words. This should suffice to make us very wary about drawing too rigid a distinction between the so-called Protestant slant in ecclesiology, with its insistence on "local-ness" and autonomy of individual churches, and the so-called Catholic slant which would put primacy on universalism and inter-dependence. The Standing Committee of the Christian Council of Tanzania, meeting in November 1974 (a month after the Catholic bishops' statement), unanimously agreed to this position:

While confirming the call of the AACC that churches in Africa make every systematic effort towards self-reliance in finance and manpower, we the Churches in Tanzania would like to dis-associate ourselves from the recent call of the AACC for moratorium and we feel very strongly that such an action is not appropriate. We believe in the Universal Church brotherhood and on this ground we approve the present system of giving and taking, i.e., sharing of God's resources: hence we are prepared to give, accept and esteem any assistance to or from fellow Churches within or outside Africa provided they [assistances] are genuinely given for the advancement of the Churches' activities in this country.[12]

Let us recall here the remark we made when discussing the Catholic bishops' statement, for that remark is just as valid in the case of those non-Catholics who reject the moratorium call. We said that such a rejection is based on the conviction that it is possible for the local churches to be authentically autonomous and self-determining even while continuing to receive outside help in personnel and finance. I would suggest that this is the real point in the whole moratorium debate. All are agreed that self-reliance is a good thing. But the proposers of the moratorium were basing themselves on a further conviction: that, in the actual situation of the churches in Africa, it is hardly possible to arrive at real selfhood if the churches simply continue to accept external aid.

It is all very nice to speak of interdependence, sharing, exchange, mutual respect. But we are not dealing here with just any kind of dependence which could gradually diminish with an appropriate amount of goodwill and a change of heart on the part of the overseas churches. We are dealing with a structural reality characterized by an in-built dynamism which, as long as it lasts, keeps the older churches and the younger ones interlocked in ties of basic and structural inequality. Just as in the case of the umbilical cord tying mother and child, there can be no hope of transforming the relationship of dependence until the decisive step is taken *to cut the cord.* Only this will liberate both the mother and the child and set them free to embark on a new type of relationship. The surgical operation forces the baby to become itself and to start developing a life of its own. Even though the baby will continue to need the mother, it has at least started to be on its own. The dependence that still continues is radically different from the one of the womb. The advocates of moratorium proposed such a surgical operation precisely, a temporary operation perhaps, but an indispensable and decisive one.

I imagine that those opposed to the moratorium would say that the comparison of the umbilical cord is wrong and inappropriate in the first place. They will prefer images that express a less total dependence, like the image of sister churches, or the one of Elder Brother and Younger Brother.[13] But let us not waste time in such disputes about images. A comparison is simply a comparison, not a proof or demonstration. Moreover, as the Latins say, it always limps anyway. The real point in the discussion is: What type of dependence are we dealing with? And what strategy is best suited to change it?

THE DEPENDENCE OF THE CHURCHES IN AFRICA

If my little experience is anything to go by, then I should want to suggest that we do not minimize the radicalness of the dependence of the churches in Africa on outside help. It is of the "life-or-death" type, nothing less. The image of the umbilical cord seems, for me, to suit the realities best.

When I became bishop of Lilongwe in 1972, the diocese had seventeen parishes.[14] To run them there were some seventy-six priests, of whom only ten were local priests, and sixty-six expatriates. This is just an example. But it is evident that the "priestly ministry" in such a diocese was *structurally* dependent on outside help. If those sixty-six expatriate priests had left all of a sudden, it would not have been the same diocese at all insofar as priestly ministry was concerned (and God knows to what extent our whole church life and activity is still dependent on the priest!). This is just one item in the whole system of dependence. But let us take another. The budget for the diocese (for the year 1971) had been 96,650 Kwacha (a Kwacha is theoretically equivalent to ten English shillings). Receipts from various sources were supposed to cover this budget. One source was the contributions from the local Christians through tithes and other collections. For that year, all the local contributions put together amounted to just K16,388. This means that the balance of K80,262 had to be received as aid from outside. If we had not received that K80,262 that year, the life and work of the diocese would have stood at a standstill. (The budget for just the upkeep of priests' communities was K23,517!).

Such figures speak for themselves, and I would challenge anybody who would claim that Lilongwe was the worst example in Africa! I would invite that person to have a look at the official figures released by the "Pontifical Works" in Rome, the department from which the bulk of funds that keep the churches in Africa going come annually. This is the central office to which all Catholic communities of the world send their aid for the missions. The amount thus received is then distributed to the missions all over the world. In the year 1975 this Roman Office distributed in all a sum of $50,004,621.[15] Of this amount a full $20,725,093 went to help the churches of Africa. In the preceding year, the Office had received from the five continents contributions totalling $48,397,707. How much did Africa contribute in this exercise of "interdependence" and exchange? It gave $160,715. (And of this amount $117,025 was from South Africa alone, while Zaire followed with $15,921. The rest of Africa gave the remaining amount.)

We can quibble about the exactitude of such figures. Some might, for instance, insist that the amount shown as Africa's contribution gives only a minimal idea of the actual amount of self-help that is actually going on in the African communities: the Roman statistics simply do not, and cannot, take these into account. That is quite correct. But that is not the point. Those figures simply show that there is no meaningful comparison between what the African churches can contribute to the universal church and what they receive in exchange. Their contribution is just a token, which the other churches do not really need. But what Africa receives is its very lifeblood without which the African churches could not possibly continue to exist.

SOME REMARKS AND OBSERVATIONS

This is perhaps a warning that we Africans should not allow ourselves to be carried away by our own rhetoric. It is all very well to talk about the church as a family where the members of the old churches and the young churches are equal partners in promoting the welfare of the church, and that they bear that responsibility as equals. What equality is there, on the financial level, between the United States with its contribution of $21,000,000 and Africa with its $160,000? Can the two sides meet and talk about church finances on an equal footing? Is their "responsibility" really equal?

Of course we may answer that in the life of the church money is not everything; it is not even the most important type of riches. The vitality and freshness of faith in the young churches is by far a greater thing before God than millions of dollars. Nobody questions that. But then, so what? Does that necessarily impress our "elder brothers"? Perhaps in these modern days there is a growing number of Christians in the older churches who are finally discovering that the materially poor churches have immense spiritual treasures available to the whole church, and who are convinced that because of these treasures the young churches should be respected and not be treated simply as "poor relatives" by the materially wealthy communities. While we may hope that such laudable sentiments will keep spreading, we still have to remember that for the big majority of our fellow Christians, importance in the House of God is still measured in terms of how many missionaries you have sent out to convert the poor pagans, and how much money you give annually for those miserable creatures of God. It would be news to such people to learn that those converted pagans think they have immense ecclesiastical riches to offer. And when they heard that, would there be much chance that they would degrade themselves to the point of begging for those treasures? In our world those who have money find it hard to believe in the worth of other treasures.

However, that is all beside the point. The young churches might succeed in offering their spiritual riches, and be respected for that. This does not change the situation. The problem is that these treasures are, as it were, the products of Christ's church which is now present and at work in the mission lands. The trouble is that, as things stand, this very presence and effectiveness of that church (which is responsible for those famous riches) is dependent on a continual injection of personnel and money from the older churches. To what extent is the "exchange" equal, when one side (the African churches) depends for its very life on the other side? It is not right to minimize the implications of the dependence in personnel and money under which the young churches are laboring.

The churches in Africa hope that, with a change of heart, it will be possible for their elder sister churches to give help without strings attached to those gifts. "Financial help coming from outside must be integrated into projects planned and to be worked out by the local churches. . . . " This hope is not illusory. The donor agencies and the older churches must be recommended for the sincerity of their efforts to give "without their right hand knowing what their left hand is doing." On several occasions African bishops have gone out of their way to praise the disinterestedness and respect with which donor bodies like the German church's Misereor and Missio serve their brethren in the missions. And the same could be said of many other sister churches. Still, given what we poor human beings are, we should not underestimate the difficulty involved in the attempt to give without any strings attached. It is easier said than done.

Here it is not sincerity or goodwill that are in doubt. You can have all the goodwill in the world, but the fact is the process of offering help hides in itself the temptation to "monitor" the route taken by this help and the effects it produces. After all, the gift is part of the giver. We are perhaps asking too much when we want our donors simply to offer their help and then leave the local church the full liberty to plan and work out the projects for which this help was requested. Again, it would be unrealistic to want the help of missionaries for the service of the local church without granting them a fair share in the formulation of pastoral policies, or enough freedom to offer their suggestions—even their constructive criticism. But we must remember that our helpers have the backing of material and expertise resources which we do not. How fair is "fair share" in influencing pastoral policies, when one partner is more equal than the other?

As for material resources in general, it is obvious that the one who has the money has the power—and "power corrupts." Perhaps in our case of religious and holy operations, there will be no deliberate taking advantage. But certainly, whoever offers help includes the right to be heard. And whoever accepts aid, forfeits by the same token a measure of independence. There are many ways of bringing to bear subtle types of blackmail, veiled threats of victimization and "punishment," which often accompany the most disinterested helping hand. We in Africa do not need to be reminded of that.

CONCLUDING SUGGESTIONS

The foregoing remarks should not be taken as meant to discredit the heroic efforts that both the African churches and our sister churches from abroad are making to bring about self-reliance. They only meant to show how this desired aim cannot be bought at a cheap price. Coming of age, for all its excitement, is a painful process. It asks for costly ruptures with a past in which life seemed secure and comfortable. It is a striking out into the unknown.

Is there real hope that the churches in Africa can eventually come of age? I think so. But there are conditions. From what we said earlier, it will now be clear that the main source of our dependence is the fact that our churches are still trying to copy the churches from overseas. Unconsciously we are attempting an impossible feat: to become self-reliant not with our own resources, but with outside resources.

Perhaps those of us who are leaders in our churches should resolutely open the way for a new experience: the liberation from the slavery of outside norms and standards. This is not easy. We are pressured from all sides into conformity and emulation, trying to prove that we are just as good as (if not better than) our sister churches abroad or the missionaries who preceded us. If in former days there was a certain material standard of life and style of living which was associated with the overseas pastoral workers whom we are replacing, we feel constrained to maintain that level for fear of "losing face." If our church used to maintain impressive institutions and establishments, we are loath to let go of them: it will be a shame to admit that the church can no longer afford all that, now that it is in the hands of the local people. And so we burden ourselves uselessly with things which we really do not need and which our churches can ill afford. Such a self-imposed slavery is the main obstacle to self-reliance.

The key to selfhood is to base the church's life and activity on the active participation of the majority in the church: those who constitute the People of God. Let the needs of the majority, their aspirations and problems, determine what our pastoral priorities will be. Let the possibilities and the limitations of their actual life dictate the structures and the shape of our institutions and organizations. Let their ways of thinking, feeling, acting, their standard of life, and their material, intellectual, moral, and spiritual resources be the basis for the activity in the church. Then this majority will stop being a passive body. They will become active, and through their very activity will determine from below, from inside, the real shape of the church. Such a church is capable of becoming self-reliant.

Mahbub ul Haq, when dealing with the underdevelopment of Third World countries, speaks of self-reliance as an essential ingredient in the strategy for true development.[16] What he describes there as a strategy for conquering material poverty can very well be transposed to fit our discussion about achieving self-reliance for the young churches. I offer these extracts as a basis for reflection.

There are four elements which are important in the concept of self-reliance:
—First, the society should not introduce any consumption of goods which cannot be shared by the vast majority of the population at that particular stage of development. . . .
—Second, the concept of self-reliance implies the maximum use of indigenous resources and technology. . . .
—Third, the developing countries must view their reliance on foreign assistance as the minimum that the country cannot do without, not the maximum that the country can negotiate. . . .
—Finally, the concept of self-reliance also implies that there must be a deliberate de-lining of the Third World from its past dependent relationships with the developed countries.[17]

Perhaps a serious meditation on these few thoughts can help us to formulate our own strategies for self-reliance.

In the first place, the young churches in Africa should henceforth be convinced that it is high time to embark resolutely on the austere road toward self-reliance in all things. It should be clear that, however much we may want to cherish a nostalgia for the former state of affairs, from now on the vitality and authenticity of our churches will depend on how well they learn to stand on their own feet. It takes time and effort to bring this home to our Christians. But we must be prepared to do that, even if this will create for some time a feeling of disillusionment and disappointment at being forced to be "cut to size" or being forced to come down to realistic standards and dimensions.

Second, the project of self-reliance calls for a clear and well-planned strategy. An indispensable premise in such a strategy is that the young churches of Africa cannot hope to reach selfhood unless they abandon the futile attempt to copy their older sister churches overseas. The project of self-reliance should start from a realistic analysis and appraisal of the local situation: the possibilities and resources in the local communities, but also the limitations that are there. For an adequate analysis of these possibilities and limitations, account must be taken of the majority of the people who form our churches and not the few privileged elites among us. Any plans for the future should be based on the resources of this majority.

The strategy for self-reliance asks for an adequate period of preparation. During this time efforts will be made to render unnecessary the ties of dependence on outside personnel and resources. This will be achieved through the creation on the spot of new systems for self-help and local cooperation and reliance: to effect "maximum use of indigenous resources and technology." It may then be discovered that a number of institutions and activities cannot be maintained with the available local resources. This should not lead automatically to the conclusion that outside help is necessary. Rather it should be the occasion for an honest soul-searching to find out whether indeed such things are indispensable. Perhaps they simply should be given up in favor of other more adapted institutions that stand the chance of thriving on continued local resources. There is nothing shameful in such a dropping of excess baggage; it is simply a liberation from unnecessary slavery, and for a rejuvenation of the life of the church.

Self-reliance should not mean isolation or the attitude of absolute self-sufficiency. Just as no man is an island, so too no church can be genuine and dynamic unless it is in continual vital link with other churches in a relation of mutual giving and receiving. We all need one another. But this need should not be such that for its very life and work the local church be basically dependent on others. There should rather be complementarity and subsidiarity: basic self-reliance for ordinary purposes, but dependence on others only in the measure of strict necessity: when and where local resources genuinely fall short.

We could go on describing what self-reliance means and how the churches in Africa can best set out to achieve it. But this is not necessary. What is important is to realize that the call for selfhood is a serious challenge to all of us: church leaders as well as ordinary faithful. It does not come to us on a silver platter. It is the result of honesty, self-denial, and hard work. We can only hope that Africa is capable of achieving it, and that it is not yet too late.

NOTES

1. For an idea of the Third Assembly of the All Africa Conference of Churches (AACC) which met from May 12 to May 21, 1974, see *AACC Bulletin* 7 (1974), nos. 1 and 2 and especially 3.

2. See, for example, *International Review of Mission* 64 (1974), where responses of various influential missionaries and church leaders are recorded. Diverse reactions can be seen in the reports of IDOC's *The Future of the Missionary Enterprise:* no. 9 (1974), "In Search of Mission"; no. 14 (1975), "Uhuru and Harambee"; no. 19 (1976), "Ujamaa and Self-reliance." *AACC Bulletin* and *AACC Newsletter* have continued to report interesting contributions to the ongoing moratorium debate. See, for example, *AACC Bulletin* 9 (1976), no. 1, pp. 38–40, "Focus on Moratorium" (by Rev. John Thorne); and no. 2, pp. 39–40, "Theological Education in a Post-Moratorium World" (by Gerhard Mey). For Asia, see Harvey Perkins, Harry Daniel, and Asal Simandjuntak, "Let My People Go," in *Mission Trends No. 3* (New York: Paulist, and Grand Rapids: Eerdmans, 1976), pp. 192–210.

3. See *African Ecclesiastical Review (AFER)* 16 (1974): 329–34.

4. *Acta Pontificalium Operum* (Rome: ex Sedibus Sacrae Congregationis pro Gentium Evangelizatione, 1975), pp. 74–75.

5. *Les prêtres noirs s'interrogent* (Paris: Présence Africaine, 1956).

6. In their "Statement of the Bishops of Africa," released in Rome at the end of the 1974 Synod of Bishops, the African hierarchy included this laconic sentence: "Following this idea of mission, the Bishops of Africa and Madagascar consider as being completely out-of-date the so-called theology of adaptation. In its stead, they adopt the theology of incarnation." Cf. *Africa's Bishops and the World Church,* Nairobi, AMECEA Office, p. 20; see note 9 below.

7. These are the so-called AMECEA countries (AMECEA: Association of the Member Episcopal Conferences in Eastern Africa). The statistics given here were released by the AMECEA Documentation Service on the occasion of the fifteenth anniversary of the Association in 1976. See *AMECEA Documentation Service,* Nairobi, no. 7/76/ 1, July 6, 1976.

8. Ibid.

9. This was the official report for the African continent. It was a mimeographed text which was distributed among the Synod participants from Africa. AMECEA Office later published, in a booklet, selected portions from this report, along with other documents of the 1974 Roman Synod. The booklet is entitled: *Africa's Bishops and the World Church: Relevant Documents of the Roman Synod of 1974.* We shall be quoting from this publication, and the references follow its pagination.

10. In what follows, *Report* refers to the excerpts from the Africans' official text (pp. 3–11 of the AMECEA booklet), while *Statement* refers to what is found on pp. 18–21.

11. H. Perkins, H. Daniel, and A. Simandjuntak, "Let My People Go," in *Mission Trends No. 3,* p. 209.

12. *IDOC,* no. 19 (1976), "Ujamaa and Self-reliance," p. 83. See also, in the same place, the declaration of the Evangelical Lutheran Church in Tanzania, July 1974: "Therefore this Church (ELCT) does not see the need for moratorium, because it believes in the Church Universal."

13. Cf. for example, *Report,* p. 11: "The still reigning attitude of the relationship between the Older and the Younger Churches was and is that of a *Father* and *Child.* Following the signs of our times, the relationship should now be that of an Older Brother and his Younger Brother, who is also growing."

14. The following statistics were taken from the diocesan archives of Lilongwe and the diocesan treasurer's reports.

15. See *Acta Pontificalium Operum,* pp. 79–84.

16. Mahbub ul Haq, *The Poverty Curtain: Choices for the Third World* (New York: Columbia University Press, 1976), pp. 71–75.

17. Ibid., passim.

5

Where Are We in African Theology?

Gabriel M. Setiloane (Botswana)

"Where are we in African theology?" is a question that no two persons will answer alike. The answer will depend on the experiences we have had and on the conferences and consultations we have attended.

BANGKOK, 1972

I believe the breakthrough with regard to the traditional western theological world occurred at the World Council of Churches meeting on mission and evangelism at Bangkok in 1972. One could, I suppose, be a little disappointed that it was at a conference on the despised subject of "missions" that we Africans were able to convince people that we have a definite theological orientation requiring recognition. But why not? It is through that branch of ecumenical Christian activity that our continent's religious and theological outlook has been processed and assessed.

It is true also, and for us perhaps shamefully so, that at Bangkok we made an impression on world Christian theological thinking not so much because of the African theology we propounded there, but because of the shock to the ecumenical world that our idea of Moratorium excited. As we defended Moratorium our African theological point of view was expounded and aroused curiosity. It was particularly in Europe that Bangkok excited an unusual response. Seminars and consultations on African theology became the vogue at Evangelische Akademien, and theologians like Goldweiser and Klauspeter Blaser began to write on it.

It was the impact at Bangkok of the African theological view on the ecumenical theological world that made the Faith and Order Commission of the World Council of Churches give it a place at its pre-Assembly Commission Meeting in Accra in 1973. Africa's activity, as you can read in the little pamphlet reporting this conference, was seen as a "challenge." I believe it was the first time in modern ecumenical history that an African statement was said to challenge the theological presuppositions of the world church and to question how they had been reached. Bangkok, as I see it, challenged the understanding and application of the Christian Gospel teaching regarding life in a world community. Although the challenge had been voiced previously on the ecumenical platform—at Geneva in 1966, and at Uppsala in 1968—it had never before come out with a single voice, and from a single continent. This indicated that there was a uniform African preconditioning in Christian approach and outlook. I believe that here in Accra in 1975 this African approach was spelt out theologically.

What was striking for us Africans at the conference was the discovery of the unity of our presuppositions. Whatever our African regional or ecclesiastical origins and professions—French-speaking, English-speaking, West, East, Southern Africa, Catholic, Methodist, Reformed—we could find agreement. (We still can not add "Lutheran," for we do not as yet have African theologians as such coming out of that confessional group.)

JOS, 1975

The next milestone in this development was, in my judgment, the Conference on Christianity in Post-Colonial Africa held in Jos, Nigeria, in August 1975. It is to be regretted that that Conference's report is not yet published. Particularly exciting to me were the views contained in the papers of John Kibicho of Nairobi, made previously in another context by Christian Gaba, which I find I can confirm from my research in Southern Africa, namely, that in the translation of the African names for the Supreme Being, or Deity, to Christian names there has been a devaluation ("diminution," Kibicho calls it) of the concept. This means, for example, that *Modimo,* the Supreme Deity of the Sotho-Tswane, is in fact, a much deeper concept than the Christian translation for God in the Bible or other Christian literature. At Jos, representatives of the western theological worldview are scandalized by this assertion. Of course it was very startling and disconcerting to the superiority-complexed western Christian theologians. But it is the point at which African theology is today—according to Gaba, Kibicho, and myself. Put tauntingly, it says that the western Christian theologians' "God" could easily die because he is so small and human. The Sotho-Tswane God, according to me, the Ngo people's God, according to Gaba, and the Kikuyu people's God, according to Kibicho, could never die, because *IT* has no human limitations and *IT* is so immense, incomprehensible, wide, tremendous, and unique.

THE FOURTH DIMENSION

The area on which I was specifically called upon to make a contribution at Jos was "how indigenous traditional understanding of Being persists in Christian communities in Africa today." I suspect that accounts for the vague title of my assignment at this conference. Here I think it is more worthwhile to attempt to assess the place of the present African theological activity (or revolution, as others might see it) in the history of Christian development. I maintain that African theology offers a fourth dimension to Christianity. (I do not presume to speak for the Asians nor the Latin Americans.) I look at Christian history from the African perspective, and I see from the beginning three dimensions or points of departure. The first is the early church, when theological foundations were laid by the Fathers and the Creeds were developed. It was, of course, all very Hellenistic, with the Roman Empire offering a base. It continued thus until the Byzantine split (A.D. 433), when the eastern church went one way and the western church another. We then had two dimensions. My strong cultural orientation to religion makes me suspicious that the basis of this split was cultural, namely, Greek vs. Roman.

The third dimension came with the Reformation. I see the Reformation, a function of the Renaissance, as a presentation of the Christian Gospel in an indigenous middle and northern European orientation as against the Roman Catholicism of southern Europe, which had exercised cultural, political, intellectual, and spiritual domination for centuries. It was the German in Martin Luther, seeking on behalf of himself and his people a Gospel that could satisfy them, that pitted him against Rome and its influence. No wonder the princes gave him support. Likewise, it is significant that John Calvin belonged to the part of France bordering on Germany. Is it not striking that most of France, being ethnically Latin rather than Germanic, is to this day much more Roman Catholic than Protestant? What I am saying is that the Reformation was a cultural revolution within the Christian church.

It is this cultural western Protestantism that gave rise to the missionary movement of the nineteenth century, and the Christianity that was preached to and assimilated by our fathers was of this type. It was a repetition of the missionizing of central and northern Europe where the indigenous cultures were imposed upon. For almost two centuries this type of Christianity has been passed on to this continent. We have imbibed it all.

But now can we not claim the right to expand our insights and interpretations? Our insights and our interpretations are based on our African-ness. This is the fourth dimension I speak about! From the East and West, North and South of this continent we have expressed in our native dialects and tongues: "We can be truly Christian only to the degree that we are truly and fully African." If we shed our African-ness to be Christians, we are fakes! How many times have we not been driven individually and collectively to declare with Martin Luther: "Here I stand. I can do no other!"

WHERE ARE WE CONTENT-WISE?

So much for our historical position in the development of Christian theological thought. Where are we as regards the content of what we stand for so adamantly? I will only mention the development of African traditional religion as a subject for academic study, with Ibadan and Makarere as leading centers in the 1960s. It is a pity that Bolaji Idowu's book *African Traditional Religion: A Definition* reached the printers so late (London: SCM, 1973; Maryknoll, N.Y.: Orbis Books, 1975). By then John Mbiti had already filled hungry minds in Africa and abroad with his apologetical works, coupling African religion with philosophy and much too simplistically drawing up similarities between African traditional understanding and the Christian faith. At the same time significant contributions were being made, especially in French-speaking Africa. Msgr. Vincent Mulago of Kinshasa, with his *participation vitale,* took Placide Tempel's *force vitale* to its logical and in-digenous conclusion. Fr. Engelbert Mveng of Cameroun worked in a more pragmatic manner, trying to discover African liturgical symbols. We English-speaking Africans have been deprived of the contributions of Pastor Seth Nomanyo of Togo, who pushed African theological challenges into the French-speaking Protestant World.

Content-wise I believe we have now established the legitimacy of the African claim to a unique and different theological point of view within the ecumenical Christian community because of our cultural, geographical, spiritual, social, and temperamental background. We have contributed not a little to the modern acceptance in world theological circles of the view that theology can be done only in context. Theology is a verbalization of an experience of the Divinity at work. Differences in environment mean different experiences of this one and all-pervasive Divinity at work, and therefore different verbalizations of these experiences. These ideas have been accepted.

AFRICAN MYTHS CONCERNING THE ORIGIN OF THINGS

I can speak only from my Southern African experience here, but I should be amazed if my brothers and sisters from other parts of the continent could not corroborate my conclusions. African myths concerning the origin of human beings and things make much more sense than the creation myths of Genesis, which, by the way, were *myths* (i.e., verbalizations of experience) of a particular group of people and have become universalized by Christian teaching.

Human Community

Our myths portray human beings as first existing in community; here we find an expression of the deep African understanding of community. It is this instinctive feel for community that is behind our frustration at Bangkok or elsewhere when our fellow Christians do not do justice to it. I suggest that it is this instinct for community that has made us in the All Africa Conference of Churches see no dichotomy between Christianity and the violence that liberates and establishes a just and harmonious community. When Burgess Carr sees the cross and its violence as ushering in an era of liberated people in a harmonious community, remember he is not talking about western theology, which he knows very well, but saying what he feels in his blood ("guts" the Americans would say!) as an African. Community comes before individuals or groups of individuals. And when we read the Scriptures we find that African theological understanding confirms Christian biblical teaching. Note that I do not say "Christian theological understanding," which we find adulterated in the second and third dimensions mentioned above.

African Concept of Divinity

I have already referred to the views of Gaba and Kibicho to the effect that Christianization of the African understanding of the Supreme Deity has been a devaluation or diminution of the African concept. What I have found is that African Christians do, in fact, Africanize the western Christian concept of God, and thus raise it to the level of their concept of *Modimo* which is much higher. So my sweet old Methodist Manyano woman informant at Lobots says: "We have learnt nothing new about religion from the missionaries. All they have taught us is *tlhabologo*," which means the western civilization and way of life. But we Africans are bringing something to Christianity: a view of Divinity much higher, deeper, and all-pervasive. That is why we quarrel so much with our Christian brothers and sisters at ecumenical gatherings. Our expectations of Christianity are different because we have different presuppositions and different views of the over-ruling, determining Divinity that we together confess in the Christian fold.

THE NEXT STEPS: AN AFRICAN CHRISTOLOGY

If, then, we maintain that we have a higher understanding of Divinity than obtains in western Christian theology, why are we continuing in the Christian fold? I must confess that nowadays I find an ecumenical Bible study session with my western Christian theologian brothers and sisters rather irksome and boring. The question is not only why do we remain in the Christian fold, but, as one young West African Christian said to me in Basel: "Why do we continue to seek to convert to Christianity the devotees of African traditional religion?"

The question as to why we are still in the Christian fold can be answered in different ways. For myself, first, I am like someone who has been bewitched, and I find it difficult to shake off the Christian witchcraft with which I have been captivated. I cannot say I necessarily like where I am. Second, I rationalize my position by taking the view that to be Christian I do not have to endorse every detail of western Christian theology. Instead, it is enough that I confess "Jesus as the Christ of God," i.e., as the unique, unprecedented, and, so far, unrepeated and unsurpassed human manifestation of Divinity. Note here that I do not say "God," as that might restrict. Is not the most ancient Christian Creed, dating from before the advent of the second and third dimensions, simply that Jesus the Christ is the Son of God?

As I see it, the next task of African theology is to grapple seriously with the question of Christology: Who is Jesus? How does he become the supreme human manifestation of the Divinity, the Messiah of Judaism and the *Christos* of Hellenistic Christianity? What does Messiah, or *Christos,* mean in the African context? Some German theologians were scandalized when I suggested that I would look for the Messiah-*Christos* idea in African thinking somewhere in the area of the African *Bongaka** and in the possession of individual persons by Divinity. I still believe that an authentic African Christology lies in that direction, and the future of African theology lies in digging it out and presenting it to the world.

FUTURE TASKS

John V. Taylor has had the temerity to take upon himself the task of writing a book on a theme that should have been treated by an African. He produced *Primal Vision* (Naperville, Ill.: Allenson, 1963), which is still all that most westerners, even theologians, have read on "the Christian presence in African religion." Now he has ventured into pneumatology in his *The Go-Between God* (Philadelphia: Fortress, 1973). I used to think that the theme of God the Holy Spirit needed to be treated from an African theological perspective. Often now I fear that such a treatment would be an endorsement of the Hellenistically-originated trinitarianism of the early church. In the Sotho-Tswane view of *Modimo,* can we honestly differentiate between the

---

*This term refers to an African traditional doctor, often derogatively called "witch-doctor" or "jujuman."

substance of the Divinity and the activities attributed in the western tradition to the Holy Spirit? Pneumatology, so-called, should, from an African perspective, be prepared to look squarely at and even dismantle the western trinitarian formula of Divinity.

Another area that needs our immediate attention, especially in Southern Africa where the advocates of black theology keep taunting us with being politically docile (e.g., Desmond Tutu's article "Black Theology/African Theology—Soul Mates or Antagonists?"), is that of the application of the Gospel to the problems of people in community. I believe that Desmond Tutu, like most of us South Africans, is confused as to which call he feels most deeply—African theology or black theology. Therefore he lays at the wrong door the charge of having been brainwashed to think that western value systems and categories are of universal validity. I maintain that his summons that African theology recover its "prophetic calling" is a western Christian cliché. Black theology, which he professes to embrace, has far too easily employed western Christian norms and terms like "prophetic" without examining their presuppositions.

When African theology ventures into the political area, and I agree with Desmond Tutu that it is high time it did, it will need to clarify not only its theological views regarding the all-pervasive, all-powerful, tremendous, inscrutable Divinity, but also its position toward the one dynamically related community of being—human, animal, and vegetable—and its theology of humankind as a participant in Divinity.

6

Theological Options in Africa Today

José B. Chipenda (Angola)

I remember three specific periods in my short lifetime: when people spoke of "peace"; when they chanted "freedom"; and now when they shout "liberation." The desire for peace came out of the 1939–1945 war that traumatized Europe and shook the world at large. The aspiration for freedom became a genuine demand from people in the colonies who had directly or indirectly helped Europe fight against Hitler. Now Third World people want liberation. They are joined by people who, although living in the so-called First World, share the anguish of the poor of this earth.

It is clear to us that the strategy these countries ought to develop must include control of existing wealth (as the petroleum-producing countries have shown) and a concerted action aimed at protecting the life and interests of their citizens. We very much hope that the liberation struggle will one day end with the elimination of unjust structures.

Liberation is about victims of exploitation. The Prime Minister of Jamaica told us in Nairobi in 1975:

Every weak nation exploited by a strong nation is a victim, every man and woman denied the chance to learn to read and write is a victim, . . . every family that is undernourished is a victim. Not only the unemployed, but every man and woman whose work is underpaid, irregular, or insecure are victims. . . . Every nation that is condemned to comparative poverty while a transnational corporation accumulates profits out of its national resources is a victim. Liberation is about victims, and as long as there is a victim upon the face of the earth, the process of liberation must continue.[1]

THE CHURCH AND LIBERATION

The search for liberation is compelling Christian thinkers to work. Latin American theologians join black Americans and urge Africans and Asians to come along. Although we are all from the Third World, there are some marked differences. Theologians from Latin America are committed intellectuals with imagination and without power, living in countries led by people with power but without imagination; the same can be said of South African black theologians articulating faith and hope in a politically repressive country. Theologians in Asia are eager to be identified with the suffering crowds; black American theologians are trying to force God to be on their side because the whites have wiped out the feeling of the presence of God on earth. It is worth recalling that the death of God theology was preceded by the publication of *The Secular City* and followed by the genesis of black theology.

African theologians realize that our countries are free but they are not liberated. We hear resounding sounds of our national anthems; we rejoice seeing bright and colorful flags in the sky. These are undeniable symbols of our freedom but also a reminder of the unfinished task to liberate Africa from ignorance, poverty, disease, ethnocentrism, and other "isms." We should not confuse freedom with liberation. Freedom is exemption from external control; liberation is the inner ability to handle freedom constructively. In Africa we are familiar with colonial conditions that created domination and institutionalized dependence. This situation of dependence goes on unabated. People with newly acquired power exploit nationals who are weak; by the same token the new elite has its hands tied because of the economic, political, and military support they receive from friends abroad. Students of African affairs again and again speak of neocolonialism. A. Mahleka wrote: "We are no less dependent on European traditions intellectually than we are economically."[2]

The church is no exception. John V. Taylor makes the same point with regard to preaching in Africa: "Christ has been presented as the answer to the questions a white man would ask, the solution to the needs that Western man would feel."[3] We ask ourselves whether there will come a time when neocolonial forces will cease to exist in order to give way to true liberation? Friends visiting us can easily be led to say: Africa is ripe for a theology of liberation. Liberation is needed, but we must guard ourselves from being involved in a purely intellectual game. Our theology should be rooted in the soil that produced it and connected to the commitments that underlie it.

"Liberation" in Africa is a highly political term. Recent history has taught us that theology was unable to liberate Africa. Angola, Mozambique, and Guinea-Bissau achieved their liberation through armed struggle. People in Zimbabwe, Namibia, and South Africa seem to be determined to tread along the same road. Politicians in these countries have the right to say: "If the blood of Christ is the seed of the church, the blood of freedom fighters is the foundation of our selfhood."

There are sufficient grounds for rulers in the newly independent countries to suspect the church. The church, through the centuries, has supported the status quo and stood against change. Three years before the beginning of the armed struggle in Mozambique, the archbishop of Lourenço Marques told his faithful:

Do not allow yourselves to be seduced by fantasies or led astray by evil counselors who feed your dreams of independence or utopias of economic and cultural prosperity. As citizens of the Portuguese nation for the last four centuries, it is within the framework of that nation that you should aspire to material, cultural and moral progress by cooperating honestly with the Portuguese authorities and obeying their orders.[4]

The churches' resistance to change is still fresh in the memory of our leaders. Unless the church show signs of repentance, it cannot be counted on in building new nations.

My contention is that we need a theology that does more than merely make promises; we need a theology that creates communities and impels people into action, a theology that transforms lives, changing hearts of stone into hearts of flesh (Ezek. 11:19).

Some people are already telling us that socialism ought to convince Africans to rely on their human resources:

Socialism, if it does not accomplish the destruction of God, at least it does show that the greater part of the things that are attributed to him are revealed as being fantasies of the priests, pastors, and other professional religious workers.[5]

Here is the challenge for African theologians. Socialism in Africa will try to lead human beings to live dependent only on their own resources. A great number of people in our congregations will fall prey to this message due to our failure to involve the church as a corporate body in the struggle against institutionalized racism. We should put the responsibility on Christians if religion is eclipsed in modern society. It would be more honest for us to accept the blame than to pass judgment on others. Decline in religion may come, not because religion is refuted, but because Christians have made it irrelevant, dull, oppressive, insipid.

SOUTH AFRICA

South Africa is a favorite case study. For better or worse what happens there will affect the whole of Africa. It is in South Africa that you find the most Christians per square kilometer. It is also there where black people are mercilessly victimized by whites.

The government of South Africa by virtue of its apartheid system rules the black population without the blacks having any say in the laws to which they are subject. The white government, which calls itself Christian, admits a high number of deaths in detention, forbids people of different races to marry, treats all Africans in white areas as temporary migrants, reserves skilled jobs for whites, uses the Bantustans as reservoirs of cheap labor, provides the country's people with racially segregated education, gives white South Africans one of the highest standards of living in the world, and silences any person opposed to apartheid.[6]

It is easy to shout "Liberation!" It is quite a different thing to break the chains of oppression and to guarantee

the right of the peasants to the land; the right of the workers to the fruit of their labor; the right of children to education; the right of the ill to medical and hospital attention; the right of [the unemployed] youth to work; the right of students to free education . . . ; the right of women to civil, social, and political equality; the right of the aged to secure old age; the right of intellectuals, artists, and scientists to fight, with their works, for a better world; the right of nations to turn fortresses into schools, and to arm their workers, their peasants, their students, their intellectuals . . . so that they may themselves defend their rights and their destinies.[7]

The South Africa of Albert Luthuli is changing. With the fall of the Portuguese regime, the torch of revolution has been raised by senior leaders in jail or exile and young people and students in schools and streets. The development of black theology no doubt helped prepare the ground from which black consciousness emerged. But we cannot underestimate the zeal and sacrifice of young people and students. They are paying a very high price. Since June 1976, five hundred people have died, many of them school children. Thousands have been detained and some of them have met death in detention. You all know about the death of Steve Biko and the banning of eighteen organizations on October 19, 1977.

THEOLOGICAL GUIDELINES

It is time to ponder anew how to grasp present and future opportunities. The following four guiding principles are most important for African theologians today:

First, we must understand African history and discover how God's hand is moving through it. Our continent has gone through several traumatic experiences. Whether we speak of people or of countries, every time Africans were in contact with people from other continents, the Africans were the losers. Thus the underdevelopment of Africa developed Europe, and the slave trade benefited slave owners in the Americas. What is extraordinary is that suffering has produced endurance and in the most crucial times God visited the downtrodden African people.

Africa and Africans are often found taking part in the redemptive plan of God. In the life of Jesus there are two remarkable instances worth remembering: when still a baby, Jesus came to Egypt as a refugee (Matt. 2:13–15); we were again honored, on the way to Golgotha, when Simon became the only man to help Jesus carry his cross (Matt. 27:32). The planting of the church in Acts of Apostles did not exclude Africa. An Ethiopian traveling from Jerusalem to Gaza met Philip and was baptized (Acts 8:26–39). Throughout church history the contribution of theologians from North Africa has been outstanding. In modern times, in spite of our material poverty, Africa and people of African descent show encouraging promises for the development of an authentic African theology.

Second, it is our responsibility to stress that God's revelation is addressed to all people. The lesson learned from current theological debate, which I hope Third World theologians may help sharpen, is that God is free to choose to whom he reveals himself (Acts 10:35). We can be knowledgeable or ignorant, rich or poor, tall or short, man or woman. For God we are the same. He uses peoples' gifts for his glory and honor.

Here is where the moratorium debate is germane. Our churches have had in their working programs too many items suggested by well-wishers in Europe and North America. To date the only issue discussed in the ecumenical forums that originated in our continent is the call to moratorium. Unfortunately the call was made without a well thought-out program for action. The moratorium issue, however, is as vital today as it was in the 1971 Bangkok World Council of Churches "Salvation Today" Conference and in the 1974 All Africa Conference of Churches Third Assembly in Lusaka. The call to moratorium enabled Africans to ask if it was God's design to make their continent a mission-field for Europeans and people of European descent. The moratorium closes the door on ideas tested elsewhere and opens the way for God's self-disclosure to people of every nation, race, and tribe, and the development of programs tuned to the real needs of people. We are called to respond. Just as in the past God lifted up the poor and satisfied with bread and cup the hungry of many lands, today "He calls us to revolt and fight with Him for what is just and right, to sing and live Magnificat in crowded street and council flat."[8]

Third, our theology should spring from people and go to the people. In this age of mass production, imported manufactured goods, and lavish consumption, it is easy to forget that culture is intrinsic. Amilcar Cabral pointed this out in the process of liberating Guinea-Bissau from Portuguese colonial domination: "Culture is one means of collecting together a group, even a weapon in the struggle for independence."[9] Theology that does not take culture seriously is doomed to failure.

Christian theology in Africa has represented the views of the dominant cultures and created incentives for Africans to fit into the accepted stereotypes. Authority flows from whites to blacks, from missionaries to bishops, to pastors, to deacons, to catechists, to believers. The closer Africans are to the missionaries and European experts, the more important they become in church hierarchy, in institutions of higher learning, and before secular powers. People in villages count only to inflate church membership. Their ideas and ideals are not taken seriously.

A friend of mine once described the different layers through which people are susceptible to change: trivial, technical, value system, and worldview.

The further we are from the deepest level (worldview), the easier the process of change, but the less is the impact on a person's life. On the contrary, the closer to that level, the greater the difficulty, but lasting is the effect on one's life.

This is the task assigned to African theologians. We are called to assess the present and plan for the future:

The future is not something that arrives from foreign parts independent of our own activity, like a change in the weather, but something that depends on us, at every moment; it is the claim of the present on us, the challenge to the human ability to use every moment to the full.[10]

Fourth, theology should help us to realize that faith does not come from doctrine to life. The contrary is true: faith flows from life to doctrine. Consequently our concept of the church must change. The church should not be a place people come to. The church ought to be a movement going to the people. Our pattern of thought must also change: "We need a sound spiritual frame of reference to enable us to go forward confidently to new experiences. The spirit of hope must replace the comfortable certainties of the familiar life we are about to leave behind.[11]

We do not need liberation theology as a label. What we need is true liberation, the courage to break with the past:

We have to break with our mental categories, with the way we relate to others, with our identifying with the Lord, with our cultural milieu, with our social class, . . . with all that stands in the way of real, profound solidarity with those who suffer, in the first place, from misery and injustice.[12]

Living theology in Africa will spring from the witness of Christians committed to building a just, sustainable society, who move away from things to people. Africa has the potentiality to prove that God is always in the midst of people's needs. The work of theologians is to discern God's will for people in a particular situation within a given time. For example, a serious study of letters exchanged between theologians, pastors, and members of the congregation, an analysis of Sunday sermons to ascertain whether they touch current economic, political, and social issues in Africa would be a sound starting point for our theology. In my language people say *kowini keyau* (where you find people, if there is a river you also find a bridge).

CONCLUSION

My contention is that committed theologians should discern the way of God and express it intelligently to people. Those who hear and accept it will not only feed the hungry, give water to the thirsty and warm welcome to the stranger, clothe the naked, visit the sick, and go to see the prisoners in their cells. They will then have strength renewed also to convince friends and foes alike that "man does not live by bread alone."

Theology, whatever name it may take, must express God's judgment on our culture, our race, our class, our arrogance, our preconceived ideas. It must be concerned with justice to all men and women, in all places, at all times and unequivocally affirm that in the presence of God and in Christ people matter, people count.

NOTES

1. James W. Kennedy, *Nairobi 1975* (Cincinnati: Forward Movement Publications, 1976), pp. 65–66.

2. "Debate," *Review of African Political Economy* (London), no. 6 (May–August 1976): 81.

3. Quoted by Manas Buthelezi, "Toward Indigenous Theology in South Africa," *The Emergent Gospel* (Maryknoll, New York: Orbis Books, 1978), p. 57.

4. François Houtart and André Rousseau, *The Church and Revolution* (Maryknoll, New York: Orbis Books, 1971), p. 251.

5. Translated from "Religião: A Submissão do Homem," *Tempo,* no. 372 (November 20, 1977).

6. PCR background paper on South Africa by Alexander Kirby.

7. A quotation from Fidel Castro's speech to the National Assembly of Cuba in Joseph Petulla, *Christian Political Theology* (Maryknoll, New York: Orbis Books, 1972), p. 136.

8. *Theology in Action,* An East Asia Christian Conference workshop report, September 1–18, 1972, ed. Oh Jae Shik and J. England, p. 28.

9. Amilcar Cabral,*Return to the Source* (New York: Africa Information Service, 1973), p. 59.

10. Milan Machovec, *A Marxist Looks at Jesus* (Philadelphia: Fortress Press, 1976), p. 88.

11. Jürgen Moltmann, "What Kind of Unity?" *Lausanne 77, Fifty Years of Faith and Order* (Geneva: WCC, 1977), p. 40.

12. Gustavo Gutiérrez, "A Spirituality of Liberation," *A Reader in Political Theology,* ed. Alistair Kee (London: SCM, 1974), p. 97.

7

The Task of African Theologians

Bishop T. Tshibangu (Zaire)

The general theme of this meeting is timely and pertinent: theology and Christian commitment in the present situation of Africa. Theology is actually a scientific or scholarly act of commitment. Defining it in precise and dynamic terms, we can say that it is "the science dealing with the divine destiny of humanity." This science is grounded on *God's revelation in Christ* and it is also based on *deep, thoroughgoing knowledge of human beings and the factors that condition their lives.* Such knowledge comes to us from philosophy, the human sciences, and the basic sciences dealing with the universe.

A great step was taken in the Final Statement issued by the Ecumenical Dialogue of Third World Theologians in Dar es Salaam (1976). It stressed the need for Christian theology to develop along lines other than those exemplified in western tradition. This brought to a successful conclusion the efforts to legitimize the elaboration of a native African theology.

STAGES IN THE ELABORATION OF AFRICAN THEOLOGY

Let me briefly mention some of the high points in the effort to elaborate an African line of thought in theology.

One of the high points in African consciousness-raising found expression in the anthology entitled *Des prêtres noirs s'interrogent.* [1] A similar initiative can be found in the work of the African Culture Society (S.A.C.), which is sponsored by the group *Présence Africaine* under the direction of Alioune Diop. For several years it has been sponsoring efforts to promote African religious thought and theological research in the strict sense.

This group helped to organize a meeting of African philosophers and theologians during the Second Congress of Black Writers and Artists, which took place in Rome in 1959.[2] It also organized a study poll of African Christian intellectuals in 1962 while Vatican II was in session. The chief highlights of these reflections were then published in 1963 in the volume entitled *Personnalité africaine et catholicisme.*[3] S.A.C. has also organized two colloquiums on African religion. The first, held in Abidjan in 1961, dealt with African religions in general.[4] The second, held in Cotonou in 1970, dealt with African religions as a source of civilized values.[5] In September 1977 another meeting was held in Abidjan under the sponsorship of S.A.C. and with the support of UNESCO.

A third set of initiatives has been sponsored by the All Africa Conference of Churches. In 1969 it sponsored a meeting of African theologians at the University of Ibadan.[6]

A fourth set of initiatives has been sponsored by the Catholic Theology Faculty of Kinshasa. In 1959 its teachers and students tackled the basic question of the possibility of an indigenous African theology. The issue crystallized in 1968 during the sessions of the Fourth Theological Seminar in Kinshasa. Several communications of that seminar were particularly noteworthy: they dealt with the problem of an African theology in the light of Vatican II, world theology, and African theology.[7]

Since 1967 the Kinshasa Theology Faculty has also conducted a Center for the Study of African Religions (CERA). This active Center publishes *Cahiers des Religions Africaines* twice yearly. Since 1977 it has also published *Revue Africaine de Théologie.*[8]

All these initiatives have brought us to the point where we are now. The possibility of an African theology is no longer a question in principle. The problem now is to work out this theology in a real and effective way.

This task imposes certain conditions on African theologians, who must now channel their theological effort and commitment in a sound and organized way.

OBLIGATIONS OF AFRICAN THEOLOGIANS

1. African theologians must be fully aware of the fact that their Catholic work calls for real spiritual commitment. There can be no theological effort without commitment. One must raise questions about one's own life and about the spiritual destiny of the people with whom one is associated. This presumes a real ability to ask fundamental questions. The theologian must be a person of deep faith and a solidly metaphysical life. The theologian cannot do any useful, worthwhile or relevant work unless he or she accepts personal involvement in the theory and practice of life while making every effort to maintain intellectual and moral sincerity and scientific objectivity.

The example of great theologians in the past and present day confirms this fact: e.g., St. Augustine, St. Thomas Aquinas, K. Barth, K. Rahner, H. de

Lubac, and P. Tillich. They became great theologians because they tackled deep metaphysical questions and committed themselves wholly to their task. They accepted the demands of thought and action imposed by their own concrete situation. African theologians must be aware of this obligation to commit themselves to the situation and the issues of their time and milieu.

2. The African theologian must be equally conscious of the intellectual demands imposed by theological work. As I pointed out above, theology is a scientific discipline grounded on knowledge of revelation and its content and also based on knowledge of the reality of human beings and the universe. This means, first of all, that the theologian must possess theological knowledge in the strict and formal sense. Vatican I defined it thus: "Reason illumined by faith which, with the help of God, seeks to gain a deeper understanding of the mysteries. It does this by learning all it can by way of analogy from nature, by exploring the relationship between the different mysteries themselves, and by considering the ultimate end of humanity."[9] It also means that the theologian must strive to possess the deepest and most accurate scientific knowledge of humanity and the factors that condition it.

If African theologians want to be rigorous and to be taken seriously, they must be fully conscious of these intellectual obligations. They must be able to go beyond simple commitment. For even if the latter is correct, it may be intuitive and difficult to formulate. Theologians must be able to propose matters in a valid and convincing way to other human minds.

3. The third obligation imposed on African theologians is that of their own social commitment. They cannot live as beings apart because they must bear responsibility for their own personal destiny and that of others. They must be involved in their community and their social participation must be as active as possible.

This participation will put them in a position to gain a deeper grasp of the cultural issues posed by their community and the living conditions of their contemporaries. It will help them to pay due attention to the questions raised by the appearance of new values in a given society, by its characteristic perception and conception of things and events (i.e., its typical epistemological viewpoint), and by the facts and events related to its socio-cultural evolution and development. If Christian thinkers are not wholly involved in the ongoing process of their society, they can hardly claim to be authentic African theologians.

4. Closely associated with this overall commitment is the obligation of ecclesial involvement. African theologians must live in fidelity to ecclesial truth. They must of course possess discernment so that they can know exactly what is defined as certain truth by the church. But they must equally cultivate courage and take risks in exploring, pondering, and expressing the theological conclusions that derive from their authentic research.

The churches of which African theologians are members also have a role to play. They must have confidence in their theologians unless there is good reason to feel otherwise. They must support them on the intellectual level and the level of religious practice, encouraging their research, avoiding hasty condemnations, and being careful not to voice fears and reservations for purely a priori reasons.

If the above conditions are met, African theologians can undertake the research that faces us with a real chance of handling it successfully.

TASKS TO BE UNDERTAKEN

In his overall study of the questions facing African theologians today Professor N. Mushete indicates that a wide variety of questions require attention.[10] Some have to do with the spirit and traditional values of African religion. Some have to do with national and cultural integration; some have to do with current social development. Some face the Christian conscience in general, but have not yet been resolved by the churches.

1. Insofar as the spirit and traditional values of African religion are concerned, we do well to recall the essential elements of African religion. H. Aguessy describes them as follows:

African religions are basically characterized by the radical flaw or lack that marks the universe. In this spirit they seek to render worship to a force or a supreme being through the mediation of the realm of the ancestors, who guarantee the integrity and vitality of the community. This effort is grounded on certain principles that are at work from one end of Africa to the other:
—the unity, community, and hierarchy of orders and beings in the universe;
—the link of solidarity between the ancestors and their descendants;
—the reincarnation of deserving ancestors;
—the indissoluble link between the visible and the invisible and, more specifically, between the dead, spirits, and the living;
—the primordial importance of the act of "living."[11]

V. Mulago examines various elements that appear and concludes that the cultural ensemble of ideas, sentiments, and rites is based on the following:

a. belief in two worlds, the visible and the invisible;
b. belief in the communitarian and hierarchical character of these two worlds;
c. interaction between these two worlds, since the transcendence of the invisible world does not erase its immanence;
d. belief in a supreme being, the Creator and Father of all that exists.[12]

These basic principles entail certain values. Described in summary form, they are bound up with: *(a)* Cultic veneration of the ancestors; *(b)* firm belief in the existence and power of mystical forces that operate in the universe and on human beings and that give direction to the destiny of both; *(c)* a vitalist philosophy which finds particular expression in the realm of marriage. There is a particular conception of the goal of marriage, and certain rules flow from that; *(d)* an intensely felt sense of solidarity between the members of a family, a community and, today, a nation. This solidarity has a real impact on the organization of religious life in the strict sense, on societal life in general, and on relationships between the members of the nation.

The question facing theologians is whether these values are to be maintained and revitalized as they now stand, or whether they are to be given a new form or even rectified.

Insofar as the values received from Christianity are concerned, the question is whether African theologians should not link them with the data of traditional African religion in order to resolve any problems. This would entail such matters as the following: *(a)* awareness of sin and the meaning of sin: the notion of moral good and evil and the criteria involved; *(b)* sacramental efficacy in relation to the ritual efficacy seen in traditional religion; *(c)* belief in the real existence of spirits of the dead and their influence on the living.

An example of such a study is that by the Nigerian theologian, Modupe Oduyoye, entitled *The Vocabulary of Yoruba Religious Discourse.*[13] The author examines certain features from a philological and linguistic point of view and then compares them with features of the Christian teaching. Some of the data examined are: *(a)* the notion and representation of *divinity* among the Yoruba; *(b)* the understanding and representation of *sin* and *repentance* on the "psychophysical" level, and the resultant notions of *pardon* and *absolution* for repented faults; *(c)* the notion and description of *sacrifice* in the Yoruba religion; *(d)* the meaning and understanding of *prayer.*

Oduyoye completes his study with an examination of some of the mystical or metaphysical representations dealing with *time, the origin of humanity, life, and death.*

Insofar as the relationship of basic African philosophical and religious concepts to the present moment in history is concerned, one can find discussions in the works of such people as Rev. J. Mbiti[14] or Abbot V. Mulago.[15]

In the 1968 Colloquium on African Theology at Kinshasa a whole program of research was spelled out in detail. Focused around the *idea of life,* four areas of investigation were mapped out: (1) life; (2) intermediaries; (3) humanity; (4) the milieu where human beings participate in life.

2. The general evolution of the African situation poses many questions to theologians. There are questions concerning one's personal attitude. A theology of concrete socio-political commitment is needed if we are to

appreciate values that are in a constant state of flux, determine the proper criteria for passing moral judgments on new social phenomena, and morally evaluate the means to be used in pursuing the aims of development.

These questions have a large socio-political dimension, which is of particular concern to *black theology*. The latter takes in a whole range of questions raised by various efforts and topics now under discussion: e.g., the quest for full political independence and liberation; the proper definition of the goal of development and its material and moral conditions; the specific nature of African anthropology; the proper direction for the African cultural system to take and the proper evaluation of its various manifestations in philosophy, literature, art, music, drama, and the plastic arts.[16]

3. African theologians must also help to clarify and eventually resolve the theological questions that have not yet been solved by the churches.

In some instances an African approach may reveal that the questions are *false questions* or questions *badly framed.* In other instances it will have to offer some contribution toward the ultimate solution.

Besides more specific questions, we can suggest the importance of such major problems as the following: *(a)* the ecumenical problem of encounter between the Christian churches; *(b)* the problem of rapport between Christian principle and non-Christian religions; *(c)* the problem of the relationship between "nature" or the "universe" and the supernatural.

As one can readily see, the program of research to be undertaken is a vast one. We must organize theological effort and commitment on a large scale if we are to undertake the program and carry it out successfully.

NOTES

1. *Des prêtres noirs s'interrogent* (Paris: Présence Africaine, 1956).

2. See *Synthèse de la sous-Commission de théologie,* II Congress of Black Writers and Artists (Rome, 1959), *Présence Africaine* 24–25, no. 5, pp. 407–08.

3. *Personnalité africaine et catholicisme* (Paris, 1963).

4. *Colloque sur les religions* (Paris, 1962).

5. *Les religions africaines comme source de valeurs de civilisation* (Paris: Présence Africaine, 1972).

6. *Pour une théologie africaine,* coll. Clé (Yaoundé, 1969).

7. See *Revue du Clergé Africain* 24, nos. 2 and 3–4 (1969).

8. Address: Faculté de Théologie Catholique à Kinshasa-Limeté, Zaire.

9. Vatican I: "Ratio fide illustrata, cum sedulo, pie et sobrie quaerit, aliquam Deo dante mysteriorum intelligentiam eamque fructuosissimam assequitur: tum ex eorum, quae naturaliter cognoscit, analogia, tum e mysteriorum ipsorum nexu inter se et cum fine hominis ultimo."

10. See N. Mushete, *La théologie en Afrique, d'hier à aujourd'hui* (Kinshasa, 1977).

11. H. Aguessy, in *Les religions africaines comme source de valeurs de civilisation,* p. 27.

12. V. Mulago, ibid., p. 116.

13. M. Oduyoye, *The Vocabulary of Yoruba Religious Discourse* (Ibadan, 1971).

14. J. Mbiti, *African Religions and Philosophy* (New York: Praeger, 1969).

15. V. Mulago, *La religion traditionnelle des Bantu* (Kinshasa: CERA, 1975). See also M. Buthelezi, "Toward Indigenous Theology in South Africa," in *The Emergent Gospel: Theology from the Underside of History* (Maryknoll, N.Y.: Orbis Books, 1977), pp. 56–75.

16. B. Moore et al., *The Challenge of Black Theology in South Africa* (Atlanta: John Knox Press, 1974); M. Buthelezi, "African Theology and Black Theology: A Search for Theological Method," in H. J. Becken, *Relevant Theology for Africa* (Durban: Lutheran Publishing House, 1973), p. 20f.

PART TWO

THEOLOGICAL SOURCES

The Bible is the basic source of African theology, because it is the primary witness of God's revelation in Jesus Christ. No theology can retain its Christian identity apart from Scripture. The Bible is not simply a historical book about the people of Israel; through a re-reading of this Scripture in the social context of our struggling for our humanity, God speaks to us in the midst of our troublesome situation. This divine Word is not an abstract proposition but an event in our lives, empowering us to continue in the fight for our full humanity [see Chapters 8 and 9]. . . .

The God of history speaks to all peoples in particular ways. In Africa the traditional religions are a major source for the study of the African experience of God. The beliefs and practices of the traditional religions in Africa can enrich Christian theology and spirituality [see Chapter 10]. . . .

The independent churches have developed through their long history a type of worship, organization, and community life rooted in African culture and touching the daily life of the people [see Chapter 11]. . . .

For Africans there is unity and continuity between the destiny of human persons and the destiny of the cosmos. African anthropology and cosmology are optimistic. The salvation of the human person in African theology is the salvation of the universe. In the mystery of Incarnation Christ assumes the totality of the human and the totality of the cosmos [see Chapters 12 and 13].

—*Final Communiqué, Pan-African Conference of Third World Theologians*

8

The Biblical Basis for
Present Trends in African Theology

John Mbiti (Kenya)

In the last ten years or so, it has become fashionable to talk about "African theology," "African Christian theology," "Christian African theology," "*Theologia Africana*," etc.; the market is now flooded with articles that try to define these terms. Some people are even afraid that any of these terms connotes a pollution or syncretism of theology (as they understand it in the western traditions of the church). Others question whether Africans are capable of producing anything that could be termed "theology." Still others think that ready-made theology has to be imported to Africa and simply "indigenized there." I have no wish to enter into a debate with any of these positions. I will use the term "African theology" in this paper, without apology or embarrassment, to mean theological reflection and expression by African Christians.

The Bible has been translated in part or in full into nearly six hundred African languages[1] and has become the basis of African Christianity, even though the literacy rate ranges from about 7 percent to 85 percent of the population in African countries. It may seem to be a contradiction that while African Christianity is biblically grounded, many of the 185 million Christians on our continent today cannot read. The Bible is a closed book for those who cannot read it: they only hear it read or recited to them; nevertheless, through the translation and increasing use of the Scriptures the biblical world has been integrated with that of the traditional African world at all levels. The Bible is distributed extremely widely throughout what we may call "Christian Africa," i.e., the southern two-thirds of the continent and Madagascar.[2] Its potential and actual influence in shaping African theology and Christianity is tremendous.

There are three main areas of African theology today: written theology, oral theology, and symbolic theology. Written African theology is the privilege of a few Christians who have had considerable education and who generally articulate their theological reflection in articles and (so far few) books, mostly in English, French, German, or another European languages. Oral theology is produced in the fields, by the masses, through song, sermon, teaching, prayer, conversation, etc. It is theology in the open air, often unrecorded, often heard only by small groups, and generally lost to libraries and seminaries. Symbolic theology is expressed through art, sculpture, drama, symbols, rituals, dance, colors, numbers, etc.

My paper will confine itself to written theology. Since about 1960, a considerable literature, mainly articles, has built up. In preparation for this paper I was able to draw upon some three hundred such articles and books by African theologians, most of which were published in the last five years or so. Written African theology is at present very much on the increase. It would be extremely valuable to have a bibliography of this literature, so that scholars and students could find their way.[3]

We shall now look at a number of areas in which the Bible is the basis of theological reflection for African Christians.

BIBLICAL THEOLOGY, HISTORY, AND RELIGION

We can discern some emerging trends from recent and contemplated publications. In 1968 Professor Kwesi Dickson, one of Africa's leading biblical scholars, published the first several volumes entitled *The History and Religion of Israel*,[4] which, though intended primarily for school use, are based on sound scriptural scholarship. These writings arise from Dickson's conviction that "it would be inexcusable to fail to give biblical teaching pride of place in this quest" for African theology.[5]

Professor Harry Sawyerr published in the same year his *Creative Evangelism*, which is also biblically grounded.[6] Sawyerr pleads for what he calls "sound doctrinal teaching" and liturgy in the "new encounter" of the Gospel with Africa. In its approach the book is very traditional and Anglican both in "doctrine" and "liturgy." Sawyerr has maintained his biblical emphasis, dealing with such themes as Paul's missionary work, sacrifice and worship, sin and forgiveness, salvation and God.[7]

Biblical Revelation and African Beliefs, edited by Dickson and P. Ellingworth, was first published in 1969.[8] The title expresses the importance African theologians intended to attach to biblical scholarship when they met in Ibadan, Nigeria, in January 1966, where the papers for this book were read. However, the contents of the book have very little biblical material, except for one essay on eschatology.

My own *New Testament Eschatology in an African Background* appeared in 1971, focusing on the question of eschatology and relating New Testament insights with African concepts.[9] On this same theme I have also published shorter articles.[10]

The late Dr. Byang Kato's *Theological Pitfalls in Africa* appeared in 1975.[11] It is replete with scriptural references and is intended to "guard against the destructive effect of heretical ideas," as Dr. Billy Graham tells us in the Foreword (p. 5). Kato intended that "the primary purpose of this book is to sound an alarm and warn Christians on both sides of the argument concerning the dangers of universalism" (p. 16). He felt that "the stage is well set for universalism in Africa" (p. 11) and went on to list the "ten significant factors (. . .) encouraging and fostering these trends." The author launched a most bitter attack on myself (pp. 56ff. et passim), Professor E. B. Idowu (pp. 96ff. et passim), and ecumenism (pp.129ff.). At the end he proposed ten points on how to safeguard what he called "biblical Christianity in Africa" (pp. 181ff.).

Dr. Kato's passionate attack on fellow theologians and the ecumenical movement arose partly out of insufficient understanding on his part. I had the opportunity of discussing with him some of the issues, on December 9, 1975. At the end he apologized to me for having unjustifiably attacked me and promised to rewrite and change the relevant parts of his book. Ten days later, on December 19, 1975, Dr. Kato drowned on the shores of the Indian Ocean in Kenya. I learned a year later that before his tragic death Dr. Kato had actually written the parts he promised to revise, and the publisher of the book undertook to incorporate them into subsequent printings of the book. I give this personal note about Dr. Kato as an indication that he had no malicious intention in this book; he apologized to me and in the same spirit I am sure he would have made personal apologies to those others whom he had attacked. His death was certainly a major loss for African theology . . . and may God rest his soul in peace.

Other biblical publications by African scholars have begun to come out through the Daystar Press in Ibadan. Modupe Oduyoye (manager of Daystar Press) published *When Kings Ruled and Prophets Spoke in Israel* (1977), which deals with the biblical account "from the call of Samuel to the fall of Samaria." This is a valuable book for schools by one of Africa's leading linguists. Other current books from the same press include: *Essentials of Bible Knowledge* by S. L. Fawole; *The People of the Book* by M. Oduyoye (dealing with the life and religion of the Jewish people before and after the Babylonian Exile); *Old Testament History and Religion* by Daniel Wambutda (dealing with the period from the establishment of the monarchy to the fall of the northern kingdom); *Cry Justice: Conversations with Old Testament Prophets* by Bishop F. O. Segun; and *The Secret School of Jesus* by J. A. Ajibola. (Other titles are cited below.) These publications give greater weight to the Old Testament than to the New, and their immediate readership is mostly school, college, and seminary students. African Christians have much interest in Old Testament accounts of Jewish cultural, religious, and political life, and these books are certainly very helpful in increasing our understanding of the Bible.

There are some important developments in the area of Christology, as summarized in a paper by Kofi Appiah-Kubi at the first consultation of African and Asian theologians, held at the Ecumenical Institute, Bossey, Switzerland, in June 1976. He incisively observed that the concepts of Christology of traditional African Christians are practical, dynamic, living, and based on real life experience. Their concepts of Christology, he says, revolve around genealogy and the rites of passage—birth, baptism, Eucharist, and death. Such titles as Mediator, Redeemer, Savior, Liberator, and Healer are pregnant with meaning for these indigenous African Christians.[12]

There are also short christological studies by Gabriel Setiloane[13] and myself.[14] John Pobee has a forthcoming book on Christology. Since he is a New Testament scholar, we can expect a scriptural basis for this work.

COMMENTARIES AND DEVOTIONAL LITERATURE

Commentaries and devotional literature form another vast field, and we can touch on it only briefly to indicate some emerging trends. No doubt there are many publications circulating locally that are not widely known.

In 1966, (now) Bishop E. Mshana published *Fidia ya Wengi: Marko no Injili Yake,* a Swahili commentary on the Gospel of Mark.[15] Other recent publications include *Studies in Second Corinthians 1–6* by Osad Imasogie [16] and *The Epistle to the Ephesians* by S. T. Ola Akande.[17]

There have been many Bible studies given at various gatherings of Christians, a few of which are summarized in published forms. For example, at the inauguration of the All Africa Conference of Churches (AACC) in Kampala in 1963, Bible studies were given on "Freedom and Unity in Christ."[18] These addressed themselves to several themes, including freedom, unity, the Body and the Trinity, worship, ethics, politics, and social relationships. Professor Jacques Ngally published "Bible Studies from an African Perspective" in the *AACC Bulletin* of January–February 1975;[19] here he presented what the AACC Theology Department prepared for the Fifth Assembly of the World Council of Churches in Nairobi in November–December 1975. These all too brief studies covered "the revelation of the Son of God" as "Christ crucified" and Jesus' mission to "liberate" and "unite." In another article, "Jesus Christ and Liberation in Africa: a Bible Study," Professor Ngally gave further meditations on Jesus and liberation from disease, hunger, wealth, tyrants, legalism, tribalism, and racism.[20]

I understand that Edward Fashole-Luke is attempting to produce an African commentary (or series of commentaries) on the Bible. At this moment I have no up-to-date information about this grand (but not new) idea.

In the devotional field we have Bolaji Idowu, *Job: A Meditation on the Problem of Suffering*;[21] Zecharias Fomum, *God's Love and Forgiveness*;[22] and J. S. Mbiti, *The Voice of Nine Bible Trees*.[23]

THE BIBLE AND AFRICAN PREACHING

I have mentioned "oral theology" as a major concern in African theological process. The Bible is the basis of African preaching, as we can all testify from our own experiences. However, we have extremely little documentation on how and to what extent the Bible is used in preaching. There are a few indications, but these come only from overseas scholars and not from African theologians.

Dr. Harold Turner studied the uses of the Bible by the Church of the Lord (Aladura), the results of which he published in *Profile Through Preaching* (Edinburgh: Edinburgh House Press, 1965). This is a very revealing study, though out of one case we cannot formulate conclusions for the whole of Africa. Turner's investigations showed "that both independent and older African churches . . . all make greater use of James than of most other parts of the New Testment," and the Aladura church "made use of the whole Bible in its preaching." He also observed that "many portions of the Scriptures that we tend to pass over or ignore are taken seriously by African Christians."[24]

Horst Buerkle has made important observations: that for the African preacher, "the persons and events of both Testaments are always near to the preacher and his congregation, as if they were part of their own time"; that "the attempt to reproduce biblical history through illustrations drawn from local African scenes is a common practice"; and that "the African preacher confronts us with the relevance of the symbol."[25]

Another expatriate investigator of African preaching, R. Albrecht, observed that among the Haya Christians (Tanzania), "sin" occupied 21 percent of the sermons. Other topics included God's work of creation (10 percent), various attributes of God (10 percent), God's love and grace (15 percent), and God's presence through "new means" (18 percent).[26]

My own limited investigation of African sermons clearly indicates that the whole Bible is used and that links are frequently made between the biblical world and African heritage as well as contemporary life. The Christian hymns strongly reflect biblical knowledge and teaching; theological views are also expressed through song and dance.

But a great deal remains to be done by African scholars regarding the Bible in African preaching, hymnology, liturgics, and the arts.

THE BIBLE AND AFRICAN THEOLOGY IN GENERAL

There are many other areas of theological reflection in which the Bible is taken as the basis. We can mention a few examples. In the field of *ethics*, we have the article of Bishop Manas Buthelezi, "Theological Grounds for an Ethic of Hope," in which he examines the important element of hope in the Gospel, demonstrating that "the Christian ethic is essentially an ethic of hope."[27] Others who have written on Christian ethics include B. Bujo[28] and N. Tese,[29] both relating African morality to the Christian faith. E.C.O. Ilogu has written on Christian ethics in the Nigerian context;[30] Bishop J. Kibira on grace and law in the pastoral context;[31] O. U. Kalu on ethical questions of development[32] and on corruption in African countries.[33]

The question of *sin* is also receiving attention, viewed partly from biblical and partly from African perspectives and background. We mention the articles of Harry Sawyerr on sin,[34] Harriet Sibisi Ngubane on "purity,"[35] and S. Mbonyinkebe on sin in central Africa.[36]

The theme of *salvation* has, through evangelism, been made almost synonymous with the Gospel. African theologians are beginning to examine this concept. The tendency is to look at both the scriptural basis for salvation and African concepts relating to it. Contributions have come from, among others, Professor Sawyerr,[37] Dr. K. Enang, who relates salvation to community,[38] O. Bimwenyi, who relates the discussion to the departed as well,[39] and J. S. Mbiti, who discusses the meaning of "Our Savior" and "salvation" in African contexts.[40]

The Christian approach to health and the practice of healing are beginning to receive serious attention from scholars, although for a long time healing has been fully integrated into the life of many Independent churches. Although it was overwhelmingly dominated by expatriates, the "Upumulo Consultation on the Healing Ministry of the Church" in September 1967 was a major recognition of African interest in the Christian dimension of health and healing.[41] Kofi Appiah-Kubi has, more recently, begun to do serious research in this area and we await his findings.[42] The theology of Christian healing lends itself readily to scriptural basis.

The theme of *liberation* has become very popular among African theologians, especially in Southern Africa and in the All Africa Conference of Churches. One must, however, point out that even though there is much biblical basis for this theme, African discussion of liberation has so far continued without or with only a few scriptural references.[43] This neglect in Africa of the biblical backing of the theology of liberation is a very alarming omission that calls urgently for correction; otherwise that branch of African theology will lose its credibility.

Another growing discussion is on the relation between *church and state* in the African setting. The urgency of this debate has intensified in recent years, as the first generation of independent African political leadership began to give way to another and sometimes more militant (if not military) leadership. The latter sometimes feels threatened by other sources of power, of which the church is or could be one. There is a growing amount of literature, with contributions by Africans like Bishop Desmond Tutu on the question of church and nation,[44] Bishop Eliewaha Mshana on nationalism,[45] Bishop Henry Okullu on church and politics,[46] Bishop C. Mwoleka on his support for "Ujamaa" socialism in Tanzania,[47] Zaire's bishops' wrestling with the church and authenticity,[48] etc. Some of the discussion has sound biblical basis, but some makes no direct reference to biblical insights.

We have to recognize the value and use of the Bible in the *formation and identity of many African Independent churches.* Their founders have used the Bible as justification and inspiration; the beliefs of these churches are normally formulated on a biblical basis; they use the Bible for the legitimation of their existence and identity; and it is often the Bible that gives them the basis for establishing close ties with the African traditional world.[49] Here, then, we see practical theology arising out of the use of the Scriptures in African Christianity and sustaining a continent-wide movement that has been labelled "renewal" and "African Reformation."

There is a vast field of theology in relation to *African religions.* Literature by Africans is mushrooming on the relationship between Christian faith and the African religious heritage. This area deserves a separate full treatment. Trained African theologians—in theological seminaries and departments of religious studies—pastors in the villages, and the vast number of ordinary African Christians are all showing great interest in this topic in one way or another. A few feel that African religiosity is demonic and should not be allowed to enter the life of the Christians or the church. Some regard African religion as having prepared the ground for the ready and rapid acceptance of the Christian faith. Some wish to revive and retain African religion in place of any other religion. The majority are at the practical and pastoral levels where Christians live with the realities of both the Christian faith and their traditional religiosity. I have not yet seen a serious and exhaustive academic work done on this relationship between the Christian faith and African traditional religiosity. There are innumerable articles and reports and consultations; and there are books and articles by African scholars on African religion itself—many of which are valuable and relevant. But the theological examination of this inter-religious relationship has yet to be done. It is to be hoped that the Scriptures will play their full role in that exposition. So far there is little use of the Bible in the debate.[50]

CONCLUDING REMARKS

My topic is open ended: there is no real conclusion to it since it addresses itself to an ongoing process of African theological work. That the Bible is playing a major role in African theology there is no doubt, as we have attempted to illustrate in this paper. It exerts greater impact on oral theology than is apparent in the extremely limited published material. Any viable theology must and should have a biblical basis, and African theology has begun to develop on this foundation. Edward Fashole-Luke is right in reminding us that "the Bible is the basic and primary source for the development of African Christian theologies."[51] Nothing can substitute for the Bible. However much African cultural-religious background may be close to the biblical world, we have to guard against references like "the hitherto unwritten 'African Old Testament' "[52] or sentiments that see a final revelation of God in the African religious heritage.[53]

Equally serious is the tendency for some theological debates to be propagated without full or clear biblical grounding. We have already cited the case of the theology of liberation. To this we could add the "moratorium" debate; the plea made by Father Charles Nyamiti for the "adaptation" and "application" of (primarily western) theology to make it African theology or "the basis" for it;[54] the "Ujamaa theology" based on "African socialism, advocated by theological student C. Lymo;[55] so-called "relevant theology" being propagated in South Africa, which is primarily a ready-made European theology turned into a consumption commodity for Africans;[56] and various discussions of the relationship between the Christian faith and African religious heritage. In these areas, biblical grounding has been either weak or lacking altogether.

Some of us are getting tired of seeing all sorts of articles and references under the big banner: AFRICAN THEOLOGY (or some similar wording). The substance of these articles often turns out to be advice on how African theology should be done, where it should be done, who should do it, what it should say, ad infinitum. Some of these self-made theological advisers, whether they be African or foreign, have little or nothing to produce beyond their generous advice; and others want to play the role of theological engineers who meticulously sabotage spontaneous theological output by African Christians.

Theology is not produced by advice alone, and those who have enough advice to give about it should first use their advice for themselves; let them produce theological works and let these works speak for themselves. I say this to both African and overseas Christians. We are tired of being advised. Let the Bible be our human adviser and the Holy Spirit our Divine Adviser. African theology is being produced, and it will continue to be produced, irrespective of what may be done to muffle it. We must move with the times and get on with the work of theologizing. After all, we have all the tools and sources necessary for the fulfillment of this task. Like the African proverb that says that "the eyes of the frog do not stop the giraffe from drinking water in the pond," neither the critical, sceptical, or advice-filled eyes of others should prevent creative theologians from engaging in theological output.

I discern remarkable signs in the development of African theology. In this development the Bible is playing a crucial role, even if not in every case. African Christianity has the Bible at its forefront, and the Bible is shaping much of its development both explicitly and implicitly. Oral theology, which is largely a prerequisite to written theology, is also strongly grounded on the Scriptures. As long as African theology keeps close to the Scriptures, it will remain relevant to the life of the church in Africa and it will have lasting links with the theology of the church universal. African theologians must give even more attention to the Bible than is sometimes the case. As long as we keep the Bible close to our minds and our hearts, our theology will be viable, relevant, and of lasting service to the church and glory to the Lord to whom be honor, dominion, and power unto the ages of ages. Amen.

NOTES

1. Information available at the time indicated that by mid-1972 the Gospels were translated into 561 African languages, the New Testament into 310, and the whole Bible into 138. See D. B. Barrett et al., "Frontier Situations for Evangelism in Africa, 1972," in *The Gospel and Frontier Peoples,* ed. R. Pierce Beaver (Pasadena, Calif.: William Carey Library, 1973), pp. 233–310.

2. The United Bible Societies reported that in 1975 they distributed a total of 14,371,000 Bibles, Testaments, and other portions of the Scriptures in Africa. This was slightly more than what they distributed in the whole of Europe (East and West), namely, 13,785,000. These figures do not include distribution through other agents. See *Bulletin: United Bible Societies, World Annual Report 1975,* nos. 102/103, First and Second Quarter 1976. An interesting but brief article, "How the Bible is Used in Africa," by J. M. Mobogori, appears in *African Challenge: Major Issues in African Christianity,"* ed. K. Y. Best (Nairobi: Transafrica Publishers, 1975), pp. 111–18.

3. There is a general and valuable bibliography, though overwhelmed by expatriate and overseas authors: *Christianity in Tropical Africa: A Selective Annotated Bibliography,* by P. E. Ofori (Nendeln, Liechtenstein: KTO Press, 1977).

4. K. A. Dickson, *The History and Religion of Israel* (London: Darton, Longman and Todd, 1968–). Also in the New Testament field, *The Story of the Early Church as Found in the Acts of the Apostles* (London: Darton, Longman and Todd, 1976).

5. K. A. Dickson, "Towards a Theologia Africana," in *New Testament Christianity for Africa and the World*, ed. M. E. Glaswell and E. W. Fashole-Luke, in honor of Harry Sawyerr (London: SPCK, 1974), pp. 198–208.

6. H. Sawyerr, *Creative Evangelism: Towards a New Encounter with Africa* (London: Lutterworth, 1968).

7. See further details of H. Sawyerr's writings in Glaswell and Fashole-Luke, ed., *New Testament Christianity*, pp. xix–xxiii.

8. K. A. Dickson and P. Ellingworth, eds., *Biblical Revelation and African Beliefs* (London: Lutterworth, and Maryknoll, N.Y.: Orbis, 1969). The French edition, *Pour une théologie africaine* (Yaounde: Ed. CLE, 1969), contains summaries of the discussions at the Consultation, which the English does not have.

9. J. S. Mbiti, *New Testament Eschatology in an African Background* (London:Oxford University Press, 1971).

10. J. S. Mbiti, "New Testament Eschatology and the Akamba of Kenya," in D. B. Barrett, ed., *African Initiatives in Religion* (Nairobi: East African Publishing House, 1971), pp. 17–28; "Eschatology," in Dickson and Ellingworth, eds., *Biblical Revelation and African Beliefs*, pp. 151–84; "Eschatologie und Jenseitsglaube," in *Theologie und Kirche in Africa*, ed. H. Buerkle (Stuttgart: Evangel. Verlagswerk, 1968), pp. 211–33.

11. B. Kato, *Theological Pitfalls in Africa* (Kisumu, Kenya: Evangel Publishing House, 1975).

12. K. Appiah-Kubi, "Jesus Christ: Some Christological Aspects from African Perspectives," in the consultation report, *African and Asian Contributions to Contemporary Theology*, ed. J. S. Mbiti (Bossey: Ecumenical Institute, 1977), pp. 51–65.

13. G. M. Setiloane, "Confessing Christ Today," in *Journal of Theology for Southern Africa* 12 (September 1975):29–38; see also "Christus heute bekennen: aus der afrikanischen Sicht von Mensch und Gemeinschaft," in *Zeitschrift für Mission* 2, no. 1 (1976):21–32.

14. J. S. Mbiti, "Some African Concepts of Christology," in *Christ and the Younger Churches*, ed. C. F. Vicedom (London: SPCK, 1972), pp. 51–62; see also *Christ and Spirit*, ed. B. Lindars and S. S. Smalley (Cambridge: Cambridge University Press, 1973), pp. 397–414.

15. E. E. Mshana, *Fidia ya Wengi, Marko na Injili Yake* (Ransom for Many: Mark and His Gospel) (Dodoma: Central Tanganyika Press, 1966).

16. O. Imasogie, *Studies in Second Corinthians 1–6* (Ibadan: Daystar Press, listed for 1976–1977 publication).

17. S.T.O. Akande, *The Epistle to the Ephesians* (Ibadan: Daystar Press, listed for 1977–1978 publication).

18. *Drumbeats from Kampala,* United Society for Christian Literature (London: Lutterworth Press, 1963), pp. 17–21.

19. J. Ngally, "Bible Studies from an African Perspective," in *AACC Bulletin* (Nairobi) 8, no. 1 (January–February 1975):33–36.

20. J. Ngally, "Jesus Christ and Liberation: a Bible Study," in *Ecumenical Review* 27, no. 3 (July 1975):213–19.

21. E. B. Idowu, *Job—A Meditation on the Problem of Suffering* (Ibadan: Daystar Press, listed for 1976–1977 publication).

22. Z. Fomum, *God's Love and Forgiveness* (Ibadan: Daystar Press, listed for 1977–1978 publication).

23. J. S. Mbiti, *The Voice of Nine Bible Trees* (Kampala: Church of Uganda Press, 1973).

24. H. Turner, "The Contribution of Studies on Religion in Africa to Western Religious Studies," in Glaswell and Fashole-Luke, *New Testament Christianity*, pp. 168–78.

25. H. Buerkle, "Patterns of Sermons from Various Parts of Africa," in D. B. Barrett, ed., *African Initiatives*, pp. 222–31.

26. R. Albrecht, "Profile through Presence: God in Contemporary Haya Sermons," in *Africa Theological Journal* (Makumira, Usa River, Tanzania), no. 4 (August 1971):40–55.

27. M. Buthelezi, "Theological Grounds for an Ethic of Hope," in *Black Theology: the South African Voice*, ed. B. Moore (London: Hurst, 1973), pp. 147–56; the same essay is in *A New Look at Christianity in Africa* (Geneva: WSCF Books, 1972), pp. 72–80.

28. B. Bujo, *Morale africaine et foi chrétienne* (Kinshasa: Editions de la Faculté de Théologie Catholique, 1976).

29. N. Tese, *Munga éthique en un milieu africain. Gentilisme et christianisme* (Ingenbohl, Switzerland: Impr. du Père Théodse, 1975).

30. E.C.O. Ilogu, "Christian Ethics in Nigeria's Non-Christian Society," in *West African Religion* (Nsukka), no. 9 (1971):28–35. The ideas are further taken up and developed in his book *Christianity and Ibo Culture* (Leiden: Brill, 1974), pp. 118–69.

31. J. Kibira, "Law and Grace in Pastoral Practice," in *Credo* (Durban) 18, no. 2 (1971):22–38.

32. O. U. Kalu, "Theological Ethics and Development in an African Context," in *Missiology* 4, no. 4 (1976):455–63.

33. For an example, though not theological, L. Bolaji, *Anatomy of Corruption in Nigeria* (Ibadan: Daystar, 1970).

34. H. Sawyerr, "Sin and Forgiveness in Africa," in *Frontier* (London) 7, no. 1 (Spring 1964):60–63.

35. H. S. Ngubane, "Some Notions of 'Purity' and 'Impurity' among the Zulu," in *Africa* (London) 46, no. 3 (1976):274–84.

36. S. Mbonyinkebe, "Brèves reflexions sur la conception traditionelle du péché en Afrique centrale," in *Cahiers des Religions Africaines* (Kinshasa) 8, no. 16 (1974):155–65.

37. H. Sawyerr, "Salvation Viewed from the African Situation," in *Presence* (Nairobi) 5, no. 3 (1972):16–23.

38. K. Enang, "Community and Salvation in the Nigerian Independent Churches," in *Zeitschrift für Missionswissenschaft und Religionswissenschaft* 60, no. 4 (1976):276–91.

39. O. Bimwenyi, "Le problème du salut de nos ancêtres ou le rôle salvifique des religions négro-africaines: le Christ-pôle d'attraction de toutes choses," in *Revue du Clergé Africain* (Mayidi, Zaire) 25 (1970):134–50.

40. J. S. Mbiti, "Some African Concepts of Christology," and "Some Reflections on African Experience of Salvation Today," in *Living Faiths and Ultimate Goals: A Continuing Dialogue,* ed. S. J. Samartha (Geneva: WCC, 1974, and Maryknoll, N.Y.: Orbis, 1975), pp. 108–19.

41. *The Report of the Umpumulo Consultation on the Healing Ministry of the Church,* Lutheran Theological College, Mapumulo, Natal, September 19–27, 1967.

42. K. Appiah-Kubi, "The Church's Healing Ministry in Africa," *Ecumenical Review* 27, no. 3 (July 1975):230–39. See also A. Sibomana, "Attitude à l'égard de la maladie en Afrique noire," in *Monchanin* 9, no. 4 (1976):24–29; J. S. Mbiti, "African Traditional Medicine and Its Relevance for Christian Work," in *So Sende Ich Euch,* ed. von Otto Waack et al. (Stuttgart: Evangel. Missionsverlag, 1973), pp. 310–18; and V. A. Nwosu, ed., *Prayer Houses and Faith Healing* (Onitsha, Nigeria: Tabansi Press, 1971).

43. For example, B. Moore, ed., *Black Theology,* articles on liberation in the *AACC Bulletin: Lusaka 74*; and *AACC Bulletin* 7, no. 6 (November–December 1974), *Focus on Liberation*; J. B. Chipenda, "Theology of Liberation," in K. Y. Best, *African Challenge,* pp. 50–55. Cf. D.M.B. Tutu, "Black Theology/African Theology—Soul Mates or Antagonists?" *The Journal of Religious Thought* 32, no. 2 (Fall–Winter 1975):25–33.

44. D.M.B. Tutu, "Church and Nation in the Perspective of Black Theology," in *Journal of Theology for Southern Africa* (Braamfontein), no. 15 (1976):5–11.

45. E. E. Mshana, "Nationalism in Africa as a Challenge and Problem," in *Africa Theological Journal* (Makumira, Usa River, Tanzania), no. 1 (February 1968):21–29; and "Church and State in Independent States in Africa," in *Africa Theological Journal,* no. 5 (December 1972):31–45.

46. J. H. Okullu, *Church and Politics in East Africa* (Nairobi: Uzima Press, 1974); and short reports or articles in *Target* (Nairobi), various issues.

47. C. Mwoleka, "Trinity and Community," in *AFER (African Ecclesiastical Review)* (Eldoret, Kenya) 17, no. 4 (July 1975):203–6.

48. "Déclaration de l'Episcopat du Zaïre," January 1975, private circulation. The issues raised are a continuing debate in Zaire.

49. D. B. Barrett, *Schism and Renewal in Africa* (Oxford, Nairobi: Oxford University Press, 1968), pp. 127–34 et passim.

50. The literature on this theme is vast.

51. E. W. Fashole-Luke, "The Quest for African Christian Theologies," in *Third World Theologies,* ed. G. H. Anderson and T. F. Stransky (New York: Paulist, and Grand Rapids: Eerdmans, 1976), pp. 135–50.

52. J. Milimo, "African Traditional Religion," in *A New Look at Christianity in Africa*, pp. 9–13.

53. E. W. Fashole-Luke refers to "Dr. Samuel Kibicho of Kenya, who claims that Africans had the full revelation of God before the arrival of Christianity" (note 51 above, p. 142). This is in connection with the essay of S.G. Kibicho, "African Traditional Religion and Christianity," in *A New Look at Christianity in Africa*, pp. 14–21. I personally do not see justification for leveling this accusation against Kibicho as far as that essay is concerned.

54. C. Nyamiti, *African Theology, Its Nature, Problems and Methods* (Kampala: Gaba Publications, 1971); and *The Scope of African Theology* (Kampala: Gaba Publications, 1973). He further defends his position in "An African Theology Dependent on Western Counterparts," in *AFER* 17, no. 4 (May 1975):141–47.

55. C. Lymo, "Quest for Relevant African Theology: Towards an Ujamaa Theology," in *AFER* 18, no. 3 (June–July 1976):134–44. The same sentiment is aired by C. Mwoleka, "Trinity and Community."

56. H. J. Becken, ed., *Relevant Theology for Africa* (Durban: Lutheran Publishing House, 1973). Most of the essays in this collection are contributed by non-Africans, and the whole book is posed in terms of imposing western theology upon African theologians.

9

Continuity and Discontinuity Between the Old Testament and African Life and Thought

Kwesi A. Dickson (Ghana)

The story of the study of the Old Testament witnesses to quite a variety of approaches and presuppositions. There was in particular one approach that exercised the minds of the leaders of the early church: Marcion's teaching occasioned a great deal of debate concerning the value of the Old Testament as part of the church's Scriptures. It was Marcion's opinion that the God of the Old Testament could not be the God of the New Testament: the former was bloodthirsty and immoral, while the latter, the Father of Jesus Christ, was the true God. Marcionism forced the church to define its Scriptural canon, but as a way of looking at the Old Testament it has persisted, surfacing again and again till our own day. Three illustrations of this may be given, two of them in relation to European scholarship, and one having to do with the Third World.

The nineteenth-century German scholar, Friedrich Daniel Ernst Schleiermacher, revived Marcionism with his contention: "The relations of Christianity to Judaism and Heathenism are the same, inasmuch as the transition from either of these to Christianity is a transition to another religion."[1] In our own century, Adolf von Harnack, the great church historian, was on the one hand able to argue against Marcionism; he observed that it would have been disastrous for the early church to have adopted Marcion's position with regard to creation (Marcion postulated a Demi-urge). On the other hand, he agreed with Marcion that the Old Testament did not deserve canonical status: "To have cast aside the Old Testament in the second century was an error which the church rightly rejected; to have retained it in the sixteenth century was a fate which the Reformation was not yet able to avoid; but still to keep it after the nineteenth century as a canonical document within Protestantism results from a religious and ecclesiastical paralysis."[2]

Schleiermacher and Harnack were not the only European scholars to have taken basically Marcionist stands; there is no doubt that there has been a certain amount of uneasiness toward the Old Testament. This attitude can be explained, at least in part, by the fact that increasingly scholarship was moving away from earlier methods of study that sought to understand the Old Testament allegorically or to read into it a Christian meaning. To insist that the Old Testament tell its own story in its own literal and philological-historical terms is to come up against a quaintness that could well lead to the adoption of a Marcionist position.

The third illustration concerns Christian mission activity in the Third World. In *The Old Testament in the World Church,* G. E. Phillips refers to the view that India's ancient religious traditions should be substituted for the Old Testament in the context of India, thus making the New Testament the fulfillment of India's religious aspirations.[3] Why should the Old Testament not give way to the very rich Hindu Scriptures? From one point of view this position has much to recommend it. After all as far back as 1500 B.C. the Hindus believed in the Great God Varuna, the Lord of the High Heavens, of whom the Vedic hymn says:

> Only the Existent One breathed calmly,
> self-contained,
> Nought else but He there was,
> nought
> else above, beyond (Mandala 10, Hymn 129).

Even though later Hinduism adopted a multiplicity of gods, it is not easy to forget the earlier tradition that extols Varuna, as in this hymn:

> Him let us praise, the golden child
> That rose in the beginning, that was born the Lord,
> The mighty Varuna who rules above,
> Looks down upon these worlds, His kingdom,
> As if close at hand (Hymn 121).

Why should a tradition that embodies such thoughts not be made India's Old Testament. After all, was it the Christian church that first defined the Old Testament canon? Was the Old Testament canon not defined by Jewish leaders following the fall of Jerusalem in A.D. 70 in order to safeguard Jewish orthodoxy? If the church had felt obliged to define the Old Testament canon, might it not conceivably have arrived at a canon that was not coterminus with the present Old Testament canon?

Upon closer examination, this attitude, which was championed by some Christians in Asia, turns out to be of a piece with the neo-Marcionism espoused by Schleiermacher and Harnack. For it assumes that the Old Testament is not essential to the story of God in human history; it is from that point of view as unsatisfactory as the European neo-Marcionism.

These three illustrations have been given (1) to place our topic in a wider context, and (2) to give some indication of our awareness of the pitfalls that an African student of the Bible should watch for. If in Africa an increasing number of people are desirous of making biblical study relevant, this is to be seen as contributing to the history of inquiry into the nature and contents of the Bible.

The available evidence suggests that in Africa the predominant attitude to the Old Testament is different from that in the three illustrations. Several scholars have documented the predilection for the Old Testament in the independent churches, in particular. Bengt Sundkler has observed that in the Zionist churches in Southern Africa the Old Testament tends to be the basis of belief, and that where "the differences between the Old and New Testament standards are felt as a problem, . . . the Old Testament standard is generally accepted";[4] furthermore the Old Testament is sometimes so interpreted as to make it conform to Bantu practices. H. Turner has shown in his *Profile Through Preaching* that the Old Testament occupies an important position in the preaching of leaders of some independent churches.[5] This attachment to the Old Testament is in contrast to the Marcionist and neo-Marcionist attitudes already referred to, though it must be allowed that this attachment has not always meant a correct understanding of the text; sometimes what amounted to misinterpretation has been used to support desired developments.

It is the reasons for this predilection for the Old Testament that we wish to examine briefly; in the process we will cite specific religious ideas and societal arrangements where similarities with the Old Testament are discernible.

There are various explanations for the attachment to the Old Testament demonstrated by African Christians, and by some independent churches in particular. First, to a certain extent the legalistic approach to the Gospel adopted by the early missionaries to Africa often led to the reception of the Gospel as law rather than grace. This understanding of the Gospel and the Christian life encouraged attachment to the Old Testament, where a legalistic attitude is readily encountered. Not only does it contain a sizeable body of regulations, but also the Deuteronomic tendency to equate acceptability before God with scrupulosity in ritual has, thanks to the Old Testament editors, been made to color much of the Old Testament. And when one realizes that the observance of ritual and other regulations occupies an important place in African traditional life and thought, the attachment to the Old Testament becomes understandable. In this connection Oosthuizen has observed that regulations and sanctions are constantly appealed to in African societies; when this attitude is carried into the church, justification for it is found in the Old Testament.[6]

Second, that the Old Testament has political appeal for the downtrodden and the dispossessed is undoubted. The oppression-salvation theme is one that should be expected to enthuse many in Africa, particularly Africans in those parts of the continent where political rights are denied them by oppressive racist rulers. It is not surprising that on the evidence of Sundkler the central figure in the Old Testament for the Zionist churches in Southern Africa is Moses the liberator, political leader, and law-giver.[7]

Third, Mbiti's observation that Africans take their religion with them wherever they go could with justification be modified, with Israelites replacing the Africans; for the ancient Israelites did not divorce religion from life.[8] In our article "The Old Testament and African Theology" we cited three illustrations of this holistic approach to reality: rights of property, tailoring, and agriculture are areas in the Old Testament in which religion operates.[9]

There are also several other aspects of Old Testament life and thought that would seem very familiar to Africans. Reyburn has said categorically that "African life and thought share in many ways the cultural life of ancient Israel."[10] There are similarities in the concepts of time, human destiny, sacrifice, the relation between deity and the land, death and the hereafter, etc. At a later stage we shall attempt a comparative analysis of two areas—the theology of nature and the sense of community—to assess the similarities.

Here we do want to stress, however, that caution needs to be exercised in drawing parallels between the Old Testament and African life and thought. The one drawing parallels must have seriously studied both the Old Testament and African traditional beliefs; J. J. Williams's *Hebrewisms of West Africa* well exemplifies erroneous equations.[11]

Predilection for the Old Testament, then, must not be equated with a correct understanding of its meaning. In studying the Old Testament it is essential to realize from the beginning that we are dealing with a particular story relating to a particular people at a particular time. The Old Testament is a Hebrew phenomenon, and scholars rightly insist that the guidelines for its study should take account of this. Even where comparative study would allow the placing of the Old Testament in its general Ancient Near Eastern milieu, scholars are careful to remind us that there is no proto-Semitic religion of which the ancient Israelite tradition is merely an expression, and that what most characterizes the Old Testament is not what it had in common with other traditions in the ancient world. In other words, the study of the Old Testament begins with the recognition that it was the people of Israel who interacted with God in peculiar circumstances, and that the relevance of the Ancient Near Eastern traditions for understanding the Old Testament must not be allowed to detract from the distinctiveness of this collection of documents from ancient Israel.[12]

The discussion so far has been a necessary preliminary to the question of continuity between the Old Testament and African life and thought. Is there in fact a continuity? It is possible, we believe, to postulate three levels of continuity: *theological, religio-cultural,* and *interpretative,* or *hermeneutical.*

THEOLOGICAL CONTINUITY

Despite the fact that the Old Testament is a particular story, it has a particularity that contains the seeds of universality. Not only does the particular, by the very fact of its being such, have a universal significance. Also, and more specifically, in the Old Testament we find an attitude that amounts to an invitation to those outside the Israelite tradition to see themselves as sharing in that tradition. After all, the great truth that Israel's story demonstrates is God's involvement in history, so that the old Israel, the new Israel, and the *goyim* (nations) are in effect within the same situation: that of God's rule over the world. The Old Testament does indeed display an open attitude, which may not have as yet been fully assessed by scholars; but a preliminary look indicates a tradition which, even if it was not the most publicized, was nevertheless striking for its rejection of an exclusivist attitude toward the *goyim*. The exclusivist attitude is perhaps most readily associated with ancient Israel and is indeed prominent in the Old Testament: in the injunction that the Israelites should not adopt the customary practices of their neighbors (Deut. 14:1; Lev. 19–29; Lev. 21:5; Deut. 14:3–20; Deut. 18:9–14) and that failure to heed this would result in their being severely punished (Deut. 8:19–20); in the refusal to accord reality to the other people's gods (Isa. 44:6f.); in the issues that pitted the prophets against the Onoride dynasty (1 Kings 16:21ff.); in the exilic attitude that considered singing the Lord's song in a strange land to be an impossibility (Ps. 137); and in the confrontation with the Greeks in the time of Antiochus Epiphanes, the subject of the book of Daniel.

Nevertheless, the open attitude is perhaps even more striking, for example in the first eleven chapters of Genesis. To begin with, God created humankind (i.e., man=*adham*=humankind). The human being was created in the image of God. The exact meaning of this is still debated; in any case, if Genesis is not very explicit on the nature of the image of God, it is far more explicit on the role to be played by human beings: to multiply, fill the earth, subdue it, and to have dominion over every living thing (Gen. 1:27ff.). Then follows a section that details human disobedience: Adam and Eve disobeyed God and were driven out of the Garden of Eden; Cain killed his brother Abel in a fit of jealously; God punished the wicked by sending a flood that killed all except Noah. With Noah God made a new beginning; a new covenant was made (Gen. 9:16) according to which God promised "to remember the everlasting covenant between God and every living creature of all flesh that is upon the earth." Thus chapters 9 and 10 of Genesis are meant to affirm that the diversity of humankind is the result of God's act.

Next we have the story of the Tower of Babel, emphasizing that the human creative urge can be misdirected. People had the naive desire to be great, and the cultural history embodied in this story seems to show that in this cultural expression lies human rebellion against God. Cultural development per se is not what is under attack here; what is excoriated is cultural development shot through with pride. The story of the Tower ends in disaster, but the disaster is only apparent because a new beginning is made with Abraham, who receives the promise: "I will bless those who bless you, and him who curses you I will curse; and by you all the families of the earth will bless themselves" (Gen. 12:3). Once again the promise of grace for humankind is given.

For our purpose, two main ideas issue from this brief analysis of Genesis 1–11. First, despite human waywardness and willful disobedience human-kind continues to be in the covenant of grace; second, religion and culture can be debased by human pride and disobedience. In these two ideas we see a dialectical response to human cultural assertion: a yes and no to religio-cultural striving. As already pointed out the no tends to resound more loudly in the ears of students of the Old Testament, but any impartial student of the Old Testament would admit that the yes is significant, if only because it exists side by side with a clear no.

To pursue the yes response a little further, in quite a few passages the Old Testament makes the point that all—including Israel—are in sin and under the judgment of God (Amos 9:7); in some memorable passages Isaiah and Jeremiah speak of God's using non-Israelites to serve his purposes—the chastisement of Israel (Isa. 10:5f.; Jer. 27:5f.). Indeed, here and there we find hints that God may even accept pagan homage. The Melchizedek story in Genesis (14:17–24) is of much interest in this connection. It is a story notoriously difficult to interpret, to be sure, but there are certain aspects of it that seem to relate very closely to the issue being discussed here. Mel-chizedek was the priest of God Most High, which is probably a reference to the Baal of Heaven known in Phoenicia and elsewhere; he blesses Abraham in the words: "Blessed be Abram by God Most High, maker of heaven and earth." It is clear that Melchizedek comes close to the belief in the one God of the whole earth such as Israel held. That is not the only interesting element in the story. Abraham gave Melchizedek "a tenth of everything," which implies recognition of Melchizedek's sovereign right. As von Rad has observed, "such a positive, tolerant evaluation of a Canaanite cult outside Israel is unparalleled in the Old Testament."[13]

In fact, an even more startling evaluation of non-Israelite cult is made by the prophet Malachi in the fifth century B.C., when he says: "For from the rising of the sun to its setting my name is great among the nations, and in every place incense is offered to my name, and a pure offering; for my name is great among the nations, says the Lord of hosts" (Mal. 1:11). This passage, taken together with some earlier verses in the same chapter, almost amounts to saying that if God is involved in the history of human beings (1:2f.) whom God has created, then God is involved in human religions. This would be a revolutionary idea, and not surprisingly Malachi's words are sometimes so interpreted as to remove from them any suggestion that under certain circumstances God would find the worship of non-Israelites more acceptable.

In fact, it is possible to see in Malachi's words the climax of a long development in Jewish prophecy of an open attitude to other peoples. The early monarchy period saw the assimilation of non-Israelite practices and ideas, such as kingship, architecture (Solomon's Temple was built according to a Phoenician pattern), agriculture (such metaphors as Israel as God's bride, and those of the vine and vineyard are related), and wisdom (e.g., Israel's wisdom book of Proverbs borrows the *Teaching of Amenemope,* an Egyptian work). Then in the prophetic period we hear Amos disabusing the minds of his people of their understanding of the significance of the Day of the Lord. Isaiah of Jerusalem utters those haunting words:

> It shall come to pass in the latter days
> that the mountain of the house of the Lord
> shall be established as the highest of the mountains,
> and it shall be raised above the hills;
> and all the nations shall flow to it,
> and many peoples shall come, and say:
> Come, let us go up to the mountain of the Lord,
> to the house of the God of Jacob (Isa. 2:2–3a).

Many more passages could be cited from the prophets to show that these champions of Israel's traditions were not so blinded by their orthodoxy that they could not admit that God had power to act outside national boundaries. Ancient Israel produced not only Nehemiah and Ezra, but also Deutero-Isaiah and the author of Jonah.

In spelling out the open attitude as advocated in certain parts of the Old Testament we have pinpointed one possible way of postulating a continuity between the Old Testament and African life and thought. God, according to this Old Testament tradition, is God of the whole earth and is concerned with Israel *and* the *goyim*. Among the latter God is also at work. All are finally accountable to God.

RELIGIO-CULTURAL CONTINUITY

It has been suggested by several writers that at some time in the past there was physical contact between black Africans and Jews who had come to the continent in search of trading partners. Thus J. J. Williams has argued, in his *Hebrewisms of West Africa,* that it is this contact that explains apparent resemblances between the Old Testament and religion and life among the Ashanti of Ghana.[14] We have elsewhere argued that Williams's comparisons are superficial.[15] In some circles there has been a tendency to jump quickly to the conclusion that there is a connection between black Africa and the ancient world on evidence that can only be described as insufficient. Thus J. B. Danquah argued in *Revelation of Culture in Ghana* that there was a connection between Ghanaian and Sumerian culture,[16] and in his *The Akan Doctrine of God* he flirts with the notion of the Akan God-name *Nyame* being in reality the Hebrew *Yahweh*.[17] Other writers have adopted the view that African culture takes its origin from Egyptian culture alone, e.g., Eva Meyerowitz[18] and C. G. Seligman.[19] It is all too easy to insist on contact and influence to the neglect of the possibility of independent development. Posnansky, recently of the University of Ghana, has taken issue with Seligman, arguing that black African customs surrounding kingship may in fact have developed independently and not have had their origin in Egypt.[20]

That various elements in the African religio-cultural ethos recall ancient Israelite beliefs and practices cannot be denied. Reyburn lists Levirite marriage, the relationship between sin and sickness, and the power of the curse.[21] A great number of similar attitudes, ideas, and customs are discernible. We shall examine only two.

First, African religions entail a *theology of nature* which has not been fully studied and evaluated. Usually the gods of Africa are interpreted as "nature gods," and on the surface, at least, it appears that they are: the Supreme Being is the creator of all things, giver of sun and wind and rain; spirits have their abode in rivers, rocks, mountains, and trees; medicines are extracted from roots and leaves; and charms are usually made of physical substances. Nature, then, is the background against which religion is expressed and deity contacted. Now the Old Testament (and indeed the New Testament also) includes much that is in accord with such practices and beliefs. There is the belief that human beings, by the use of magical arts and practices, can control gods and demons, and this belief persisted till a late date: Deuteronomy, dating probably from the seventh century B.C., forbade the community to indulge in such practices (Deut. 18:9f.). That Deuteronomy found it necessary to condemn such practices is indicative that at the popular level they were respected and employed.

It is equally notable that certain natural objects were considered sacred in Old Testament times. Thus at Shechem there was a sacred oak in the sanctuary (Josh. 24:26), and its existence can be traced according to tradition to Abraham's time (Gen. 12:6). In fact, the oak of Moreh at Shechem was the focus of a Canaanite cult which was evidently indulged in by the Israelites. The wells at Beersheba were probably used as sacred waters (Gen. 21:25f.); in Amos 5:5 and 8:14 the prophet seems to be decrying such an attitude toward these wells. Among sacred stones was the Serpent's Stone at which Adonijah made sacrifices (1 Kings 1:9). There was also the stone used by Araunah the Jebusite as a threshing floor (2 Sam. 24:18–25). David bought this stone and made it the base of an altar to God. Yahweh himself was conceived and appropriated by some as a kind of nature deity: he is closely associated with Sinai or Horeb, a mountain so sacred that at certain times it was forbidden to set foot upon it (Exod. 19:12f.). As late as the time of Elijah this mountain was venerated. Yahweh is represented as God of storm and fire: he revealed himself to Moses in the Burning Bush. When Elijah engaged the prophets of Baal in a contest his sacrifice was taken by fire. In the sixth century Ezekiel saw Jerusalem burned by fire that came from Yahweh's chariot wheel. Yahweh routed Sisera and his men through the storm that immobilized their chariots (Judg. 4–5).

Scattered throughout the Old Testament there is abundant evidence of beliefs and practices of a kind that would be readily understood in Africa. However, it is doubtful whether the distinctive evolution of post-exilic Yahwism would have taken place unless from the very beginning Yahweh had been something other than a nature deity. In both accounts of creation it is made clear that God is not nature. In the beginning there were God and "material." A philosophical mind might see a dualism here, but the Hebrew mind was not concerned. God, for the Hebrews, was not to be confused with the material universe; the world resulted from the Creator's action upon the "ordered chaos." And Deuteronomy forbade Israel to indulge in those practices characteristic of the milieu to which Israel and its neighbors belonged.

It will have become clear that in the theology of nature there is continuity, but at the same time discontinuity, between the Old Testament and African life and thought. This pattern of continuity and discontinuity is to be observed also in the area of social relations as illustrated by the *sense of community*. In Africa the concept of corporate personality is well known and needs very little elaboration. It is exemplified in the family, which is both nuclear and extended (the latter form is more pronounced), and in the clan system, which technically unites all members of a clan, no matter how widely separated physically. More strikingly, the community in the African sense is made up of the unborn, the living, and the dead. The unborn child is already a citizen of the spirit world and is believed to be one of the departed members of the family or clan. Cults are paid to the dead, cults that inculcate a sense of solidarity and security, through integration of a worldview, and that constitute a regulatory moral force.

It is not entirely correct to say, as some do, that in African thought individuals have no dignity of their own or meaning in themselves. It is true that individuals are not free to make decisions against custom; however, not only are individuals believed to be especially endowed with distinctive souls and destinies by God, but also individuals must themselves make their destinies successful by acquiring and maintaining good characters. Such beliefs are fairly widespread in Africa.

Similarly, among the ancient Israelites the concept of the solidarity of the group played an important role in their societal arrangements. Thus the destruction of Achan, of the members of his family, and even of his nonhuman belongings, because he had broken the law of the ban, would not have been classified by any of his contemporaries as cruel, inhuman, and irrational (Josh. 7:1ff.). The Achan story highlights the basic group to which every Israelite belonged: the family or *beth* (house). The family was patriarchal and extended, as illustrated when Genesis tells us that Jacob's family comprised three generations (Gen. 46:8–26). Then there were the clan (*mishpachah*), which would consist of several families, and the tribe (*shebet*), a collection of clans. Corporateness, then, whether within the family, the clan, the tribe, or finally the nation, was a fact.

The available evidence would seem to suggest that the dead, in the consciousness of the living, were part of this corporateness. Officially, it would seem that no cult was paid to the dead; however, the dead were owed certain duties that were taken seriously (1 Sam. 31:12; 2 Sam. 21:13–14; etc.), and it may thus be said that they were honored in a religious spirit.

With regard to the place of the unborn in this group consciousness, the evidence is uncertain. However, three passages may be cited in favor of the possibility of such a belief: Genesis 17:7f., the blessing by God of Abraham and his descendants; 2 Samuel 7:1ff., the so-called Zion or Davidic covenant, which speaks of succeeding generations from the line of David as irreversibly part of the covenant with David; and, from the New Testament, Hebrews 7:4–10, where Melchizedek gave Abraham his priestly blessing when Abraham had given tithes to Melchizedek. In both the receiving of blessing and the giving of tithes by Abraham the author of Hebrews includes the yet unborn priestly descendants of Levi.

All this could be spelt out in greater detail, but enough has been said to suggest a similarity of outlook between Africa and ancient Israel as regards the sense of community. Indeed, in both ancient Israel and Africa there is a failure to recognize certain limitations inherent in this concept of group consciousness. The attitude toward the enemy illustrated this. Certain Old Testament passages show an awareness of the need to act in love toward the enemy (Exod. 23:4f.; Prov. 25:21–22); these passages nothwithstanding, love seems easily suppressed, particularly where the integrity of the nation is at stake. Hence the many passages in Deuteronomy regarding the need to exterminate the non-Israelite populations of Palestine. Similarly, in Africa, despite the belief among many of its peoples that all people were created by the Supreme Being, intertribal, and sometimes also intratribal relations, can often be bitter.[22]

However, there is much in the Old Testament that represents a rising above these limitations. The teaching of prophets like Amos and Deutero-Isaiah shows an awareness of that love of God which transcends the national boundaries of Israel, as we have already observed. Even if Israelite thinking was divided on this issue—and the division spills over into New Testament times when the church struggled with the question of Gentile admission—the very fact that there is this insistent strain of openness ensures that Israel's history could not be written without due prominence being given to this attitude, which to a certain extent marks a discontinuity with the traditional African understanding of community.

INTERPRETATIVE, OR HERMENEUTICAL, CONTINUITY

There was a time in the history of biblical interpretation when the Old Testament was deemed to be so special that it could not be interpreted in the same way as other works of literature. The author of the Old Testament was held to be the Holy Spirit; some even considered that the Masoretic points of the Hebrew were inspired. This kind of attitude did affect the interpretation of the text insofar as it discouraged questions regarding the limitations of the authors. The Reformers, who did not hold a rigidly formal doctrine of inspiration, nevertheless, in their interpretation of the Old Testament, tended to adopt the criterion of whether or not the books were expressions of the work of Christ. With the coming of the Enlightenment in the eighteenth century formal reason was enthroned, and since divine authority was claimed for reason there was no hesitation in adopting a critical attitude toward the Old Testament. Some recognized reason to the exclusion of revelation, others did not. In our time there is a diverse array of tools for studying the Old Testament (and indeed the Bible as a whole), and the influence of sociology, psychology, the phenomenology of religion, etc., has been recognized. The employment of these and other tools has resulted in a much broader understanding of the meaning and value of the Old Testament.

Earlier the point was made that the Old Testament is a distinctively Hebrew phenomenon, so that one of the tasks of the interpreter is to study the Old Testament against its original, authentic setting; the original intention of the text must be sought. However, the humble scholar would admit that the meaning of the text in its true historical setting is not always discernible, though this does not argue against making the attempt to so understand the text. Side by side with this approach, another task of the interpreters has come to be recognized: in approaching the text, they must keep in mind the questions and problems of their own period. In other words, interpreters approach the text with their own presuppositions; they do not divorce themselves from the questions and problems that concern their generation. For in confronting the Old Testament the interpreters are seeking directions for their own time; they are seeking to clarify their own situations. In this connection it has been observed: "The particularity of the mode of biblical revelation—the witness of a specific people at a particular point in history—suggests that the medium is the message, namely, that God's word is intended for identifiable situations rather than to be taken as amorphous, generalized truth having little to do with the specifics of the human condition."[23] It is in view of this that consideration is being given by the West African Association of Theological Institutions to the production of a Bible commentary; this is why James Cone argues as forcefully as he does in his *A Black Theology of Liberation* for a biblical basis for the present black social and spiritual revolution.

In this dimension of the interpreter's task we see another kind of continuity between the Old Testament and African life and thought; for in confronting the Old Testament Africans cannot, and must not, leave behind the questions and problems that matter to us. Thus the text and the African—or the black American, or the Latin American, or the Asian or the European—are bound together. A few years ago T. A. Beetham expressed the regret that African students "can still come away from their lecture-room after studying the first two chapters of Mark's Gospel—with its account of the touch of Jesus of Nazareth on different kinds of illness, including mental sickness—without having come to grips either with the failure of their own Church, despite its hospitals and clinics, to exercise a full ministry of healing or with the success of some Independent Churches in this respect."[24] In particular, the theologians who have a church affiliation and who are concerned with expounding biblical texts in their preaching are invariably challenged—and rightly so—to interpret the text in relation to some specific relevant situation or other.

This kind of continuity, we regret to say, has not been taken very seriously by African theological educators and students; it has not been as much in their consciousness as the religio-cultural continuity. In fact, it is only in the last few years that the protagonists of African theology have shown any interest in this biblical aspect of the matter.

To recognize and act on this hermeneutical continuity is, paradoxically, to come up against a discontinuity, for this mode of interpreting the Old Testament, approaching it with questions and problems relating to one's own time, brings African interpreters face to face with Christian theology; they are forced to measure the answers they find against the teaching of Christ. After all, one of the crucial areas of biblical study is the relation between the Old and New Testaments. Consensus of scholarly opinion is against that Marcionist and neo-Marcionist view that advocates the removal of the Old Testament from the Scriptures.

This is not the place to discuss the various ways of establishing the relationship between the two Testaments; we shall confine ourselves to some general comments. It is generally accepted that the New Testament takes up the ideas found in the Old Testament regarding the relations between God and humanity and brings them to fruition in the life and work of Christ. This is an important insight, but it tells only part of the story, for it is being increasingly recognized that the Old Testament is more explicit in certain vital areas of religious thought. Thus the nexus binding religion and life is spelt out in greater detail in the Old Testament. When the World Council of Churches held its meeting at Bangkok on the theme "Salvation Today" and raised such important issues as the place of material welfare in human salvation, some of the key biblical passages for study came from the Old Testament. Also, the Old Testament paints the majesty of God in more glowing colors; the visions of God in Jeremiah and Isaiah, to cite only these two prophets, put us before the throne of God's overwhelming majesty in a way few biblical passages do.

Thus, on the one hand, the Old Testament has considerable religious value in itself, and on the other, it is inextricably bound up with the New Testament. Hence the Old Testament is brought under the close scrutiny of the New Testament. The implications of this for our topic are clear: the continuity between the Old Testament and African life and thought should be exposed to the cross-event, which for Christians is judgment on whatever insights might be gained by looking at the Old Testament and African life and thought together. And the radical nature of the cross-event spells discontinuity. Yet in this cross-event Christ's involvement with society is clearly seen; for the radical nature of the cross serves to underline the extent to which God would go to identify himself with humankind in the totality of human circumstances.

NOTES

1. Friedrich Schleiermacher, *The Christian Faith,* 2nd ed., trans. H. R. Mackintosh and J. S. Stewart (Edinburgh: T. & T. Clark, 1928), par. 12.

2. Adolf von Harnack, *Marcion, Das Evangelium vom freunden Gott,* 2nd ed. (Leipzig: J. C. Hinrichs Verlag, 1924), p. 217.

3. A. E. Phillips, *The Old Testament in the World Church* (London: Lutterworth, 1942), pp. 14–21.

4. Bengt Sundkler, *Bantu Prophets in South Africa* (London, New York: Oxford University Press, 1964, reprinted), p. 277.

5. Harold W. Turner, *Profile Through Preaching* (Edinburgh: Edinburgh House Press, 1965).

6. G. C. Oosthuizen, *Post-Christianity in Africa* (London: C. Hurst and Co., 1968), p. 169.

7. *Bantu Prophets,* pp. 107, 277, 334–36.

8. J. S. Mbiti, *African Religions and Philosophy* (London: Heinemann, 1971, reprinted), p. 2.

9. K. Dickson, "The Old Testament and African Theology," *Ghana Bulletin of Theology* 4 (June 1973):31f.

10. *Practical Anthropology* 7, no. 4 (July–August 1960):153.

11. J. J. Williams, *Hebrewisms of West Africa* (London: George Allen and Unwin Ltd., 1930).

12. See M. C. Vriezen, "The Study of the Old Testament and the History of Religion," in *Supplement to Vetus Testamentum* 17, Congress Volume (Rome: E. J. Brill, 1968), pp. 1–24.

13. Gerhard von Rad, *Genesis,* 2nd ed. (London: SCM, 1963), ad loc.

14. Williams, *Hebrewisms,* p. 27 et passim.

15. *Legon Journal of Humanities* 1 (1974):23ff.

16. This manuscript has not been traced since the author's death.

17. J. B. Danquah, *The Akan Doctrine of God* (London: Cass, 1968).

18. Eva Meyerowitz, *The Divine Kingship in Ghana and Ancient Egypt* (London: Faber & Faber Ltd., 1960).

19. C. G. Seligman, *Races of Africa,* 3rd ed. (London, New York: Oxford University Press, 1957); *Egypt and Negro Africa* (London: Routledge, 1934).

20. See Posnansky's article "Kingship, Archaeology and Historical Myth," in R. O. Collins, ed., *Problems in African History* (Englewood Cliffs: Prentice-Hall, 1968).

21. *Practical Anthropology* 7, no. 4 (July–August 1960).

22. M. J. McVeigh, *God in Africa* (Cape Cod, Mass.: Claude Stark, 1974), p. 45.

23. R. A. Bennett, Jr., "Africa and the Biblical Period," in *Harvard Theological Review* 64 (1971):483–500.

24. *Christianity and the New Africa* (London: Pall Mall Press, 1967), pp. 106–7.

10

The Value of African Religious Beliefs and Practices for Christian Theology

Mercy Amba Oduyoye (Nigeria)

The "African" religious beliefs and practices referred to in this paper are specifically those of black Africa, that is Africa south of the Sahara, excluding the racist white minorities of the south and other immigrant groups. I am also excluding the beliefs and practices of Islam and non-indigenous religions like Hinduism and the Bahai faith. This is not to say that I am unaware of what Mbiti calls "contact religion." Most Africans, says Mbiti, do not see any contradiction in holding a mixture of beliefs and practices. Indeed it is this mixture that makes this paper possible.

Religious pluralism is found in Africa as elsewhere on the globe. The popular description of Africans as "notoriously" or "incurably" religious is belied by Africans who call themselves atheists or humanists. Secularization is a factor on the African scene. There are those who are to a greater or lesser degree Islamized or Christianized.

There is also a group that we may refer to as "traditionalists." Some of these are simply theorists, but there are masses of people in Africa who hold to the traditional religious beliefs and practices of their forebears to the exclusion of the missionary religions. Their religious customs blend with their social life and are at the base of all their institutions and festive celebrations. It is the traditionalists who will form the subject of this study. It is their religious beliefs and practices that we designate as "African."

Modernization has had a disruptive and weakening effect on African life and thus on African religion. At the same time it is evident that the missionary religions together with modern technology have proved inadequate to our needs. Since the old appears unable to stand on its own and the new by itself is proving inadequate, we should expect some creative syncretism to develop in Africa.

A living Christian faith in Africa cannot but interact with African culture. In fact there is being developed an interpretation of Christianity and specifically of Christian theology that one may describe as African. The intention of this paper is to draw attention to the fact that the process needs to be accelerated if African Christianity is to escape being a fossilized form of nineteenth-century European Christianity.

AFRICAN RELIGIOUS BELIEFS AND PRACTICES

It is now accepted by most African Christians that it is time to study the religion of our forebears. This has arisen out of the recognition of the poverty of the liturgy and theology emanating from European and American Christianity. They do not touch the African soul at its depths. Here we will consider various African traditional beliefs and practices, giving particular attention to those relevant to African Christian theology.

a. African belief in the divine origin of the universe is shared by Christianity. In African religion, as in Christianity, God leaves humankind in charge of the world, as a *steward.* In both African and Christian myths of origins, humankind becomes the center of the universe. But human beings wantonly exploit the world's physical and human resources to an extent that even God cannot tolerate. The African recognition of the divine spirit in nature and of the community of spirit between human beings, other living creatures, and natural phenomena could reinforce the Christian doctrine of creation as well as contribute to Christian reflection on ecological problems.

b. Related to the belief that humankind is the custodian of the earth is Africa's conviction that the past, present, and future generations form *one community.* Africans therefore try to hold in tension the demands of the traditions of the elders and the necessity to build for the future. This communal sense has far-reaching implications, for example, in attitudes toward land rights. In Africa there is nothing so difficult to alienate as land; it has to be preserved for the coming generations. "I conceive that land belongs to a vast family of which many are dead, few are living, and countless members are unborn."[1] If immigrant European exploiters of Africa had understood and respected this we would not today have the horrible Bantustans in South Africa. If Africans themselves had remembered that land is the gift of God to the people, and thus in modern times to the nation, development projects involving land use would have had a better chance of success.

Africans recognize life as life-in-community. We can truly know ourselves if we remain true to our community, past and present. The concept of individual success or failure is secondary. The ethnic group, the village, the locality, are crucial in one's estimation of oneself. Our nature as beings-in-relation is a two-way relation: with God and with our fellow human-beings. Expand the communal ideology of clans and ethnic groups to nations and you have a societal system in which none is left in want of basic needs. It is an extension of this belief that has led some African politicians to declare that the independence of their own countries means nothing as long as there remains on African soil one state that is still under colonial rule. This is one of the underlying principles of Pan-Africanism. We prosper or perish together as a people. Nkrumah, in concluding his autobiography, said, "Our task is not done and our own safety is not assured until the last vestige of colonialism has been swept from Africa."[2]

The world is in need of religious tolerance, based on a recognition of one God from whom all movements of the spirit take their origin. A belief in one God who is the source of one human race renders all racism and other types of ethnocentricity and exploitation of persons heretical and blasphemous. With its mythology based on African traditional beliefs, African Christianity may be in the vanguard of this movement. Can African Christians contribute new symbols and myths for promoting justice and reconciliation? Can covenant meals, symbols of sharing and of the acceptance of communal responsibility, begin to happen more meaningfully in the church? Can more people "break bread" together not only on their knees but in their homes, sharing in the utilization of national resources?

The role of ancestors in the life of Africans becomes important in enabling them to remember their source and history. To deny history is to deny one's roots and source of self-identity. It is also to deny the fact that we embody in ourselves both the past and the future. Ancestral cults serve the purpose of keeping people from becoming rootless and purposeless, blown about by every fickle fashion and ideology. The ancestral cults have been the custodians of the African spirit, personality, and vivid sense of community demonstrated in socio-religious festivals.

The teaching that God is the Originator of all humanity and, as a corollary, that there is one human family, is held by Christianity, but it stands in dire need of reinforcement. The movement from nationalism toward universalism will be promoted by making available to the world Africa's vision of the unity of the individual person and of humanity. Africa's contribution can enable us to utilize creatively the tension between the universal and the particular and to develop the theology of the unity of humankind.

c. A sense of *wholeness of the person* is manifested in the African attitude to life. Just as there is no separation between the sacred and the secular in communal life, neither is there a separation between the soul and the body in a person. Spiritual needs are as important for the body as bodily needs are for the soul. This is basic to African medicine and psychiatry. Moreover, for a wholesome life people not only have to be at peace with themselves, but also must be fully integrated into the community. The African contribution can help purge the Christian religion of the separation of the human being into body, soul, and spirit.

d. The International Women's Year stimulated a lot of discussion which to me was basically an inquiry into whether *women* are an integral part of humanity or merely appendages to the male. The present freedom of African women to express dissatisfaction with their secondary roles and often non-roles is said to have been brought by Christianity and westernization. I agree that there has been some progress in economic activity and politics. But as far as the cultic aspect of religion goes, women now as before are relegated to the background. The cultic events in which women take complete charge are few and far between. The fact that women do the dancing and cooking for festivals does not, to my mind, compensate for their exclusion from the "holy of holies" in the festivals. The limitations placed on women's participation in religious practices is further aggravated by the irrational fear of blood. It is an area wide open for study. Further work on women in African religion will be a great contribution to global women's issues.

African women have a traditional belief in the benefit of sacrifice for the community. Sacrifice, taken seriously, can lead to social reforms and to lifestyles that are less wasteful and more mindful of humanity's stewardship of life and ultimate dependence on the Source-Being. But I have difficulty in understanding why it is the prerogative of only one sex to sacrifice for the well-being of the community.

e. Christianity will have to take seriously the African belief that God delegates authority to intermediary beings. In Africa there is a widespread belief in the *"divine right of kings,"* which is often sanctioned by African religions. The ruler is almost invariably a cultic person, and his or her person is considered sacred. Against this background, certain modern political leaders have instituted what have come to be known as "benevolent dictatorships." Without the sanctions that provided the checks and balances in the traditional system, these have always ended in chaos. African organization had its own constitutional processes for removing rulers who abused tradition. The divine rights of rulers worked in traditional Africa when belief in the Supreme Being was taken seriously and decision by consensus was actively pursued. The people's role in their own development is slowly being recognized by current African politicians. The days when the ruler took a unilateral decision to declare what the people needed are slowly passing—one must say rather too slowly.

f. Covenant-making is a characteristic of African life. A ruler, for example, is always a covenanted or constitutional monarch. There is always a reciprocal oath-taking between the ruler and the ruled, who are often represented in the associated ceremonies by the elders of the community.[3] There are also oaths and covenants between friends and others that bind members of exclusive clubs within the community.

When these oaths are taken seriously they are more binding than any signature made on legal documents. A person who flouts *Nsamansew* (the last will and testament of a person) is sure to be called quickly to the spirit world to render an explanation. The process of oath-taking always contains a religious element; one always swears by a divinity who thus becomes the chief witness to the transaction. Covenant meals seal reconciliation and purification ceremonies, since one cannot conceivably work to the disadvantage of another with whom a kolanut has been shared. We should investigate what makes African traditional oaths and covenants more binding than the Lord's Supper.

g. Africa has a realistic attitude toward the *power of evil*. If we recognize that the collective evil produced by humanity is strong enough to "materialize" into a force to reckon with, then we shall see racism and other kinds of exploitation for what they are and be able to develop the appropriate weapons to fight them. Certain humanistic claims that humanity may be educated into eschewing evil leads us down a very long road to the humanization of our societies. What is evil is to be exorcized. Here again is a possible meeting point of Christian theology and African belief.

h. *Reconciliation* has a central role in African religion and practice. Broken relations are never allowed to go unhealed. Sacrifices are performed and communal meals held to restore normalcy. In both African religion and Christianity, when life is sacrificed, when it is given back to God, it is made sacred and harmony is restored. This belief is embodied in the Christian doctrine of atonement. A fresh statement of this belief, which makes use of African ideas of sacrifice and covenants, will enable African religion to make another contribution to the religious development of humankind. Here again, by analyzing the theological elements of Christianity and of African religion, one can indicate areas where African religion will be supportive of Christian theology and contribute to its restatement in terms relevant to the African context.

i. Most *rites of passage* performed by Christians in Africa have been enriched by African culture. Marriage, naming ceremonies, and burials are good examples. Yearly festivals involving cleansing and the driving away of misfortune are current in Africa. There are sacrifices to cleanse or to bless the individual or group after a trauma—birth, death, disease, plague, accident, etc. These have been woven into liturgies of Christians in the form of thanksgiving services for almost any situation. On the other hand, Christians have shied away from puberty rites and other rites of initiation into adulthood because they have misgivings as to whether a Christian's allegiance to the church (and Christ) does not conflict with age-group allegiance and membership in secret societies. Initiation to adulthood, however, is initiation into full responsibility in one's community; it is the culmination of a long process of socio-political education. There should be further discussion about the relationship of these initiation rites to Confirmation and recognition rites prevalent in some Christian denominations.

j. Other traditional African *liturgical practices* are most apparent among the African Independent churches. These are the churches that have been founded by African Christians and that, not being bound by the stately liturgies and theological sensitivities of the West, have developed lively liturgies with music and prayer forms that are authentically African. Some of the older Christian congregations, both Roman Catholic and Protestant, have awakened to this and are fast renewing their liturgies along the lines that are relevant to African religiosity. Drumming, dancing, extemporaneous prayer, dramatic methods of conveying the word of God, and stunning cultic robes are being observed among African Christian congregations. More use is being made of symbols and of spiritual healing and exorcism. There is a strong sense of community among members of the Independent churches, and in the urban situation they become the new "extended family." The songs that western Christians developed in their nationalistic spirit and racial pride are dropping out of the repertoire of African Christians as they become aware of the songs' non-Christian character. For example:

> Can we, whose souls are lighted
> with wisdom from on high:
> Can we to the benighted the Lamp of life deny?

Such hymns are rarely heard in African congregations today; they are being replaced by African tunes with words that come out of the depths of the African soul or from the common source of Christianity—the Bible.

THE AFRICAN THEOLOGICAL TASK: SOTERIOLOGY

The word "syncretism" has become a bogey word, used to frighten all who would venture to do Christian theology in the context of other worldviews and religions. But is syncretism not in fact a positive and unavoidable process? Christian theology and practice have always interacted with the religious and philosophical presuppositions of the various periods. Practices like the observance of Sunday, distribution of Easter eggs, and the festival of the Nile in the medieval Coptic church are instances of the acculturation of Christianity. Evidence of this process is increasing in Africa.

Since the theme of salvation features so prominently in African religion, I would like to offer some reflections on the question of salvation for African Christianity. Both in the New Testament and in the early church, the way people interpreted the significance of Christ was closely related to what they saw as their greatest need. Christ was all things to all men, to quote Paul. The names given to Jesus of Nazareth in the Bible were all titles that held significant salvific content. He was the Son of Man who came to take up the elect of God. He was the Son of God, the Logos who was at God's right hand in bringing order out of chaos. He was Lord but, unlike our Caesars, he was the suffering servant. To some he was a Zealot, a nationalist, but one who forgave his enemies and prayed for them. To the sick he was a doctor and to the sinful he spoke as God.

These and other titles were the responses of those who had faith in his uniqueness or at least in his significance for the development of human history.

He attracted a wide variety of people, from simple manual workers to the intellectuals of the Jewish world. It was from soteriology that Christology developed. I believe that for theology to be relevant to African culture it has to speak of salvation.

Our salvation theology has to feature the questions of racism and liberation from material need. It has to emphasize the need for communal decisions as against totalitarianism. Above all, salvation is to be seen as salvation from evil, both individual and structural. At several points our Christian theology can be aided by African religious beliefs and practices.

THE AFRICAN CONTRIBUTION

Africa's approach to the basic religious problems facing humankind—creation, survival, human relations, the existence of a spirit world, etc.—was as meaningful and relevant to the pre-scientific age in Africa as were similar approaches all over the world. These approaches, which we designate primal worldviews, are at the base of all religions and effectively continue to influence the ordering of society and of individual life. African religious beliefs and practices have provided, and continue to provide, Africa with a philosophical fountainhead for the individual's life and for the ordering of society. African traditional religion emphasizes the common origin of all humanity. It is the source from which a person's sense of dignity and responsibility flow. The search for security invariably begins here and for many it is also the last resort. Far from being redundant or anachronistic, African religious beliefs and practices have shown such a remarkable ability for staying relevant that Africans have a responsibility to share their basic tenets with the rest of humanity. This will be a task of recalling the peoples of the whole world to basic principles of human community and the religious basis of life even though some think these principles have become outmoded or are a hindrance to the advancement of humanity.

We must note that since "traditional" life was permeated in all its aspects by religion, any appeal we make to traditional values and practices is ultimately religious. Also we must bear in mind that the basic element in religion does not consist of practices of cultic places and persons but the beliefs that are manifested through them. So that even when modernization has modified ceremonies and other cultic practices, human beings will continue to depend on the beliefs as a rock on which to build. So, for example, the belief in the living-dead, in the existence of spirits, and in magic and witchcraft are a part of the Africans' recognition that life is not entirely materialistic. These beliefs are an expression of the yearning for life after life. Since the Supreme Being is believed to be the Source of Life, the search after the life-force is itself a groping for a closer and more personal relationship with Being Itself.

To contribute more effectively to the religious development of people, African Christian theologians have a duty to theologize from this context and incorporate the authentic African idiom into Christian theology. Utilizing African religious beliefs in Christian theology is not an attempt to assist Christianity to capture and domesticate the African spirit; rather it is an attempt to ensure that the African spirit revolutionizes Christianity to the benefit of all who adhere to it.

NOTES

1. Kwame Nkrumah, *Ghana* (Edinburgh: T. Nelson and Sons Ltd., 1959), p. 10.

2. Ibid., p. 240.

3. R. S. Rattray, *Ashanti Law and Constitution* (Oxford: Oxford University Press, 1929), p. 82.

11

Indigenous African Christian Churches: Signs of Authenticity

Kofi Appiah-Kubi (Ghana)

One of the most prominent features of modern Africa has been the emergence of the so-called Independent churches—which I prefer to call "Indigenous African Christian churches." These are churches founded by Africans for Africans in our special African situations. They have all African membership as well as all African leadership. Some were founded by Africans in reaction to some feature of the Christianity of missionary societies; most were founded among those people who had known Christianity the longest.

The use of the term "Independent" for these churches connotes a certain condescension. It suggests that there is some more important reference point outside these churches. Thus my preference for the term "Indigenous African Christian churches."

REASONS FOR EMERGENCE

Reasons given for the emergence of these churches and their activities within the African societies are normally narrowed down to political, economic, and social deprivation and racial discrimination. However valid these may be in some cases, the present research among some of the Indigenous churches in the Akan society in Ghana presents a different picture altogether.

On the basis of the data of the present research, I contend that spiritual hunger is the main cause of the emergence of the Indigenous African Christian churches, and not political, social, economic, and racial factors. In these churches, the religious needs of healing, divining, prophesying, and visioning are fulfilled by Christian means.

Spiritual experience is the pivot of most African religions. Healing, prophesying, and divining revolve around the supreme idea of spirit possession. In these churches the Akan Ghanaians seek a way of Christian expression, struggling for the selfhood of the church, and asking to be allowed to worship as Akan Christians. They do not want to be turned into Europeans before they can worship.

The most significant and unique aspect of these churches is that they seek to fulfill that which is lacking in the Euro-American missionary churches, that is, to provide forms of worship that satisfy both spiritually and emotionally and to enable Christianity to cover every area of human life and fulfill all human needs. These churches maintain that to satisfy Akan needs, Christianity should not only integrate all the good elements found in Akan culture, but also find means to unite Christianity and daily life in such a way that the first inspires the second.

In Akanland a revaluation is occurring, with emphasis on the traditional values, in an attempt to capture the capacity and the right to practice the full arc of Akan culture. There is desperate search for identity, an identity that has roots in tradition and reaches for a unity with which to face a pleasant and honorable future.

There is a conscious attempt on the part of the people to revive or perpetuate selected aspects of the Akan culture, which is considered more satisfying than western patterns. By this noble and bold attempt these churches are meeting a need grossly ignored by the intellectualized Christianity of the missionary kind.

MAIN CHARACTERISTICS

For these Indigenous African Christian churches Jesus Christ remains the supreme object of devotion. He is the Savior, the Baptizer in the Spirit, the Soon-Coming-King, and the Healer.

In contrast to a cold, frigid, professionally-aired Christianity that is mainly interested in form, these churches are free, emotional, and to some extent fanatical in their Christian worship. Several of the churches are charismatic, lay, egalitarian, and voluntaristic in contrast to the established, professional, hierarchical, prescribed religion of the missionary churches.

They view the divine as transcendent and immanent at the same time. The kingdom is to appear on earth—a new heaven and a new earth in this world. The belief is "this-wordly" rather than the "other-worldly." They think that salvation is for the elect; there is hope for the children of light and complete damnation for the children of darkness.

The majority of the churches are messianic. Salvation is brought about by a redeemer, who is the mediator between the human and the divine. The leadership tends to be charismatic and endowed with supernatural powers.

The members are said to be the channels through whom the supernatural gifts of the Holy Spirit may be transmitted to help others at their moments of greatest need. Some are endowed with the word of wisdom, others with knowledge, faith, the working of miracles, prophecy, the discerning of spirits, tongues and interpretation of tongues, or the gift of healing—indeed all nine charismatic gifts listed by Paul in 1 Corinthians.

The insistence of the churches that all the supernatural gifts are available even today in Ghana sets them apart from other Christians who chronologically restrict such charismatic gifts to the time of the Apostles or the early Christians.

The Indigenous African Christians believe their experiences to be part and parcel of the normal life for all Christians in all nations today. It is their greatest desire therefore to see all the supernatural gifts of the Holy Spirit renewed and properly functioning in the lives of contemporary Christians.

Every member is urged to become an evangelist to his or her neighbors and friends—a system of "priesthood of all believers." The believers are urged to enter the valley of human sin and suffering with the compassion of Jesus, bringing supernatural help to those who face problems without knowing that God loves them and desires to meet their needs.

The Bible is central to their religious and daily life. They have great love for reading the Bible, a love rarely found even in clergy or religious people of other churches. Members are quick to state that their religious practices are truly Christian, justifying themselves by the Bible. They read the Bible eagerly, souls hungry for the word of God, devouring and savoring every word. They read the Bible so assiduously that they have been nicknamed "the people with the dirty Bible."

For them the Bible is not just a historical record but a blueprint for life. They tend to be fundamentalists in this regard. To them the biblical message is simple, direct, and eminently personal. They are urged to listen carefully to the voice of God through the Spirit in prayer, which seems to say "God knows all your problems and will provide for your needs in due season." One does not understand this intellectually.

Unfortunately in Ghana as well as in other African countries, especially among the leaders and some sophisticated members of the established churches, these Indigenous African Christian churches conjure up nothing more than images of emotionalism, fanaticism, religious mania, illiteracy, messianic postures, credulity, and panting after miracles. I am convinced that this public image no more reflects the true nature of these African churches than the Inquisition or the massacre of St. Bartholomew's Day reflects the essential quality of Catholicism.

REASONS FOR THEIR ATTRACTION

The teachings of the Indigenous churches have attracted many adherents among the Akans, who believe that for any religion to be meaningful, it must be practical, dynamic, and problem-solving. Despite the negative criticism of the misinformed and uninformed, these churches are growing by leaps and bounds in numbers and strength.

While one major denomination after another reports seriously declining memberships and incomes, as well as declining overseas missionary staffs and supports in these days of Moratorium, the Indigenous African Christian churches are Africa's fastest growing body of Christian believers, indeed a third force in African Christianity beside Protestantism and Catholicism.

Thus serious researchers into activities of these churches and concerned leaders of the established churches ask: "What attraction do these churches have to the general public who flock to their doors?" "What are the common denominators in these healing churches, and what are they really reacting against in the imported western models?" These are indeed crucial questions and require serious analysis.

Since it incorporates elements of the Christian religion, worship in these churches is quite familiar to converts from mission churches. At the same time, the African elements—particularly the supernatural powers of the prophets and the healing miracles that counteract the forces of evil, disease, and witchcraft—are sought by those unhappy and dissatisfied with the strictly western nature of most of the mission churches.

Another important area of attraction is the importance these churches place on veneration of ancestors, who are said to be the custodians of law, morality, and ethical order of the Akans. The mission churches, while overlooking the Akan ancestors, urge their members to venerate St. George of England, St. Andrew of Scotland, or St. Christopher of the Vatican, who are very much removed from the converts' daily wants and anxieties.

In addition to the attractions of a religious nature, there are social attractions to these churches. Especially in the urban areas where anomie reigns supreme, the churches provide solace for the lonely. There is a fraternity where individuals are encouraged to regard one another in a certain sense as siblings; hence the use of the terms "brother" and "sister" by members who are in no way related. The members are encouraged to behave as a family, to support and sympathize with one another. The churches stress traditional values such as respect for age and obligation toward family members. The members are also encouraged to marry from within their congregations.

The churches meet the strongly felt need for small groups of people supportive of the disadvantaged and the disappointed. In this respect the Indigenous African churches are very important for the social and psychological life of the people since their congregations provide small reference groups in relation to the wider society for their members.

The churches help individual urban Akans to overcome the stresses and strains of the urban and industrial life. Those who would be described as deviants and psychiatric cases in some societies are often accommodated by these churches and helped to become useful members of the society.

Alcoholics and drug and cigarette addicts are also helped to overcome their psychological incapacities. In fact, in Akan society it has become a joke among the youth that when one refuses to smoke or drink alcohol one is often asked: "Are you saved?"—meaning simply, "Are you a member of one of these Indigenous African churches?"

To prevent their members from falling victims to the wild life at night clubs, the churches allow for full expression of emotional outburst through drumming, clapping, dancing, and spirit possession. The practice of comforting the despairing and the uncomforted is one of the hallmarks of the churches' attractions.

The churches offer spiritual and supernatural protection to members through the help of the prophets or the spiritual leaders. They attract people with such needs as employment, promotion in business, education, marriage, and political career.

Most of the people interviewed believe strongly that the churches offer the essential spiritual resources to help them achieve a satisfactory life's destiny, which is crucial to every Akan regardless of education or social standing. This includes wealth, children, and freedom from the fear of evil powers and witchcraft.

But the most important single reason why people join the Indigenous African Christian churches is *healing*. This came out quite clearly in the research. To the question: "Why did you join this particular church?" people invariably and quickly replied that they had been ill for a long time, they had tried all forms of treatment to no avail, they were directed to, for example, Prophet Prah, and, behold, they are fit as a fiddle: "Praise the Lord, Halleluja!"

In dealing with psychosomatic problems these churches are very successful through the powers, techniques, and willingness of the spiritually endowed leaders and members. They are also successful with chronic diseases considered incurable by western technological medicine.

More often than not in the churches I visited the set pattern for recruitment was something like this: the original convert in a family or a village was cured of some incurable disease during a healing service or an annual convention. He in turn informed his people by giving a testimony of what the Lord had done for him through the work of prophet so-and-so.

In the established churches, medical practice has become so specialized and secularized that the ordinary pastor has been radically excluded from service for the sick; thus healing and worship have become separate. In the Indigenous African churches there is a reintegration of healing and worship. This corresponds with the Akan understanding, for religion in the Akan concept must be concerned with the health and fertility of human beings, animals, and land.

I was generally told that the prophets did not want to start their own churches but rather to use the gift of healing bestowed on them by the grace of God in already established Christian services. It was repeatedly reported, however, that after the patients had been healed they were mocked by the other members of their churches and so were often left without churches. This forced several of the prophets to form their own churches for their healed patients. This was the case of the Life and Salvation church, which was attached to Prophet Prah's Divine Healing and Miracle Ministry. Prophet Prah told me that he performed healing services in general churches and had no intention of founding his own church until the needs of his neglected, despised clients forced him to that action.

THE INDIGENIZATION OF WORSHIP

If the churches in Africa are to grow and develop, they must be allowed to take root in the soil of Africa where they have been planted. In this Africanization process the Indigenous African churches have made a breakthrough and have a great deal to teach the missionary churches.

The Indigenous African churches, through careful and concrete adaptation of certain cultural elements into their worship, have made Christianity real and meaningful to their African adherents. The following are a few of the areas where the Indigenous African churches have adapted, and in some cases blended, the African culture with Christianity to root Christianity in the soil of Africa.

The Naming Ceremony

Among West African peoples the concept of corporate responsibility is very strong. This is especially manifest at birth, marriage, sickness, and death. The birth of a baby is the greatest blessing for the family, and to a large extent for the community as a whole. The Akans attach a special importance to the day on which the child is named. This day is generally the seventh or eighth day after birth. In fact, the new baby does not really belong to the family until the eighth day, when the child's continued existence would seem to indicate that it has really come to stay. The general assumption is that if by the seventh or eighth day the child still lives, then the ancestors, the gods, and the Supreme God have blessed the child for the family. At times it is simply said that the Ghost-mother has relinquished the child into the world of the living.

Traditionally Akans name the child after the day of its birth. For example, a Friday-born male child is called Kofi, a Saturday-born male is called Kwame, and a Sunday-born male is called Kwasi. A Saturday-born female is called Amma, and a Sunday-born female is called Akosua.

The giving of the personal name has been adopted with small modifications by some African Independent churches in Ghana and elsewhere on the continent. My present example is drawn from the practice of the church of the Messiah in Ghana. As in the traditional practice, among the members of the Church of the Messiah, the baby is taken to the temple on the eighth day. The father of the child presents about three names to the spiritual father (the priest) who, through meditation, selects the right name for the child.

The spiritual father then drops water three times into the child's mouth, saying, "The whole congregation will be a witness to your life, and when you say 'Yes' it is 'Yes' and 'No' must be 'No.' Let your Yes be Yes and your No, No." Taking salt, the spiritual father continues: "This day I give you salt, and according to the Bible you are the salt of the earth, but if the salt loses its taste, how shall its saltiness be restored? It is no longer good for anything except to be thrown out and trodden underfoot. Therefore from this day may your life be like the salt and may all trials and temptations which may be in your way be wiped away now and forever."

Finally, taking the honey (an alcoholic beverage is used in the traditional Akan custom), the spiritual father says: "This day I give you honey which is the witness of all humankind. May this honey wipe away all trials and temptations. Now Kofi Appiah-Kubi, we do not give you this name for you to be lazy, but rather that you should take up the cross of Christ and follow him in the wilderness, in the bush and in the villages. In the name of the Father, Son, and Holy Spirit, Amen."

Marriage

The African Independent churches recognize to a large extent the traditional system of African marriage. Instead of employing gold rings, wedding cakes, and other expensive articles used by the missionary churches, the Aladuras, for example, use eight different symbols. In place of the ring, they use the Bible. The couple grasp the Bible presented by the minister as the seal and sign of fidelity. Because of the hardiness and constant fruit-bearing of the banana plant with its large clusters of fruit, this plant is used to signify the profound hope of all African marriages—many children. The coconut is used to signify maturity or the secret blessing of God. Just as no one knows how the milk gets into the nut, so no one knows how the two are chosen by God for marriage. An orange is presented to symbolize a sound body and mind; bitter kola nuts symbolize long life and the wisdom and knowledge of God. Salt is given with the words "You are the salt of the earth; may you never lose your savor, but be a benefit to society." Honey is a sign of sweet marriage relationships with no bitterness, and finally a seven-branched candelabrum represents the prayer that the eyes of Almighty God and the living Lord may ever be upon the couple.

Position of Women

It has hitherto been believed by many travelers, missionaries, and writers, and even by some uninformed or misinformed modern scholars that the African woman is kept in a lowly state, that she is in fact, little more than an animal, a property to be bought and sold, enjoying neither sympathy nor respect. This notion coincided with the patriarchal structure of the western mission churches, with the result that ordination of women to the priesthood is non-existent in the mission churches.

The African Independent churches have outstripped the missionary churches in this area. There are many women church leaders and prophetesses. In West Africa, for example, most of our traditional shrines have women priestesses (e.g., Nana Oparebea of the Akonodi shrine at Larte).

There are also some women founders of churches; for example, Alice Lanshina of Lumpa church in Zambia, Captain Abiodum of Cherabim and Seraphim, and Alice Tania of the church of the Twelve Apostles in Ghana.

Music and Musical Instruments

The hymns and songs of most African Independent churches are often remarkably short and simple. They tend to be one-, two-, or three-line refrains. The contents embrace confessions, prayers, and praises, with constant refrains of "Amen," "Halleluja," and "Praise God." Some of these hymns have been composed by the church members themselves; others are taken directly from the mission churches.

A few examples will suffice here:

> Jesus your grace abounds,
> Jesus your grace abounds,
> You have brought the wayward home.

> I patiently wait for my Lord.
> I have become like a new-born babe.
> I patiently wait for my Lord.
>
> Thank him, thank him,
> Thank your king,
> For he is good,
> and his mercy is bountiful.

Most of these hymns are sung with drum accompaniment, hand-clapping, and dancing. They are also given a typical African touch in rhythm, tempo, and style. Like most African music, they are sung as duets or trios, with several refrains and repetitions of particular lines.

The African Independent churches have wholeheartedly accepted the use of locally made drums. The use of drums has been frowned upon by the missionary churches as pagan and therefore devilish. In fact, until recently no Christian could with impunity use any musical instrument in church except the piano and the organ, neither of which is built in Africa. Those who played the guitar were considered hooligans and unbelievers by members of the mission churches, and even today guitars are seldom allowed in churches of missionary origin. The African Independent churches use horns, rattles, and what may be called an African piano, in addition to drums and guitars of all sizes.

Sister Mary Aquina, in an article on the Rhodesian Zionists, remarks that the members of this church support their use of drumming and dancing with biblical quotations. In a sermon she heard, based on Psalms 149 and 150, the preacher said:

We Zionists please God with our drumming. In Psalm 149, verses 3 and 4, we read: "Let them praise his name with dancing, making melody to him with timbrel [translated as drums] and lyre [translated as the African piano]. For the Lord takes pleasure in His people. . . ." Here we are told to use the drum and the African piano, because we are told both drum and African piano please God. The Bible is our witness that we please God with our drumming. But many do not understand what we are doing and they think that we are playing. Look also at Psalm 150. There we read: "Praise him with trumpet sound; praise him with timbrel and dance." This proves that we teach only what is written in the Book. The Bible is our teacher.

Singing and drumming are usually accompanied by dancing. Dancing is mentioned together with singing in the Bible; in fact, David danced before the Ark of the Covenant.

12

The Theater in the Search for African Authenticity

'Zulu Sofola (Nigeria)

There is no doubt that the cultural renaissance that has stubbornly insisted on authentic African experience has included African Christianity. Questions are being asked by those whose sensibility tells them that Christianity is less than well rooted in African soil. Africanization has now become the vogue, and frantic attempts are being made to dress Christianity in an African garb, without, however, stripping off the dress in which it cloaked itself on its way to Africa from Europe. There is, therefore, a grotesque image standing on the altar of Christianity, an image that shocks the African believer and baffles the European missionary. The question now is, what shall Africans do to resolve this complex situation? How can Christianity be authentically rooted in African soil?

Here we will attempt to offer some approaches from the viewpoint of the theater artist. Theater is a medium of artistic expression where all aspects of the human experience are mirrored in a dynamic, living form. A metaphorical image of reality, it reflects the total cosmic, moral, and metaphysical order of the life of the people.[1] It is an arena where human beings are presented in a cosmic totality, acting and reacting to forces around them and within them, perceiving and being perceived by those interacting with them, and by those in the audience who experience with them the enigma that is the common lot of humanity. For human beings possess a consciousness that propels them into involvement in a universe bigger than themselves, as they restlessly question their own reality, the meaning of existence, and the forces that seem to manipulate them and the universe. The theater at its best is an arena where the pursuit of ultimate truth presents itself rid of bigotry, religious

126

dogmas, and fanaticism. Though playwrights stand between the characters and the audience, they communicate their artistic vision and insights through the characters who must experience life as the individuals they are, not according to what playwrights themselves believe. The drama of life is presented in a fluid and dynamic form for the purpose of binding, cleansing, rejuvenating, and communicating the communal moral and cosmic order for the edification of the human soul and the elevation of its intellectual wellbeing.[2]

In this paper Africans will be presented first in their own world, guided by their own definition and perception of cosmic reality and moral order, by their understanding of the place of humanity in the scheme of things. The Nigerian scene will be the central focus, a paradigm of the African world. In the second place, Africans will be presented through the medium of the theater within a world of artistic reality well rooted in African soil. Plays will be used to portray the African world as encapsulated by the playwright. This will be done in the hope that African Christians may see, through this dynamic contemplative medium, what perhaps their absorption in European Christianity ordinarily prevents them from seeing. Examination of the African world in its various manifestations is needed to equip the Africanization of the Gospel with the necessary building blocks. The theater, being a living entity, will help to focus the minds of theologians on the African world and people, a prerequisite for the search of African authenticity within the church.

THE AFRICAN WORLD

The African world is an integrated cosmos with a unique fluidity that makes unbroken continuity possible. It is a state of perpetual transmutation, which Wole Soyinka refers to as a state of transition.[3] The cosmos is seen as possessing a nerve center that holds all aspects of existence in place, but which, at the same time, gives each being free access to self-determination and volitional involvement in life without jeopardizing the existence of others. There is a certain mystic union which encourages amicable coexistence of all forces, and which at the same time makes truncation or indefinite suspension of transmutation impossible. This is the essence of the dark center where the mysterious continuum of transition and intertransmutation of life, both essential and material, occurs.[4] Thus all things, good and bad, come from the same source. There is a continuity in movement, a perpetual transition, cyclical in nature, eternal, yet not dichotomous as in the European view of the cosmos. The present is the meeting point between the past and the future, the past is transmuted into the present, and the present is in passage to the future. Thus those already born are the ancestors, and the living are the unborn in a passage of transition. There is a strong cohesiveness that binds all aspects of existence. But Africans are not unaware of cosmic tension and turbulence. There is great fluidity, but there are crucial points of crisis at certain stages of the process of transmutation. These stages, are viewed seriously as they have a decisive influence on the meaning of existence and the realization of its fulness. These crisis points of special concern to Africans seem to be seven in number.

1. Everything existed *ab initio* in essence and as one great Entity, a Force, which itself was not created and which has in its Being all that is. From it all things came and into its body shall all beings return. Each creature existed first in essence as a part of the Initial Essence before it evolved into an individual entity. The first stage of crisis in the process of transmutation occurs, therefore, at the point where the individual entity evolves and commences its journey. The matter is clear in the case of human beings, for it is at this point that individuals in essence participate in the making of their destinies. In essence, kneeling or standing before the Supreme Essence, they state what they would like to become in their material manifestations on earth. This stage is crucial as it will determine the nature of the series of reincarnations they will undergo before they are finally reunited with the Supreme Essence. For this reason spiritual partners are given to them. In the presence of these spiritual partners the individuals in essence engage in mutual contracts with the Supreme Essence. The latter sanctions the contract and the individuals are then ready for their journey to earth. We note that unlike the teachings of the Christian, European cosmic view, individuals here are actively involved in molding their own destinies. There is a free, mutual participation at a point where in Christian theology the individuals' destinies are forced upon them, with the resultant disharmony and strife.[5] There is consequently, in the European worldview, a tendency for individuals to engage in a continual war with the cosmos as they strive to get possession of what they believe Fate has robbed them of. The integrated cosmic whole falls apart in the European world because individuals are separate entities existing on their own, grabbing what they can at the expense of other beings. Christianity, coming to us through Europe, brings this self-centered spirit and the rejection of amicable coexistence, and the African soul rejects it.

2. The second crisis point in the process of transition or transmutation takes place at the gate of heaven. This is the point where individuals, after choosing their destinies, confront the first set of beings. What happens at this point determines to a great extent the fulfillment of the dreams that they made known to the Supreme Being, and for which both they and their spiritual partners have commenced the journey to earth. What happens here can, moreover, turn a good life into a miserable one, threaten a good destiny, and make an individual destined for a long life into one with a short life.

The complex nature of this situation is compounded by the fact that the destiny is often forgotten by a person after birth, though the oracular art can be consulted for recollection and redirection. The spiritual partners might not be able to make the individuals turn to the nerve center of their being to rediscover what they said in essence before the Supreme Deity. The result would be a total disarray of life, for all subsequent transitional stages depend on what occurs at this point.

3. The next crisis occurs when the essence is transmuted into flesh. The seriousness with which Africans view this stage is reflected in their insistence on peace and quiet during the night. The stage of transmutation into flesh is achieved in the act of sexual union. The essence at this crucial point undergoes a transmutation into a physical being, and is then deprived of much of its mystic and spiritual quality. We can understand why African communities express their concern over this moment of transition and surround the act with taboos and general environmental conditions that must be observed. Since night brings time for deep communion with the Supreme Deity, time when the human soul seeks rejuvenation through a return to the fount of life, time when the Initial Essence strives to renew in creation what was lost in the day's activities, it is only natural that this crucial stage of transmutation should occur when all is at peace. What happens at this point is believed either to enhance or disrupt the destiny, and the sexual act is therefore not a mere physical, erotic act, but a crucial moment in the process of transmutation.

4. Following the stage of transmutation into flesh comes the period of gestation climaxed by the ejection of the child into the physical world. As was true for the individual essence in the process of its separation from the Supreme Essence, so now the essence in flesh remains a part of the being of the mother until at birth it becomes a separate individual ready to face its own journey through life. This journey will last until death brings an end to this particular component in a series of reincarnations that are to be undergone before the essence finally reunites with the Supreme Being. This period is filled with traumatic experiences and fearful expectations of joy. As the Umu-Ezechima put it, the *Ashi* or *Nkwa* of both child and mother are occupying the same zone at the same time. The mother is aware of her own *Ashi,* or destiny, but that of her unborn child is still a mystery.

Pregnancy is usually a time of great joy among Africans, but there is always an awareness that the mother is a receptacle for the new essence and individual whom she did not create and whose destiny she certainly had no part in making. During pregnancy there exist simultaneously two individuals whose destinies are different and whose "essences" may conflict with one another. For the unborn ancestor in passage may have unresolved problems from a previous life that may threaten the life of the mother. This factor—in addition to earthly forces of evil, such as witches—contributes to the traumas of this stage. Then, too, the mother herself may have had her own destiny interfered with, and the result might be the death of the child being sent into the world through her.

As might be expected, the crucial point of crisis in this process is the stage of labor and delivery. Often Europeans and so-called educated Africans refer to the people's concern during childbirth as primitive and superstitious, yet seen within the framework of the people's cosmic view, it is a period that deserves great concern.

5. The next point of crisis, analogous to the period of pregnancy and childbirth, is that of life here on earth and its termination through death. Life is a struggle; it is a chain of events that at times seems to aim at the destruction of the individual. Africans are very much concerned about this and engage in a series of spiritual, supernatural, and physical exercises to protect themselves. The primary concern is one's destiny. Individuals must, therefore, discover, through the proper channels, what are their particular destinies, whether anything has gone wrong at any particular stage, and if so, what they can do to rectify things. Africans have often been regarded as preoccupied with warding off evil, but Africans who concentrate on the spiritual in their quest for the true nature of their destinies do so in the belief that the concept of destiny is positive and healthy. The fact is that certain disruptive forces here on earth may prevent individuals from achieving their destinies.

After a journey on earth, with its chain of crises, death comes, bringing its own traumas as individuals push through to another level of transmutation. There is definitely a severe struggle at this point, and the ease with which the end comes depends heavily on whether it is the death destined for the individual or premature death caused by other forces. If it is the former, the spirit or essence returns to the Supreme Deity to restate or modify its destiny in preparation for a return through reincarnation. But if the death has been premature, the spirit wanders about in the forest and the community until the time destined for death occurs. At this time, as in the first case, the essence returns to the Supreme Deity for another attempt at life through reincarnation. Death, therefore, is not a termination of life, but a stage of transition. Hence the dead are not dead.

6. The sixth level of transmutation consists of a series of reincarnations during which individuals are given a wide opportunity to improve before they reunite with the Initial Essence. This stage is a complicated process that can be but briefly examined here.

There are two forms of reincarnation. The first is that in which a child is born immediately following the death of a member of the family. In this case, the child is of the same sex as the deceased member, and in most cases resembles that person. In some cases the child is conceived immediately after the person's death, or is already conceived before the death occurs. In the latter case, the person is said to have died though his physical frame is still alive, but he must die physically before the child is born, or else it will not be he who is returning. In this form of reincarnation, the deceased must return within the first year after death, preferably within the first nine months, and he must return in the same sex. The proximity of the time of death to the time of the next birth seems sufficient to identify the one who is reincarnating. The child is given the exact name of the person reincarnating, so that the person is seen as returning in his totality.

The second form of reincarnation is that of the essence of an individual of either sex for as many times as may be required to complete the destined cycle. The deceased may reincarnate at any point in time, and for this reason the oracle must be consulted to verify the reincarnation. The returning ancestor may announce his coming by pronounced characteristics that lead the family to suspect his return even before it is confirmed by the oracle. At other times he insists on being recognized through abnormal crying, restless-ness, and physical ailments that fail to respond to medical care. It is often thought that those who present themselves through distress need recogni-tion immediately, either because of a lack of attention suffered in their previous life, or because there is a ritual act of some sort that must be performed before the spirit can settle in the newborn child. Once recog-nized, the person is welcomed with songs of praise.

Although it is usually members of the immediate family who reincarnate, there are times where in-laws and very close friends return. In such cases a ritual known as "the opening of the door" must be performed; otherwise the spirit of the reincarnated will remain outside the family. Quite often a situation of this sort is ridden with problems, for the reincarnated one is often sensitive to the fact that he is not a member of the family, and withdraws or sulks much more frequently than the bona fide members of the family.

In both types of reincarnation, there may arise many complications, par-ticularly if the person returning is known to have led an evil life in his previous existence; for then the family is burdened with the rites and rituals necessary to help in the purification of the newborn child. Then, too, the reincarnated may pollute the family tree and frighten people from marrying into the family.

To the European mind this system may appear unfair and inhuman, but concern for what individual members of the family do, and what the family as a whole does, enhances family solidarity. It forces the individual to see confession, forgiveness, purification, and even expulsion as being essential to present and future life.

7. The final and seventh stage in human transmutation is the return of the essence to the Supreme Essence from which it came. The ancestor whose essence has completed its cycle ceases to reincarnate and thus seems to be

lost to the memory of the living. With the African people there is nothing like the Christian hell. What one has to suffer takes place here on earth or in the world of ancestral spirits where people may disregard one, or perform rites and rituals that might control one's reincarnation, or even transform one into a nonhuman form like an anthill or mushroom.

The foregoing analysis portrays the concepts of totality and interrelatedness in African cosmology, what Wole Soyinka calls cosmic unity unfolded through intertransmutation.[6]

AFRICAN THEATER

We shall now examine *A Dance of the Forests*[7] and *Wedlock of the Gods*[8] to show how drama demonstrates aspects of the African cosmic view. *The Gods Are Not to Blame*[9] will be considered as exemplifying the European cosmic view forced upon Africans.

A Dance of the Forests was written to celebrate Nigerian independence in 1960. Because this was an occasion for rejoicing and reflection on the glories and achievements of the past, one would naturally have expected a play of joy and hope. Instead, we have a bitter satire set in the forest. It is the concept of forest among the Yoruba in particular and the Nigerians in general that will receive our attention.

Contrary to the European notion of the forest as a place where life is renewed and rejuvenated, the forest in this play is a place of disorder, chaos, abnormality, and unsettled spirits. To Shakespeare's Europe, as in the typical classical comedy, the Forest of Arden typified the renewal of self and the restitution of lost power, amity, and love. But Wole Soyinka envisioned the birth of independence as taking place in the chaotic dungeon of the forest. To him the forest was a place of utter disorder and chaos, the direct opposite of a place of human abode, a place where the spirits of those who died prematurely lingered until the time of their appointed death released them and they could settle in the spirit world. It was the abode of those denied burial because of some abominable act, a place where spirits lingered, burdened with fear and guilt, while they wandered about destroying human life and vegetation and polluting the earth. It was likewise a place where mothers who died before an illegitimate childbirth were buried, and the forest was filled with the dreadful cries of the unborn children whose destinies were unfulfilled.

The playwright saw the country as sick with corruption, injustice, bitterness, confusion of purpose and objectives, a loss of direction, and in the clutch of a demonic presence that would destroy the new life as soon as it was born. Independence was seen as a very significant moment of transition, but the past and the present were so grim that one feared for the newly born.

The forest in this play, therefore, is not the abode of ancestors who interact with and are appeased by the living. Setting the birth of Nigerian independence in this type of forest foretold the crises which were to follow, and which confirmed Soyinka's farsightedness.

In *Wedlock of the Gods* the themes are adultery and its punishment. A young woman, Ogwoma, forced to marry against her will, resorts to adultery in a desperate attempt to avoid Leviration and has illicit relations with the man she had desired to marry. The sin must be punished to propitiate the dead, the living, and the unborn.

Adultery, within the Nigerian context, may be divided into two broad categories: legal adultery and illegal adultery.

Legal adultery. Because of the African people's desire for many children, childless marriages are treated as special cases, and actions that would normally be considered sinful are condoned. In cases where the husband is impotent, the wife is permitted to have children by a man other than her husband, with the full approval of her husband and kinsfolk. The children of this union are considered to be the children of the husband. The lover, in these cases, is usually an outsider, but at times, to preserve the family blood, the brother of the husband is allowed to assume the role of lover.

A second case concerns the remarriage of a woman whose husband dies while she is still of child-bearing age. Such a woman is permitted to take a lover who is known as the "ghost father," and the children born of this union are said to "ride on the back of the dead husband"— *"imutinye nwa na azu di."* A variant of this form of legal adultery occurs when the husband dies early in marriage, before he has any issue. The wife is then encouraged to take a lover by whom she will have the children denied to her by her dead husband, whose children they will be considered to be.

A third form of legal adultery at times occurs in the case of a married woman who is childless and wealthy. Because of the African custom of considering a woman the wife of the one who pays her dowry, such a woman can pay a dowry to another woman and thus become her "woman-husband." The wife is allowed to have a lover, and the children born will be considered the children of the childless woman and will bear her name. This is possible because in most African systems the children can bear the name of either parent. The childless woman thus ensures that she has her own children who will bury her when it comes time for her to die.

Illegal adultery. Three forms of illegal adultery are recognized, and all are considered sinful. The first form results when a married man engages in a sexual act with a married woman whose husband is still living. If the woman were unmarried, the act would not be considered sinful, for we are dealing with a polygamous system.

The second form of illegal adultery is that in which a married woman engages in an extramarital affair with a man, married or unmarried, who is not her husband. The point here is that a man's wife is his alone, as long as he is neither impotent nor dead. The third form of illegal adultery is incest between brother-in-law and sister-in-law.

The worst form of adultery is that which takes place while a woman is still in mourning for her dead husband. This type of adultery has grave repercussions on the living, the dead, and the unborn members of the family. Severe disorganization is introduced into the family: the dead husband's spirit cannot return to the world of the ancestors; his reincarnation is dreaded for it would disrupt the destinies of the one in whom he were reincarnated; indeed the entire system of transmutation is put in jeopardy. This is the type of illicit affair treated in the play *Wedlock of the Gods.* Ogwoma's act emanated from her protest against an unwanted marriage and from her desire to be united in marriage with the man she loved. According to the customs of her people, no pardon was possible, so her mother-in-law acted rightly in avenging the wrong done to her dead son. To propitiate the living, the ancestors, the gods, and the unborn, Ogwoma had to be killed and thrown, together with her unborn child, into the forbidden forest, unburied and unmourned.

The third play to be considered is *The Gods Are Not to Blame,* by Ola Rotimi. It is an adaptation of the Greek play *Oedipus Rex,* by Sophocles. Rotimi's play is of special interest here because it is an attempt to clothe the Greek cosmic view in a Nigerian garb, just as African Christians are attempting to cloak in African garb a Christ from Europe.

The striking areas of affinity with the African world found in this play are those of destiny and the effects of an individual's sin on the community as a whole. In Greek cosmology destiny is forced on individuals who are thus helplessly burdened with what they can neither influence nor alter. They may try to run away, but they cannot escape. Their natural impulse is to fight these natural and supernatural forces in order to survive. Africans, on the other hand, as we have seen, actively participate in the making of their own destinies, and irrational and intolerable arrangements of their lives rarely occur. Hence it would be inconceivable that an African would ever be destined to kill his own father and marry his own mother. Nor would an African god have ordained that a child should commit a murder in order to right a wrong which was still unrighted, but which had been committed earlier in his life. An African oracle might insist that unless the blood of the murdered one were avenged by someone, the child would have to kill. This might include the killing of his own father, but the oracle would definitely not include the marrying of his own mother.

In a case like this, the family, upon discovering what had been done, would perform the required ritual (*Igigbu*) and save the child. The child would not have been killed or thrown away to perish, an act which would have automatically ended the play as soon as it had begun. In other words, there would have been no play.

The next problem in this transplant of a Greek cosmology into a Yoruba world is that of a total stranger's inheriting the throne. Strangers were normally used as sacrificial victims in an established kingdom such as is presented in this play. That the people of Kutuje would make a total stranger, Odewale, their king would be virtually unthinkable. Though there have been times in African history where an established kingdom has invited an outsider to rule over it, this has been an emergency measure, and the kingmakers have always consulted the oracle to justify their decisions. Moreover the suitability of the invited candidate has always been investigated. As one who would link his people to their gods, he had to be free from blemish. Consequently, the kingmakers of Kutuje would have discovered the awful destiny hanging over Odewale's head, and would have rejected him. He would never have been made their king, let alone been allowed to marry his own mother. Furthermore, the African kingship system is a communal focal point for the ancestors, the living, and the unborn. The living king must reach the gods through the ancestors on behalf of the living. It is his duty to keep the life of the people intact through his own clean life and the rites and rituals he performs on behalf of the people. A stranger king would not know the ancestors, nor would they know him. As a result, his propitiatory rituals, rites, and prayers would miscarry.

However, even had Odewale consented to the murder of his father and a marriage with his mother, when he returned to be crowned king of Kutuje, the kingmakers would at that time have consulted the Ifa Oracle, and the initial problem would have surfaced once again. Odewale would then have been put to death and eliminated completely. But if by some chance he had been crowned, had married his own mother, and had had children by her, when the truth became known, he would have been killed together with the children of this monstrous union. He would not have been allowed to wander off with the children who would have been able to return to Kutuje as their father had. The community would have gotten rid of these evildoers once and for all.

Ola Rotimi seems to have been blind to the reality of the African world when he transplanted a Greek worldview into the Yoruba cosmos. His primary concern seems to have been to give the Greek characters and towns Yoruba names, to dress the characters in Yoruba attire, and to allow them to dance and talk as Yorubans with Greek soul. The play thus becomes a caricature of the Yoruba reality. *A Dance of the Forests* and *Wedlock of the Gods,* on the other hand, are plays authentically rooted in African soil, faithful to the realities of the African cosmos.

The same process as we see in *The Gods Are Not to Blame* seems to be occurring in the frantic but misdirected desire of African Christians to dress Christ in African clothes, without giving thought to the European soul with which Christ came to Africa. Unless Christ is presented to Africans in a manner acceptable to the African mentality, Christianity will remain alien and irrelevant. Christ must have an African soul, a soul that understands the realities of the African cosmos, before he can respond to our lyrics, dances, and customs. He must first be liberated from the grip of Europeanism before he can be embraced by Africans in their quest for self-realization and liberation.

NOTES

1. James M. Clay and Daniel Krempel, *The Theatre Image* (New York: McGraw-Hill Book Co., 1967), p. 25.

2. Wole Soyinka, *Myth, Literature, and the African World* (London: Cambridge University Press, 1976), p. 4.

3. Ibid., p. 5.

4. Ibid., p. 26.

5. F. M. Cornford, *From Religion to Philosophy: A Study in the Origin of Western Speculation* (New York: Harper Torchbooks, Harper Brothers, 1957), pp. 8–22.

6. Wole Soyinka, *Myth, Literature, and the African World*, p. 26.

7. Wole Soyinka, *A Dance of the Forests* (London: Oxford University Press, 1963).

8. 'Zulu Sofola, *Wedlock of the Gods* (London: Evans Brothers, Ltd., 1973).

9. Ola Rotimi, *The Gods Are Not to Blame* (London: Oxford University Press, 1971).

13

Black African Art as Cosmic Liturgy and Religious Language

Engelbert Mveng, S.J. (Cameroun)

I have been asked to speak to you about the Lagos Festival, and I have spent much time pondering how I should broach this topic. Ordinarily a festival illustrates the cultural vitality of a people, an age, or a group. Viewed from the outside, every festival is part of the mundane world and everyday life. It is thus bound up with entertainment, publicity, commercial transactions, and the meeting of different interests. That is not what interests you here, however. Viewed from the inside, on the other hand, festivals usually manifest the cultural vitality of a group. What truly interests theologians, then, is the import of this cultural life and the foundations on which it rests. So I have decided to talk to you about the essential ingredient of the Lagos Festival: i.e., black art. I shall consider this art insofar as it is a cosmic liturgy and a religious language.

To comprehend the thinking of a people, one must have solid knowledge of their language and their conception of the world. To appreciate something like the Lagos Festival, one must get down to its underlying import. That is to say, one must get down to the conception of humanity and the world that it expresses. The philosophy of Plato and Aristotle is unintelligible to those who have no idea of their anthropology and their cosmology.

Black art is essentially a *cosmic liturgy* and a *religious language.* Such language establishes a permanent link between the *destiny of humanity and that of the cosmos,* however scientific or not may be its underlying image of the world. Should we refer to this as theological language? I think it is something more than that. I think it is religious language. In any case it has to do with the essential thing, with the perduring link between humanity, the cosmos, and

137

God. Hence we must take the language of African art seriously, for it is addressed specifically to theologians.

In my book, which bears the same title as this paper (2nd edition, CLE, Yaoundé, 1974), I showed that the language of black art is anthropological, cosmological, and liturgical. I will not repeat my argument here, but I will try to make the essential points.

ANTHROPOLOGICAL LANGUAGE

It may seem banal to say that black art expresses the human being. However, the human being is a complex reality. Close study of African tradition reveals that its art expresses human beings insofar as they are *beings with a destiny*. Their destiny in this case is life flaunting its reason for being in the face of death. It is the ongoing struggle between life and death, and ultimately the victory of life over death. Human beings are beings with a destiny insofar as they are the battleground for the struggle between life and death, the combatants who take sides with or against life, and the initiates in whom the victory of life over death (or its defeat by death) is verified.

The fact is that the vocation of human beings on earth is to ensure the victory of life over death.

Black art is a language of signs and symbols that are messengers of either life or death. In my aforementioned book, I offered this analysis of colors and their symbolism in African art:

> red = life
> white = death
> black = night, suffering, testing

These three colors sum up the destiny of human beings, who are caught between life, death, and suffering.

In my book I also analyzed what I call the *solid or real body of symbols:* i.e., the serpent, the tortoise, the cowrie, the kola nut, and so forth. In African art all of these convey some message of life or death to human beings. Thus the great book of African art enables human beings to examine the visage of the cosmos and read of the names of those who are allied with life and those who are not. This is the deeper import of such symbolism.

Black art also expresses human beings insofar as they are *persons,* insofar as they bear within themselves all the elements involved in the struggle for life and its victory and serve as a network of vital relationships that gives concrete, historical reality to them as persons.

That is why African art gives expression to human beings as *monad, dyad, triad,* and *community.* As monad the human being is simply an individual, the bare outline of a person with no concrete consistency. As *dyad* the human being appears in the twofold *male-female* dimension, which gives real consistency to the human person. Here is the locus of encounter, dialogue, confrontation, choice, and freedom. It is the moment for initiations, love, and freedom. Those who have passed through the hallowed rites of initiation reach the portals of freedom and love. Human beings then move from dyad to triad: *father–mother–infant.*

Representation of the couple in African art goes back to prehistory. Egyptian art, like other styles of black art, depicts the ancestral couples. The father–mother–child triad is equally universal, expressed in figures and even more important in symbolic language.

It is in the course of the rites of initiation that the young people learn the rudiments of their artistic tradition and celebrate the mystery of life and death. Thus one can readily see why rite and art are inextricably linked together. They are born from the same source, express the same reality, and tend toward the same end.

Monad, dyad, and triad reveal the basic structure of the human person. Because this structure is essentially a network of interpersonal relationships, it is simultaneously *crowd* and *community.*

For us, then, art expresses the creativity of living communities. This does not mean that the group suppresses the individual. The two are complementary. The male-female relationship, which is the prototype of every human relationship, is grounded on complementarity.

We do well to focus for a moment on the anthropology of black Africa as it appears in black art. The *human person* is never a monad. The individual is not a person in the African understanding of the latter term; it is simply the projected outline of a person. The human being is defined as a person insofar as it is a network of interpersonal and cosmic relationships. It is the recapitulation of both the cosmos and humanity. Human beings are linked to each other and the world; they are an extension of both. Every human initiative effects fulfillment, insofar as the cosmos once again attains freedom and awareness; and it also sets in motion the whole world system that pivots about our being. The African notion of the person is dynamic. One is all the more a person insofar as one is integrated into the world and society.

Such a view of the person has immediate consequences on the plane of ethics. Moral responsibility means taking charge of one's destiny, a destiny that is inextricably bound up with the destiny of both the cosmos and the human community.

In African art it is apparent that the male-female relationship is not accidental, it is constitutive of the person. Rather than being primarily a matter of law and right, it is in the order of nature. The same holds true for a person's relationships with fellow human beings and the cosmos. All our actions have a cosmic and social dimension. Our responsibility before God is primarily a matter of our responsibility toward ourselves, our fellow humans, and the entire cosmos.

Such a conception of the person can greatly aid any theological expression of *faith*. What theologians call "Christology" is nothing else but an attempt to express the mystery of Christ in terms of the anthropology that is part of the theologian's own tradition. Judeo-Hellenistic tradition, for example, describes the mystery of the incarnation in terms of the mystery of the *Word-made-flesh*. The vocabulary used stems from that tradition. African tradition prefers to talk about the mystery of the *Son of God* becoming the *Son of Man*. It is a mystery of "humanization" or "humanification," if you will.

Now as we saw above, real human beings are a network of interpersonal and cosmic relationships. Thus the incarnation enables Christ to assume all of humanity and the cosmos. Strictly speaking, he realizes a *new creation* that contains a new humanity, a new heaven, and a new earth. That is why a *sacrament* is the cosmic manifestation of the incarnation. It is the Son of God turned into the *water* of Baptism, the *bread and wine* of the Eucharist, the *anointing* that consecrates, and the *words, gestures, and rites* that sanctify.

Getting back to African art, then, we see that our consideration of its anthropological dimension has led us directly to its *cosmic* and *liturgical* dimensions.

COSMIC LANGUAGE

If black art expresses the human being, it also expresses the world insofar as the world is bound up with human destiny. Indeed the world is conceived in the image of human beings. The language of art deciphers the great book of the world, which is written in the letters of life and death and addressed to human beings. The struggle between life and death does not take place solely in the heart of human beings; it fills the entire cosmos. All that exists—spirits, cosmic forces, natural elements, living and dead human beings—are mobilized in this struggle. They are found to be either on the side of life or on the side of death. The importance of the symbolism of black art is that it enables us to look at the great book of the world and find out the names of those allied to the two camps. We thus can find out who our friends and who our adversaries are.

In creating a work of art the artist creates a new world and humanizes nature. Black African esthetics takes the cosmic battlefield where life and death confront each other and transforms it into the Elysian Fields where life chants its victory over death. Every work of art breathes a whiff of immortality into inert and mortal matter. Every rite, dance, piece of music, and work of plastic art is a cosmic celebration of life's victory over death. It is a cosmic liturgy.

That is why all the forms of traditional art are complementary. It is the human body that unites them in liturgical celebration, that brings together gesture, word, dance, music, dress, ornamentation, tatoo, makeup, mask, architecture, time, and space. Through artistic expression human beings become the soul of soulless things and the voice of voiceless things. They become *earth, air, fire,* and *water.* They are at once body and spirit, a microcosm in the heart of the macrocosm.

To write the book about black African esthetics would be to write about creative wisdom. For us esthetics is not in the order of sensuousness linked with concupiscence. The laws of esthetics are the laws of *life* and *love.* The beautiful is love incarnated, objectified, and personified. And for us love is always the victory of life over death.

Thus the language of African art is eminently *religious,* not theological. It celebrates the human adventure under the gaze of God. It celebrates the wonders of God. But it does not judge God, or describe God, or unveil God, or profane God.

CONCLUSION

The Lagos Festival, then, can be seen in its true dimensions in terms of what I have said above. Manifesting the cultural vitality of black Africans, it was a time for reflection and an examination of conscience. That is why it ended up with a colloquium on *education.* Feeling their own pulse, blacks realized that the surface waters of their vitality were in turmoil. For them artistic expression is the supreme way in which they express their victory over death. Today, in Black Africa, death takes the form of racial hatred and bigotry (South Africa), neocolonialism, economic exploitation, cultural suppression, and the spiritual suffocation of disembodied religions. If the creative genius of black people dies, it will be the end of our people. Our survival requires the restoration of our cultural sovereignty. That is why education is so important.

Some visitors at the Lagos Festival were struck by the youthfulness and dynamism of the participants. Some were surprised by the slogans and shibboleths used: e.g., "Jazz is my religion." But every people expresses its religious experience in its own way. For us black Africans, art is our supreme mode of expression. Intellectual speculation has its merits, of course; but in every civilization art represents the peak of human creative experience.

That is why we feel that we must promote a dynamic and authentically religious art in Africa. Sacred architecture, liturgy, music, dance, and the plastic arts should help our people in their quest for dialogue with God. Thus we will be able to avoid all those "atheist" religions that have no churches, or that have churches without art, religious symbolism, music, joy, or hope.

Theological training should provide solid grounding in the artistic forms of the African tradition. African Christians should forge a Christian idiom that is deeply rooted in the tradition of black art, for black art is both religious language and a cosmic liturgy.

—Translated by John Drury

PART THREE

LIBERATION CURRENTS

We feel called to proclaim the love of God for all people within the dynamics of a conflictual history. We are committed to the struggles of our people to be free. . . .

The struggles for the transformation of socio-economic systems, the struggles against racism, sexism, and other forms of economic, political, social, and cultural oppressions, are all to be taken seriously as sources for theology. . . .

We recognize that African women have taken an active role in the church and in the shaping of our history. They have shown themselves to be an integrated part of the liberation struggle. But we cannot ignore their exclusion from our past theological endeavors. The future of African theology must take seriously the role of women in the church as equals in the doing of theology [see Chapters 14 and 15]. . . .

There are many forms of oppression. There is the oppression of Africans by white colonialism, but there is also the oppression of blacks by blacks. We stand against oppression in any form because the Gospel of Jesus Christ demands our participation in the struggle to free people from all forms of dehumanization [see Chapters 16, 17, and 18]. . . .

The focus on liberation in African theology connects it with other Third World theologies. Like black theologians in North America, we cannot ignore racism as a distortion of the human person. Like Latin American and Asian theologians, we see the need to be liberated from socio-economic exploitation. . . . African theology concerns itself with bringing about the solidarity of Africans with black Americans, Asians, and Latin Americans who are also struggling for the realization of human communities in which the men and women of our time become the architects of their own destiny [see Chapter 19].

—*Final Communiqué, Pan-African Conference of Third World Theologians*

14

The Role of Women in Present-Day Africa

Rose Zoé-Obianga (Cameroun)

PERSONAL EXPERIENCE

In the course of the past seven years since my return to my country, my role has taken on three important aspects:

1. I have been working for the church in educational programs for young people. On the administrative level, we have been involved in the formation of those who are to shape the young, by developing the existing institutions and by creating new ones that can meet the standards of modern life.

The problems have not been simple. The need has not been to create schools and colleges in order to allow teachers to improve themselves during periods of renewal financed by the West. The fundamental problem was, and still is, to desist from fostering negative values among maturing young people. The problem is how to bring to full awareness the young people of Cameroun in particular and young Africans in general, with regard to their own living and dynamic culture. We must help them meet the demands of modern life, while promoting values that are not irreconcilable with the legacy of their ancestors.

On another level I have been involved in the establishment of a church-related school in the capital, where young people are being drawn to the rather superficial side of modern life, namely the cinema, dances, sports, etc. We would not like to be accused of belittling all forms of art, but what can one say when confronted with all the modern films that are useless and harmful because they are incapable of arousing in the young sentiments and patterns of behavior worthy of the future of the country, of Africa, and of the world?

One is shocked by an attitude of heart-rending irresponsibility on the part of parents who have forgotten or who do not know that the education of children begins at home, and that, when they arrive in our hands, it is already too late to recover them.

And so we often ask ourselves: What is the purpose of a church-related school? Would it not be better to transfer to the state the duty of educating them, since we cannot provide for these young people anything specifically Christian? Then could we not get along with Sunday schools and Bible classes, etc.?

2. Next, as an elder of the church, it has been my role to participate in the administration of the parishes, of synods, and of general assemblies of our church. I have also been involved in encouraging ideas that will assist in the consolidation of our church and will enable it to respond effectively to the needs of the Christian people in Africa today. I have been working to uphold in one way or another the Christian faith in our countries, to spread the Good News of Christ, and to support the evangelization and development of men and women for their material and spiritual welfare.

3. Finally, I am one of the officers in the Association of Christian Women of our church. In this work the action is more extensive because the problems are more complex. Our association is one of the most important in our country, having more than 20,000 regularly enrolled members.

The work is immense. It consists first of all in organizing a structure that enables women to fulfill their various vocations. The women must have programs of action, evangelization, formation, and support to carry on. They also need to create relations with other feminist associations, religious or otherwise, within our country, but also throughout Africa and the whole world. Finally they need to participate in the programs of our church of which they are at the present time the principal source of vitality. Of course all this takes effort, time, and material and spiritual means.

THE GENERAL ATTITUDE OF THE CHURCH

Active roles such as the one we have been describing seem to be rare or exceptional. Women have to face those obstacles that come from within themselves, but also those from outside, from those who accuse us of being revolutionaries, dangerous subversives. Our commitment is viewed as provocative and often causes us to be abused or scorned to a discouraging degree.

In any case we must take this into account: If African society is making praiseworthy efforts to allow women to branch out into various new roles, such is not the case in the majority of our churches, on the part of most ecclesiastical leaders. This all stems from a certain conception of woman that still paralyzes many of our ministers and elders of the church. In general our opponents can be characterized as:

a. those who uphold the timeworn adage: "Women have long hair, but short ideas," which reflects a retrograde and limited view. The emergence of women, although it is still timid, these people would say, does not reflect the wishes of the majority of women in our church.

b. those who do not allow participation in the Association of Women. At whatever level, the women belong to these men, and the men can do as they wish with them. This results in a power struggle and inevitably creates a dangerous competition.

c. those who—because the women are demanding admission into management—frequently choose and appoint not the most competent women, but the most scheming, the most likely to support them in their struggles with other ministers; the criteria for choosing them is not their effectiveness.

d. those who do not admit, although there is no theological basis against it, that women can become ministers in our church. They refuse because of their personal advantage, not because they have any irrefutable proof either in the Bible or in their constitutions.

As a consequence women have been allowed to give only a spontaneous expression of their faith, one that is naive and credulous. Their ideas are of no consequence. Their point of view leaves the world indifferent. Their self-awareness seems dangerous because it could dethrone man from his pedestal.

IN PRESENT-DAY AFRICA

To commit ourselves at the present time is above all to become fully aware of our role in the church of today. We are living now in a period of latent unrest that seems to carry us along with it. People are asking the reasons for this state of confusion. On all levels there are pressing questions, most especially for women. In view of the prevailing situation, all women, each woman, should be fully aware of belonging to the church of today. It is not the church of yesterday, nor that of tomorrow, but that of today.

The church in Africa is a product of colonization. We should say that today's church is colonial or post-colonial. Just as there has never been any African theology, there has never been any appreciable involvement of African women in the church.

We must henceforth be our "own missionaries." It is up to women—and men—to listen to the questions asked in our Christian community; it is up to us to reflect calmly and courageously upon the church handed over to us by the missionaries of the West. We must point out the very real danger of keeping women out of all decision-making within our churches. For a long time, in the wake of the missionaries, African women could not recognize and appreciate the church in which they found themselves. They could not become aware of their true position with all the consequences that this position was to bring with it. Women have a legitimate place in the church today because they belong to this church. And their help is fully efficacious. The ravages have been enormous and deep. The time for inertia has passed, well passed. More than simply a critical glance is required. There must be penetration, a feminist penetration of the church.

This shift is necessary and obligatory for those committed to an authentic African Christianity. The difficulties of the enterprise cannot be hidden from anyone. To speak of the church in Africa today is to start down a very dangerous, but a very exciting path.

To play a role, to become committed, means to give up being a mere spectator. A conscientious awareness of belonging to the church today does not mean keeping our arms folded, still less applauding noisily all that is said and done. Involvement must not be limited to the lowest, most naive level. Certainly women are numerous, they sing a lot, they dance with zest, they pray with fervor, they preach with much eloquence; but what do we discover? For want of education and formation on the part of the church, they are often incapable of taking firm stands, clear-cut positions.

African women must be willing to fight the good fight. They must be willing to fight *against* their own alienation, their timidity, and *for* their influence within the church. They must be willing to fight at the side of their brothers, whose struggle would thus become efficacious as they recognize their own true worth. Isolation is not and never will be profitable to the men. No, in Christ there is neither male nor female. . . .

This will be possible only if women succeed in getting rid of certain complexes that are both paralyzing and alienating, for example, the timidity of which we spoke, the excessive shyness. These complexes should not be acceptable when it is a question of the survival and triumph of the Gospel.

To be committed is to put oneself at the service of Christ. The service that I speak of is a commitment to Christ, and not a commitment to the administrative church, to the church of the ministers. No, Christ is without mercy. There is no possible compromise. There is no room for procrastination. Christ on the Cross wants our bodies and souls. He tolerates no limitation, no lapses.

Commitment to Christ requires the liberation of African women. They will no longer be slaves: not of uncomprehending and intransigent husbands and brothers, nor of a retrogressive society, nor of alienating church structures. They are freed by their faith that opens all possible horizons to them.

Commitment to Christ presupposes a break with everything and with everybody. Family, work, leisure, all must be radically reviewed in the light of Christ's demands. And we well know that children, husbands, friends, and colleagues will almost always be obstacles to the commitment of women. The same will be true of other Christians (namely, men, whose attitude is often condescending, even scornful, negative, and demoralizing, as well as other women who have no confidence in women and who will be the first to ridicule them). Indeed, other Christians can often be the worst obstacles.

Decisions are at the center of power. In fact any person who can make decisions holds power. We point up the fact that—because of the deliberate absence of women from decision-making within our churches—true control is in the hands of men only. And they do not want to let go.

CONCLUSION

In conclusion, if the modes of our various commitments are personal, even quite individual, they must lead us necessarily to responsibility, that is to say, a taking in hand of our individual destinies with regard to Christ and our participation in the tasks of the church.

We must get to know our problems, those of our Associations of Women, those of our churches, in order to judge them and discuss them properly, and finally to offer suggestions and adequate solutions.

To succeed in convincing our brethren we must therefore cease to play the role of figureheads and pawns whom men push around at will in the effort to show that we are forever incapable. Thanks to our mutual support, women will participate; they will give proof of unsuspected ability in making decisions.

Let the Africans, men and women, not behave in such a way as to show the world a mask that hides Jesus Christ.

—Translated by Aimée Bourneus

15

Women in South Africa: The WAAIC

Constance Baratang Thetele (South Africa)

AFRICAN INDEPENDENT CHURCHES

The African Independent Church movement comprises black men and women who got tired of being regarded as objects by their white missionary leaders. They seceded from the churches led by whites, whom they had come to recognize as racists who had invaded their culture, destroyed their historical traditions, perverted their institutions, and made them landless vagrants in their own country.

It is generally accepted that the phenomenon of religious fission and the development of sects is universal and has been a significant part of Christian tradition in Europe and the United States as well as among Third World peoples. What is especially significant for this process in South Africa is that it is a reaction to missionary efforts that attempted to assimilate elements of traditional African beliefs. Adrian Hastings suggests that the following factors have led to the appearance and growth of the African Independent churches:

1. Justification for secession provided by missionary theology
2. Lack of scope within the mission churches to allow for ritual and concretization of the sacral
3. Multiplication of Christian missions in one area
4. Need for small neighborhood worship groups to give a sense of security
5. A pattern of tribal life encouraging decentralization and fission
6. Areas of felt need for which the mission churches made no provision

150

7. Bar to senior promotion of native ministers within white-dominated churches
8. Color bar of the larger society also reflected in the churches
9. Disorientation with rapid social change, especially among the uneducated in the urban areas
10. No scope for African leadership in political, civic, and individual fields

All of the above factors were present in South Africa, whereas they apply in more limited ways to other parts of Africa. The proportionately high rate of proliferation in South Africa can be understood in light of the multiplication of these factors, all working concurrently.

The Independent churches in South Africa in many ways are both pre-revolutionary and actively revolutionary at the same time. They are pre-revolutionary in the sense that they do not operate according to a set plan or strategy in trying to move society toward a definite goal. But they are revolutionary in their impact on the fabric of the society, creating a change that provides the dispossessed people with a sense of hope and a vision for the future. They offer a place in society where people can begin to sense their role as creators of their own histories, rejecting a passive acceptance of the status quo and beginning to work out alternatives to dehumanization.

WAAIC

The Women's Association of African Independent Churches (WAAIC), a sister organization of the African Independent Churches Association (AICA), represents initial efforts to break out of traditional functions in order to confront difficult issues in a more revolutionary way. The thoroughly pervasive nature of this movement offers hope that a new character and thrust may emerge at the grassroots level that will lay the foundation for a new fabric of society.

At the start, membership in WAAIC was limited to women whose husbands were ministers belonging to AICA, though later it came to include all interested women. In 1968, Els te Siep was appointed by the Christian Institute as an advisor to WAAIC; three full-time staff women, also of the Christian Institute, were to organize in-service training for leaders. Emphasis was placed on literacy, cooking, and sewing and knitting. The trained leaders would in turn organize neighborhood classes.

Every member of WAAIC was expected to pay a subscription fee ot 20 cents a month in addition to the membership fee paid on admission. WAAIC also maintained what was called the Cent Fund, where each member donated one cent per week to be used for support of widows and orphans.

The first efforts of WAAIC were concentrated on *literacy classes.* Anyone with a minimum of five years primary school was considered a teacher, with the women voluntarily offering their homes as classrooms. Forty small groups developed, mostly in Soweto (South Western townships). At first the medium of instruction was the vernacular but then gradually moved to English. The volunteer teachers taught whatever they felt most competent to teach, starting from reading in the vernacular, English, and Afrikaans, to more complicated work like grammar and composition (in all three languages) as the students progressed.

One of the techniques used to get the students to practice the skills at home was to get them to compile pamphlets describing all the day's WAAIC activities and then read their reports in class the following day. This not only gave experience in communication but also served to unify the organization and provide a forum for a constant exchange of ideas.

Cooking classes dealt with preventing illness, finding and preparing cheap but nutritious foods, and applying better cooking methods. They also dealt with health care in general, hygiene (including physical exercises), education of the children, and sex education.

Sewing and knitting classes were very popular with the older women. WAAIC provided sewing and knitting machines as well as wool and fabrics. Whatever was made was sold. The profit would then be used to buy new materials or else be contributed to the general budget of WAAIC.

The differences between the WAAIC programs and the more conventional approach of the Board of Christian Education are apparent in the following comparison:

Roles (who learns)

Board of Christian Education (conventional): Certified teachers, counselors, administrators, and students. All roles have well-defined expectations.

WAAIC Programs (alternative): Teachers, administrators, parents, community members, students. Anyone who has something to teach. Certification relaxed. Role distinction blurred.

Curriculum (what is learned)

Board of Christian Education (conventional): District or circuit-prescribed curriculum. Knowledge is broken into subject areas.

WAAIC Programs (alternative): Wide variation in educational substance dictated largely by interest of learners. May encompass areas usually taught in school, but can also extend into many other areas.

Motivation (why it is learned)

Board of Christian Education (conventional): Extrinsic motivation. Learning is intended to fulfill requirements and pass tests. Authority is vested in teacher/minister.

WAAIC Programs (alternative): Intrinsic motivation. Learning results from interest or need to learn a skill or to develop knowledge. Authority is vested in student. The student decides.

Methods (how it is learned)

Board of Christian Education (conventional): Emphasis on reading, writing, listening. Group presentation by teacher is common, with some audiovisual aids and some discussion.

WAAIC Programs (alternative): Methods vary as widely as the curriculum. Reading, writing, and listening are not excluded, but emphasis is on doing and experiencing. All senses are involved.

Location (where it is learned)

Board of Christian Education (conventional): In the church school building (classrooms) or in the church hall. There are some field trips, but they are exceptional.

WAAIC Programs (alternative): Wide variation in location of learning: private homes, forest, libraries, businesses. Instruction in formal classrooms is the exception rather than the rule.

Time (when it is learned)

Board of Christian Education (conventional): Instruction typically occurs between 8 A.M. and 4 P.M. The day is segmented into periods or modules.

WAAIC Programs (alternative): Learning takes place any time, depending on the nature of the learning task, with infrequent scheduling and no time segmentation.

Through WAAIC the women have found that dealing with the practical matters of leading a "better quality life" offers a most meaningful ministry.

WAAIC members distrust the whites and have insisted on maintaining their independence from white domination, thus preserving the heart of the collective sentiment inherent in their formation. These women have been able to move forward in significant ways never before accomplished by other women's groups within African society. Through a cooperative venture undertaken on their own initiative, they have been able to enjoy the benefits of programs never before available. More important than the obvious material gains is the new sense of self-accomplishment and confidence.

The rapid growth of WAAIC activities has been due to the contagion and enthusiasm that such awareness brings. The difference in the quality in the lives of the women has been significant enough to attract non-Independent church groups. Thus, what started as an in-group project has already spilled over into very diverse ecumenical circles. All the classes were open to any interested women, regardless of religious belief, so that it was, and I believe still is, possible to find Independent church members alongside mission church members and non-Christians.

The activities of AICA and WAAIC are an expression of a people who have not accepted the dictates of their oppressors as "God given." Though submerged in the "culture of silence" members of these movements have become aware that cultural invasion is an instrument of domination. They have not allowed invasion to alienate them from the spirit of their own culture and from themselves. The combination of the spirit of independence from western standards and pride in being able to help oneself is creating a new awareness that will inevitably be the groundwork for effective social change and the ultimate transformation of the society.

16

Church and Politics in Africa

Kodwo E. Ankrah (Uganda)

THE COLONIAL POWERS AND THE CHURCHES

During the colonial era, missionaries sought the protection of their governments, which then had territorial occupational power. Cooperation existed between the church and the colonial administration; the leaders, both of church and state, were foreign—often from the same metropolitan country. This type of alliance was pragmatic. The metropolitan authorities provided protection and safety.

Missionaries, merchants, and the military reinforced each other: the French in Zaire; the Portuguese in Mozambique, Angola, and Guinea Bissau; the Spanish in Latin America; the British in Rhodesia, Ghana, and Kenya; etc. This "tragic alliance" not only represented a twisted Gospel, but it usually guaranteed unfavorable treatment for missionaries when the nationals finally evicted the foreign merchants and the foreign military.

"FLAG" INDEPENDENCE AND NEOCOLONIALISM

The term "flag independence" suggests the disillusionment that has grown in the independent nations of Africa. Many had hoped that independence would transform society, but contrary to the hopes entertained, as Brockway notes,

mass poverty continued, appalling housing and primitive sanitation in towns remained, unemployment increased. A gulf grew sometimes between the people and the European-American educated elite who became the Political Establishment; new indigenous rulers tended to become bureaucrats and sometimes dictators. Corrup-

155

tion poisoned the regimes, ministers becoming rich and living in mansions which rivalled those of the previous European masters. . . . Power by dominant political cliques was strengthened, one party states were decreed, sometimes reflecting national unity, sometimes exploiting it, opposition leaders were imprisoned; governments were overthrown by army coups, sometimes radical, sometimes reactionary and supported in the background by American and Western (and we may add Eastern) agencies.[1]

For thousands of Africans, independence has brought everything but peace and prosperity. The military and the politicians have utilized coercive governmental instruments to enforce their particular brand of power. In the name of sovereignty of the state, parliaments have been suspended, constitutions have been disregarded, special powers have been assumed by the leadership, emergencies have been declared, and control of the government by the people has been abolished.

According to Nkrumah, "the essence of neo-colonialism is that the State which is subject to this, is, in theory, independent and has all the outward trappings of international sovereignty. In reality its economic system and thus its political policy is directed from outside."[2] The achievement of independence in Africa did not wipe out overnight the former roles: the provision of cheap raw materials by the colonized people to the metropolis, which in turn supplied finished products. Several studies have been made and more need to be made to analyze the causes and the extent of this dilemma, and how to prevent its continuation. Moreover, beside the old scheme between the former masters and the subjected states, new institutions are creating more serious neocolonialism: the multinational companies.

The pragmatic approach taken by many leaders in Africa is based upon the belief that without outside aid the newly acquired independence of these new nations will never grow to the full. There are others who hold that those who produce the raw materials and those who turn it to manufactured goods must have equitable utilization of the resulting profit. This latter school of thought is opposed to the existing international economic system. What position have the churches taken to the neocolonialism that characterizes our "flag" independence? The World Council of Churches has urged the churches to support the New International Economic Order discussed at UNCTAD IV in Nairobi. But the tragedy is that church leadership and theologians in Africa are not knowledgeable about this new economic order and the implications of neocolonialism. There are leaders who consider such ideological issues as foreign and contrary to the "gospelling" of the word of God.

THE CHURCH AND THE STATUS QUO

In Africa today we cannot avoid asking the question: What is the political responsibility of the church? Does the Christian way of life and its imperatives imply socio-political options and commitment? This is the same as asking whether the prophets throughout the ages have had political and social responsibilities. History is replete with evidence that the Christian message had been made into an ideological legitimation of the status quo. These are theological questions that are being raised elsewhere but not sufficiently in Africa at the moment.

a. The message was expressed in terms that gave the impression that what really mattered was eternal life, and, therefore, what really counted most was to lead a life that prepared us for eternal life. In other words, the world provided the background against which we must work out our salvation in fear and trembling and with patience to endure the problems encountered. By ignoring this world and its activities, the church indirectly blessed the operative social, economic, and political structures.

b. The doctrine of divine providence reconciled people to the world. Whatever suffering existed had been permitted by God as part of a pre-ordained design to prepare us for blissful future salvation. We should be satisfied with our lot and not be angry with what is inflicted on us. No revolution was recommended.

c. The Christian doctrine of original sin made Christians believe that depraved human nature would always breed injustice in society. It is only individuals who may be converted by the grace of God; we cannot look to human society for justice. Although this is a distortion of the Gospel, African Christians by and large have not related preaching the Gospel with the establishment of justice.

d. The notion of divine lordship was extended to legitimate hierarchical secular and ecclesiastical systems on the pattern of the master-servant relationship.

e. The Christian message has advocated, and continues to advocate, the ideal of unity and peace separated from the demands of justice. This overlooks the inequities that exist between people and communities. The church thus tends to protect the most powerful and to encourage the submission of the powerless.

There are some theologians who speak against the above interpretations of the Christian message and for a different relationship between the church and the political order. They advocate more involvement of Christians in actions for justice.

a. They insist that God is present in us as enabler, as a transforming agent, appointing us to be transformers of human life. Turning to God does not mean that we must forget the struggle against injustice. Christian preaching must provide the incentive for constructing a better human existence on earth, no matter how temporary this earthly existence.

b. Divine providence is God's redemptive will for all humanity and is manifested in movements and situations that contribute to the positive redemption of humanity. Attempts to bring redemption to humanity will have to work through the structures of society—those in existence or new ones.

c. The doctrine of original sin means that the salvation promised by Christ and proclaimed by the church has social implications, as revealed in the redemption of history from the power of darkness. Where sin abounds there divine grace abounds even more to enable us to act differently in spite of ourselves. The doctrine of original sin must not, therefore, cripple humankind's desire for justice.

d. The acceptance of the lordship of God should not be used as justification for any system that encourages one-man rule either in political or ecclesiastical government. Rather, that affirmation must mean that God in Christ has overcome sin and death and rules all: monarch as well as subject, president as well as laborer. It should mean God is Lord because of the divine victory in Jesus Christ and therefore there should be victory for all humankind.

e. The only unity that must be proclaimed and advocated is that in accord with God's will of justice. It requires the conversion of all, even to the point of restitution for the underprivileged and oppressed.

CHURCH AND STATE: A CREATIVE TENSION

The church is considered by Christians to be the instrument of God for the salvation of humanity. Christians are called to proclaim liberty and salvation in all spheres of life. This view of the church, if reflected in the behavior of its members, would mean that the church would support any movement that fostered human liberty. Indeed, many influential African nationalists were Christians who overtly or correctly helped to work for the abolition of the colonial rule. To them, colonial rule represented repressive and oppressive regimes that had to be abolished.

The presence of the church in post-independence Africa must be made manifest in the day-to-day affairs of the nation. But it is precisely such involvement of the church that irritates the politicians who feel that no one is above them once they assume leadership of the nation.

Is the role that the church plays in present-day Africa different from the role it played during the period of colonialism? The answer is in the affirmative. In the colonial period, the church accepted the popular theological teachings as expressed above. The church did not say much against the privileged economic position enjoyed by the foreign citizens of the colonial power; in effect, the church supported these economic and social differences in the belief that they offered civilizing influence on the nationals.

In the present, post-independence era, both church and state claim to be concerned about human dignity. Most governments articulate their aims in terms similar to the following statement of the Ghanaian government. It seeks to establish:

a strong and progressive society in which no one will have anxiety about the basic means of life, about work, food and shelter; where poverty and illiteracy no longer exist and disease is brought under control; and where our educational facilities provide all the children with the best possible opportunities for the development of their potentialities.[3]

It is when these cherished aims are not achieved by the state that the church becomes concerned. This concern may result in the church's making statements and taking actions interpreted as "unconstructive" criticism of the state.

Such articulation by the church and its leadership presupposes an awareness of the needs of the society and the nation. Unfortunately, however, as Bishop Okullu has remarked, "the Church has been slow in giving the guidance which African nations have needed in working out their national aspirations as independent States. Instead many a Church leader has found himself largely jumping on the band wagon and accepting opinions mooted by politicians."[4]

Where the church has not become aware of its responsibilities in society, and where the leaders repeat the popular slogans of the politicians as they repeated the popular theological doctrines in the past, church and state get along beautifully, peacefully, and amicably. However, when the church and its leadership become consciously aware of their social responsibility and begin to demand action on the part of the state, irritations begin to develop.

Such irritations are likely to arise when the church requests the government to reshape its policy to address seriously the needs of the poor rather than the rich minority; to concentrate on medical projects that benefit rural areas rather than the plush urban hospitals; to expand facilities for primary, secondary, and technical schools rather than developing highly sophisticated facilities in the universities; to develop mass housing programs for rural and slum populations rather than deluxe, modern apartments and residential housing for the rich. Then the politicians are likely to demand that the church "keep out of politics."

A further point of church-state friction sometimes arises over the question of church-operated social services. Should our church-related colleges, hospitals, and farms accept government aid? With government accepting an increasing responsibility to finance former welfare services rendered by the church, what is the church's justification for continuing to provide these expensive services? What if the state requests the church to relinquish all rights to operate such services? There have been occasions when states have completely taken over educational, medical, and welfare institutions belonging to the church. Should the church continue to claim a certain distinctiveness of service and success of operation? Can it do so without incurring the wrath and jealousy of the state?

These are minor issues. The relationship becomes critical when the state feels its sovereign power is being challenged. With its increasing advocacy of human rights, the church has come into severe conflict with the state. It is the state that should protect individual freedom. If, however, the state itself tramples on these freedoms, must not the church speak out? The church must seek to be the conscience of society and provide guidance to the state.

Both church and state are instruments of God for the purpose of achieving human welfare. The authority of both is granted by God and therefore that authority is ultimately limited by the demands of God. The prophets from Elijah to Jeremiah attest to this (see also John 19:11; Rom. 13; 1 Tim. 2:2; 1 Pet. 2:11).

The political power of the state is at the service of the needs of society and the equitable and just administration of the resources of society. Any abuse of the affairs of the society by the state must be the concern of the church, which is equally authorized by God to care for the welfare of the people. Anything that obstructs the well-being of the people must be the concern of both state and church. The church cooperates with the state in the provision of those services that enhance society's welfare. The church is required by its commitment to Christ to criticize persons entrusted by the state to look after the welfare of society when they fail or neglect their responsibilities.

The church, like the prophets of old, must be courageous enough to expose the new leadership in African states who squander our scarce resources through pomp and ostentation. It is the church's responsibility to speak to the new governments in Africa and remind them of their God-given responsibility: to care for the welfare of all men and women in the society. The power entrusted to them is a sacred one requiring wisdom, humility, courage, and compassion. It is in this light that theologians in Africa must study our local problems and the complexities of our cultures.

In brief, the progress from colonial rule to independence has placed new burdens on the church. The church in Africa must be scripturally aware of its responsibilities—to be prophets and at the same time practical in the face of the ever-changing economic order and systems. The church and the state have equal responsibility for the welfare of society, and the authority given them is to be used in a complementary way. Both institutions are under the sovereignty of God.

NOTES

1. Fenner Brockway, *The Colonial Revolution* (London: Hart-Davis, MacGibbon, 1973), pp. 572–73.

2. Kwame Nkrumah, *Neo-Colonialism: The Last Stage of Imperialism* (London: Thomas Nelson, 1965), p. ix.

3. *Ghana Seven Year Plan for National Reconstruction and Development,* 1963/64—1969/70, Office of the Planning Commission, p. v.

4. Bishop J. Henry Okullu, *Church and Politics in East Africa* (Nairobi, Uzima Press), p. 12.

17

The Theology of Liberation in Africa

Bishop Desmond Tutu (Lesotho)

THE GENESIS OF LIBERATION THEOLOGY IN AFRICA

I was asked toward the end of last year to prepare a paper for this conference of Third World theologians. Had I done my paper at that time, I might have been able to write with reasonable detachment and the objectivity much loved by academics. But this I can no longer do with any integrity. Why? The reason is that I write toward the end of 1977 in Southern Africa, in the aftermath of the death of Steve Biko in detention. I write after the extraordinary finding of the Chief Magistrate of Pretoria at the inquest on Steve's death that though he died of serious brain damage, no one was to blame for this death. I write in the wake of a massive security clampdown in the Republic of South Africa when several organizations, for example the Black People's Convention, the Black Parents Association, and even the Christian Institute, have been banned and several individuals have either been detained without trial or banned—and these were organizations and persons who were still working for a reasonably peaceful solution to the crisis in Southern Africa. I write after the major black newspaper in the Republic of South Africa, *The World,* has been banned. I write after the National Party, led by B. J. Vorster, has been returned to power with a considerably increased majority, and he has already declared that there will be no significant changes in the policies of his government. And I write too after the security forces of Ian Smith have recently killed over a thousand so-called terrorists (including women and children) in Mozambique. To write with an academic detachment and objectivity might please members of certain Senior Common Rooms, but it would be to discredit theology as the pastime of those who would fiddle while their Rome was burning.

This is the *Sitz-im-Leben* of this paper, and it gives us an opportunity to realize more clearly the genesis and nature of liberation theology. Liberation theology more than any other kind of theology issues out of the crucible of human suffering and anguish. It happens because people cry out, "Oh, God, how long?" "Oh, God, but why?" And so liberation theology is in a sense really a theodicy. It seeks to justify God and the ways of God to a downtrodden and perplexed people so that they can be inspired to do something about their lot. Those who suffer so grievously have not usually doubted that there is a God. They have not even doubted that such a God was a living God, a powerful God, and a God of righteousness and goodness. It is precisely because they have believed that their perplexity has arisen: if they had not believed, there would be no need of a theodicy. If they believed that God was neither good, nor loving, nor powerful then there would be no problem. There would just be the brute fact of their suffering forming part of the givenness of a truly harsh reality.

The cause of bewilderment is not the traditional form of the problem of evil, i.e., "Why is there suffering and evil in the universe of a good God?" No, the burning question is not "Why is there suffering?" but the more immediately pressing one of "Why do *we* suffer so?" "Why does suffering seem to single out us blacks to be the victims of a racism gone mad?" Another way of putting the same anguished cry is, "God, on whose side are you?" or even more disturbingly for some people, "God, are you black or white?"

All liberation theology stems from trying to make sense of human suffering when those who suffer are the victims of organized oppression and exploitation, when they are emasculated and treated as less than what they are: human persons created in the image of the Triune God, redeemed by the one Savior Jesus Christ and sanctified by the Holy Paraclete. This is the genesis of all liberation theology and so also of black theology, which is a theology of liberation in Africa. Black theology has occurred mainly in Southern Africa, where blacks have had their noses rubbed in the dust by white racism, depersonalizing them to the extent that they have—blasphemy of blasphemies—come to doubt the reality of their own personhood and humanity. They have often come to believe that the denigration of their humanity by those who oppress them is the truth about themselves.

Black theology as a theology of liberation has become part of the struggle of a people for their liberation. For this reason it has usually been proscribed or, at least, regarded with suspicion by the powers that be. It has become part of the black consciousness movement, which is concerned with the evangelical aim of awakening in blacks a sense of their intrinsic worth as children of God. In Southern Africa, black theology was inspired by its North American counterpart, which existed for so long implicitly in the Negro spirituals that gave heart to black slaves in the heavy days of their bondage and which became more articulate and explicit during the civil rights campaign. It was inspired too by the knowledge that so much of Africa had thrown off the shackles of colonialism. Liberation theology takes very seriously the socio-political dimensions of reality as those which, to a large extent, determine the quality not only of secular but also of religious life. Liberation theology dismisses the dichotomy of the secular and the sacred as thoroughly unincarnational and irreligious.

THE NATURE AND STYLE OF LIBERATION THEOLOGY

When the Jews were in exile in Babylon, most of them were depressed and dejected. They were disillusioned with their God who had proved to be less powerful than the Babylonian deities, since for a people to be defeated meant in the theology of those days that their God had been worsted by that of their foes. They saw around them in the ziggurats and other structures and statues impressive monuments to the triumphant gods of Babylonian religion. The Jews had been proved very small indeed. At such a ghastly hour in the history of Israel a group belonging to what is called the Priestly School produced a magnificent hymn to creation, a paean of praise to God the Creator, in the form of the "P" account of creation in Genesis 1–24. It is not to devalue this splendid piece of theologizing to describe it as a theological propaganda tract designed to awaken in the exiled Jews a renewed faith in their God as so transcendent that his mere fiat was sufficient to bring the universe into being. In the Babylonian creation narrative, Emma Elish, creation had to come about through the bloody battle between Marduk and Tiamat. But now the Jews could say, "Our God just speaks, and things happen, so there, ha! ha!"

This is an outstanding example of how theology is done in the Bible: almost always in response to the needs of a specific set of circumstances. We could multiply the examples. In the Bible theologizing never happens in a vacuum; much less is it the creation of someone who sits in splendid academic isolation and detachment. When the community was forgetting the universalism implicit in the divine promise to Abraham (Gen. 12:1–3) because of the zealous but necessary teachings of an Ezra or a Nehemiah or the Rechabites that Israel was a peculiar people, a "Ruth" or a "Jonah" was written to counteract this rigid particularism. When Christian Jews were agitated about whether they should still be circumcised, then Paul had to write "Galatians." Most of the Bible is technically referred to as "occasional" because it is "occasioned" by particular circumstances and it addresses those circumstances. The theology we find in the Bible is thus an *engaged,* an involved theology which is also existential (for it is concerned with the existence of a specific, particular group of believers).

This is the biblical paradigm that liberation theology has followed meticulously. It speaks out of and into a specific situation, in this case, the situation of political oppression and injustice, of social and economic exploitation of a specific group of believers. It seeks to make sense of their suffering in relation to what God has done, is doing, and will do. The ultimate reference point is the man Jesus who is the Word of God par excellence. Liberation theology seeks to discover what sort of God we have to deal with and whether we can go on believing in him with any sort of integrity. More than most theologies, it accepts that there can be no final theology, that all theology is provisional and cannot lay claim to a universal validity, for any relevant theology must accept the scandal of its particularity, which, after all, is the price of its relevance. And no theology can easily transcend the limitations and conditioned-ness of those who theologize. Too many of the unseemly controversies that scar the history of the church have happened because one kind of theologizing has pretended to a finality that it could not have. There is no one true way of theologizing. Even in the Bible there is a rich diversity of theologies, all existing check by jowl, theologies that may complement one another, though they also may be quite incompatible. Liberation theology claims it is part of this rich diversity; it glories in its limitations and is prepared to leave the stage to its successors once it feels it has fulfilled its task. There are far too many theologies around that have outlived their usefulness, and we ought to be ruthless in getting rid of the accumulations of centuries in our attic.

There must be different theologies since all of us apprehend God and the things of God differently; we express those apprehensions differently. Theology will change with the changing circumstances if it issues out of and addresses a particular set of circumstances, if it answers specific questions. Good answers for today will be useless tomorrow because tomorrow's questions will be different. Of course, we will have to learn from yesterday's questions and answers because in the theological enterprise it is futile and wasteful to try to start *de novo*. But we should not easily canonize the determinations of yesteryear and so make the awful mistake of identifying theology with the Gospel of Jesus Christ. Theology is temporal, the Gospel is eternal. Our understanding of that Gospel, of that divine revelation, will change constantly; that is what theology is about.

THE CONTEXT OF LIBERATION THEOLOGY

By the token of particularity, certain parts of the biblical message will be more apt for certain situations than for others. The Gospel of Jesus Christ is many splendored. Who would doubt that in hate-filled Ulster the aspect of the Gospel that is most apt is reconciliation for those estranged factions? For the victims of oppression and injustice it is important for them to hear that the God they worship is the liberator God of the Exodus who led a rabble of slaves out of bondage into glorious freedom.

Oppressed peoples must hear that, according to the Bible, this God is always on the side of the downtrodden. He is so graciously on their side not because they are more virtuous and better than their oppressors, but solely and simply because they are oppressed; he is that kind of a God. So to the anguished cry, "God, on whose side are you?" we say emphatically, "God is on your side," not as some jingoistic national deity who says "my people right or wrong," but as one who saves and yet also judges those whom he saves. God is compassionate yet the holy one who demands that those whom he saves must also be holy. God saves *from* a death-dealing situation *for* a life-giving situation. Those whom God has saved must become the servants of others, for they are saved ultimately not for their self-aggrandizement or self-glorification, but so they may bring others to a saving knowledge of God.

Ultimately God saves the oppressed for the sake of their oppressors. It has often sounded like so much sloganeering to say that oppression and injustice dehumanize both the victims and the perpetrators of the unjust system and that liberation theology is concerned as much for the liberation of the oppressors as of the oppressed. But who can doubt that this must be true when Jimmy Kruger, the South African Minister of Justice and of Police, could say of the death of Steve Biko: "It leaves me cold." What has happened to the humanity of a person who can say something so callous about the death of a fellow human being?

GOD IN LIBERATION THEOLOGY

Liberation theology has underscored that God is concerned for the liberation of oppressed victims; hence its stress on the Exodus-liberation biblical themes. But this is not the only aspect of the biblical and Christian teaching that is crucial in liberation theology.

To the victims of a system of rampant injustice it is equally important to realize that God is also the God of power, not only the God who will lead them to freedom. He is a God in charge in his universe. He is not impotent despite all appearances to the contrary, despite the fact that evil and injustice seem to be on the ascendant. He is Lord, the all-ruler of the book of Daniel and the Revelation of St. John the Divine. Nothing that happens can ever catch him off guard. He is not like the gods of the prophets of Baal whom Elijah mocked so cruelly. He has not fallen asleep, or gone on a journey, or turned aside to relieve himself so that our cries rise into an empty void; our cries do not fall on deaf or unheeding ears. No, our God has heard and seen our affliction and has come down to deliver us. And he is strong to save. Our people here in Southern Africa need to hear this.

Yes, after the events I referred to at the beginning of this paper, our people were stunned into a despair and helplessness, and it is of the utmost importance for liberation theology to declare loud and clear that God is a God of hope. "Comfort, comfort my people, says your God. Speak tenderly to her." Yes, the church must uphold the faith and hope of God's people in these dark days when there seems to be little reason for hope.

Liberation theology also depicts God as a God of compassion. Surely God can't remain aloof and untouched by our suffering as some Aristotelian unmoved mover. The Bible assures us that God is really like a nursing mother in his tender concern for his people who suffer. He longs after us, even when we are wayward, waiting for our return like the father of the prodigal waits for the return of his son. He is like a mother hen who would collect her young under the shadow of her wings, and in Jesus Christ he weeps over a beloved city. Yes, God weeps with and for us, because our God suffers the exquisite pain of a dying God.

Those who would scorn liberation theology often think that its adherents are naive in the extreme because they think that a change for the better in political and economic circumstances will necessarily usher in the golden age. This is a misreading of liberation theology. Liberation theologians have too much evidence that the removal of one oppressor often means replacement by another; yesterday's victim quite rapidly becomes today's dictator. Liberation theologians know only too well the recalcitrance of human nature and so accept the traditional doctrines of the fall and original sin, but they also know that God has provided the remedy in Jesus Christ.

THE CHALLENGE OF LIBERATION THEOLOGY

Liberation theology is no mere intellectual exercise, no mere cerebral enterprise, for it deals with matters of life and death for those on whose behalf it is being done. Liberation theology must enable the victims of oppression to assert their God-given personhood and humanity and must help exorcise from them the awful sense of self-hatred and self-disgust which are the ghastly consequences of oppression. Then these victims will not cry out for the flesh pots of their days of bondage when they stand face to face with the demanding responsibilities of their freedom. Liberation theology must help them enter into their glorious heritage as the children of God who made them free for freedom.

Liberation theology challenges those whom it addresses not to be consumed by hatred, self-pity, and bitterness, for these are as dehumanizing as the oppression that caused them. While calling them to freedom, the Gospel of Jesus Christ also calls to limitless forgiveness, not as a spineless acceptance of suffering but as participation in the divine economy of salvation. This is when the oppressed turn the tables; it is when they make up what is lacking in the sufferings of Christ.

Liberation theology exposes itself to critical scrutiny, but it must not be judged by some arbitrary, a priori criteria of an imagined intellectual respectability. Liberation theology would wish to be numbered among other theologies that have found acceptance in the rich Christian heritage. Yet we who do liberation theology believe we are engaged in something too urgent to have to wait for the approbation of the West or of those who would blindly follow western standards of acceptability and play western games using western rules. No, liberation theology must be judged by whether it is biblical, by whether it is consistent with the Gospel of Jesus Christ, by whether it is guilty of self-contradiction, and by whether it works. If it fails the test according to these criteria then it deserves to be condemned roundly for it will be offering God's suffering people palliatives rather than effective remedies.

Liberation theology becomes part of a people's struggle for liberation; it tries to help victims of oppression to assert their humanity and so look the other chap in the eye and speak face to face without shuffling their feet and apologizing for their black existence.

Those who speak about justice and sharing the resources of the earth more equitably are often accused by certain "religious" persons of being political and exhorted to pray about these things. We who do liberation theology believe such exhortation to be arrogant in the extreme for it presumes that we have not first prayed. We contend that we too have had a real encounter with Jesus Christ in prayer, meditation, Bible study, and the sacraments, and that the imperatives of this encounter constrain us to speak and to act as we do. It is not our politics but our faith that inspires us.

Liberation theology challenges other theologies to examine whether they are biblical in the sense in which liberation theology has been shown to be biblical. Other theologies are challenged to become more truly incarnational by being concerned for the whole person, body and soul. They are called upon to glory in their built-in obsolescence, not to cry out for a permanence and a universal validity that properly belong only to the Gospel of Jesus Christ.

Liberation theology challenges churches everywhere to be true to their calling to exercise a prophetic ministry in speaking up for the dumb, the voiceless, for those too weak to speak up for themselves, to oppose oppression, injustice, corruption, and evil wherever these may be found. This could be a call to martyrdom, but if God be for us who can be against us?

Let God arise and let his enemies be scattered.

18

Liberation Theology in South Africa

Allan Boesak (South Africa)

A NEW CONSCIOUSNESS

We cannot understand liberation theology, whether in South Africa, in Latin America, or in other parts of the Third World, unless we understand that it developed within a framework of a new political consciousness. People became aware, first of all, of their own situations. There was a new consciousness of themselves, of where they were, of the political, social, and economic dynamics in their situations. When people began to understand their situations, they started asking questions they had never asked before.

In the theological tradition in which I grew up, a solid Dutch Reformed tradition with its Calvinist theology, we were never given a real understanding of our situation. This tradition never gave us an understanding of ourselves, and, therefore, there was never room to ask the vital kinds of existential and theological questions that should be asked if we want to say something theologically that would make sense of our situation.

The first question that we ask when we get this new consciousness is: WHY? In asking "WHY?" we begin to discover that we have lived through a theological tradition that, although it was our own, was really never our own. It has always been controlled by people who also control the political parties, the economic and social situation, our very lives. In South Africa we have a particular situation that we call "apartheid." Apartheid is not only a political system; it is not only an economic and social system. It is also a theological reality. Perhaps the distinction of color is stressed, but just the same "apartheid" is a religion, just as all forms of racism become religions.

The new consciousness that I'm talking about, which gave rise to the development of a liberation theology in South Africa, is a human consciousness that we call black consciousness. Through black consciousness black people discover that they are children of God and that they have rights to exist in his world. Black people discover that they are part of history, and they share this history with God, which means that they are responsible to act as human persons. The situation in South Africa did not happen just accidentally. It did not just come about. The situation was created by people. It is a system that is still being maintained by people through various methods. Black consciousness says to black people that they are human, that they are children of God. Black consciousness gives black people a clear realization of the situation in South Africa and of the negation of their human "beingness." When black people see clearly that they are black and are children of God, then they can be proud.

But why is it then that this very blackness is the reason for their oppression? Black people in South Africa are not being oppressed because they are Muslims, or because they are Methodists, or because they are wayward Presbyterians or Dutch Reformed; they are being oppressed because they are black, because they are not born white. Whiteness is tantamount to human "beingness." If one is not white, one is not human. Nobody has to deal with a black person on the level of a human being. Can a Christian in a Christian country with a host of Christian churches speak and preach about the sanctity of family life and about the responsibility of parents and children and at the same time vote for a government and sustain and aid a system that gives theological justification to laws that maintain that black people cannot live together as husband and wife?

In 1973, hundreds of children were sent away from their parents in Johannesburg back to some homeland, where it was claimed they ought to be, back to grandparents or to aunts or to whatever relatives they had—but away from their parents. A reporter of one of the English-speaking newspapers asked the Bantu Administration Board, "Why are you doing this? These are children you are sending away from their parents." The white officer in charge of this operation said, "Well, you know, you must try to understand that these black women are not the same as our women. They really do not feel bad when we send their children away, because, you see, they do not see things the same way as we do. They are really very happy when we relieve them of the burden of having to care for their children so that they can work uninterruptedly for the white madams they work for." That was in 1973.

Last year the government demolished the squatter homes of people where I work and live in Bellville, in Motterdam. This move rendered thirteen thousand people homeless, even if their only homes had been shacks of tin and cardboard and wood. Another official of the Bantu Administration said, "Well, you see, you've got to understand black Africans to understand the action of the government. They do not value family life the same way as we Christian people do." Whiteness is equal to human beingness; blackness is less than that and therefore less than human. I could spend two or three hours reciting the different laws that would substantiate this statement.

When I discover that God has made me a human being though I am not white, it means that I have a right to be here; I have a right to exist; I am not less in his eyes. I believe in him. He has sent his Son for me, and when the Word became flesh, God became a human being. He became like me. He shared the same feelings that I share. When we begin to understand this, we begin to ask the question, "What am I then?" White law says that I am not a human being. What do you do when you're black and you're a Christian and the people who oppress you say that they are also Christians? They also pray and they also read the Bible. For black Christians, however, the Gospel is the incomparable word of liberation, while for white Christians it is an instrument from which they derive a theological justification for the system that oppresses blacks. How is this possible?

When we begin to ask these questions, we then begin to realize that the traditional theology, or what we call "white" theology, has never really asked these questions because it could not. It has never had any room for the questions we are asking because it never had any room for the sufferings of black people.

The simple question now becomes: Whom do I obey and to what extent? What is my duty as a Christian? If you ask that in a white church, the response is: "Let every person be subject to the government authorities."

In a white church, or on the radio, it is the most natural thing in the world for a white minister to pray for our Christian government: "Thank God for the Christian government that we've got." But when we black South Africans pray about the government, our prayer is for deliverance.

A SITUATIONAL THEOLOGY

Black liberation theology is a situational theology. All theology has always been situational; it has always been theology in context. The only new thing that we have discovered is that it is theological foolishness (and I'm not sure whether that is equal to sinfulness) to say that what is good for the situation in Germany as discovered by a good German Reform theologian is also good for the situation in North America and therefore also good for the situation in South Africa. Each theological concept develops within a particular context, and our theological thinking—the way we read the Gospel, the way we understand the Gospel, the way we interpret the Gospel, the way we interpret our situation in the light of the Gospel—has everything to do with what we eat and how many times a day we eat, what salary we earn, whether we own a home, whether we live happily with our family, and so on. The situation in which we live, the context in which we live, profoundly influences the way we do our theology.

Even Abram Kuyper (and there was a time when those of us who are good Reformed theologians used to swear by Abram Kuyper although some people swore at him) said in a very important essay on the Reformed Social Congress of 1899 that the person who is an employer will never understand the situation and the longings and the desires of those he employs because he does not share the situation in which they live.

There is a clear line of demarcation between how blacks live in South Africa, and how whites live there. Everybody knows that South Africa is not a democracy, but it is not full dictatorship either. We might become that in a few years, but now we are what I would call a "pigmentoracy," whereby people are given rights and privileges according to the color of their skin. At the very top of the social ladder in South Africa we have the white South Africans. They have everything: all the economic, social, and political privileges. They vote and they have a very high standard of living. Next there are the colored South Africans: the Asians, the Indians, etc. This is a clear, politically recognized category in South Africa, whether one is "colored," or "Cape colored," or "other colored." At the very bottom of the social ladder is what the government calls the Bantu, the *African* people.

Black consciousness makes black people look at the situation. What is a "colored"? The law says that a colored person is one obviously not white and obviously not Bantu. This means we don't know what we are. We're people of mixed blood. My mother had white skin but my father was very, very dark with very clear African ancestry. For white South Africans that's the most terrible thing to be, of mixed blood. To be a "colored" is therefore not only a political category. It is an economic and a psychological category.

Those at the bottom of the social ladder have almost nothing in South Africa, no property rights nor the right to live with their families or children. They have to carry passbooks. But the "colored," because they have some white blood, share white people's culture to a large extent and speak their language, either Afrikaans or English. We listen to their music and we share their religious concepts. We are therefore more civilized and have more rights to more things than the Africans. I may own property in South Africa, but an African cannot. I may live with my wife and my children, but an African cannot. This special situation has been a creation of the white people, who tell us who we are and where we belong. They call us the "brown" people. Black consciousness says this is nonsense.

As Christians we identify with the least in our society. Therefore we are also black South Africans and do not speak of "coloreds." We tell the government time and again that we refuse to accept privileges that they are willing to give to us but not to the rest of the black community.

This is our situation and all the elements in it have a theological significance. If we have a theology that does not take into account this oppressive situation and the hundreds of oppressive laws then we cannot be authentic. We are not true to ourselves, not true to our situation, and ultimately not true to the Gospel itself. A theology that does not take into account this situation will never be able to interpret the demands of the Gospel or to say what the Spirit has to say to the people in this situation. That is why we have a black theology; that is why it is a situational theology.

Black theology, therefore, because it comes from a situation of oppression and suffering of a people who believe in God and who ask what the Gospel of Jesus Christ has to say about the situation, is also a theology of liberation.

THE EXODUS THEME

The themes of liberation theology that have become so important to black and Native American Christians in the U.S., to people in Asia and Latin America, are the same themes that run through black liberation theology in South Africa. The exodus is also our model, but we are not really saying that we expect that through some miracle God today will re-enact the Exodus as it was acted out before. God will not do that because black people in South Africa are not going anywhere. We're staying, so we have no Red Sea to cross. But neither do we want white people in South Africa to cross any sea. We want them to stay, but not as they are now. What we need is a spiritual and a political Exodus out of the situation of oppression toward a situation of liberation, out of the situation of inhumanity, darkness, and hatred toward a situation in which we, both whites and blacks, can regain our common humanity and enjoy a meaningful life, a wholeness of life that has been destroyed.

When he began his ministry Jesus Christ did not draw a thick line between the Old Testament and the New, but rather he stood squarely within the tradition of the Exodus and the prophets of the Old Testament. The theme of liberation in the Old Testament became the same theme in the New Testament proclamation of Jesus Christ, and there is no way that you can speak of the Gospel without speaking of liberation. In the beginning of his ministry Jesus Christ makes that very, very clear in the temple at Nazareth. His quotation from Isaiah 61 goes back to what Old Testament scholars have called "the actualization of the Exodus" throughout the Old Testament. The Exodus became the basis of the action of God and the action that God expects from his people.

The Exodus is not an isolated event; it is the beginning of a movement all through history, whether it is the Israelites over against the Pharaoh and the Egyptians or the poor and the widow and the orphan over against the rich and the powerful within Israel. Jesus Christ announced and accomplished what Yahweh was doing from the very beginning. The whole book of Genesis is no more than a prologue to this central event of the Exodus that would set the tune and pace of all that Yahweh would be doing for his people right through to the New Testament. And the same God who listened to his people who called upon his name and delivered them is able and willing to do the same in our situation today if we call upon his name and believe that he will indeed liberate us.

CONCERNS OF LIBERATION THEOLOGY IN SOUTH AFRICA

In conclusion let me mention just a few concerns of liberation theology in South Africa today. First, we must understand that our concern is not merely to liberate people; it is also to liberate the Gospel. We've read the parable of the man who goes out and sows his seeds, and some fall on rocky ground and others on the road. The parable is essentially trying to indicate vulnerability of the Word and even of the reality of the kingdom.

In a certain sense, God makes himself vulnerable in his Word by giving his Word to us and saying, "Go out there and proclaim it." Few know better than the black people what has happened to the proclamation of the Word. We simply have to refer to our own history and to what is happening in my country right now. The question that black people now put to the churches and the question that we are grappling with is really this: Is the Gospel of Jesus Christ indeed the Gospel of liberation and hope for me, or is it to remain an instrument of oppression in the hands of white people to use over the blacks? That is why I say that one of the concerns of liberation theology in South Africa is to liberate the Gospel, so that that truth might come out and people might understand it.

A second concern of liberation theology is the integrity of the Christian church and its ongoing witness in South Africa and all over the world. The South African Christian church is not isolated; we are bound to the other churches by sharing the same faith, the same confession, the same baptism, and the same belief in God the Father of Jesus Christ.

A third concern of liberation theology in South Africa is that we should understand what liberation means for South Africa. One of the things that we have to fight is a long tradition of western theological dominance in South Africa. This has introduced into African thinking and way of life a kind of dualism that we had never known and an individualism that has been very detrimental, not only to the Gospel but to the church and to our very human existence. Black people have got to understand that when they say, "I've got Jesus, then I'm all right," they're not all right. They have to understand that when we believe in Jesus Christ it does not make us immigrants out of history. In fact it places us right back within the world, in the middle of history, and that is the place where we have to proclaim his name.

We have got to understand what liberation means for the African. And this means that we have got to bring back what has been a reality in African heritage and African traditional thinking for centuries, namely, the concept of the wholeness of life, which is also a biblical concept. We have to move again to the sabbatical year. One of the striking things in the passage on the sabbatical year, which is also very striking in the ministry of Jesus Christ, is the wholeness of God's liberation. It begins with the rest of the land and a renewed devotion to Yahweh, and it ends with the rest of the land. In between there are people and exiles and deaths and property; not one single aspect of the life of Israel is not touched and judged thoroughly by God's proclamation of liberation in the sabbatical year. We have to bring back this wholeness, which has been in Africa for a long, long time.

The fourth concern of liberation theology in South Africa is our own situation. We must make a proper social analysis. I believe that as real and as ugly as racism is in our country, it is not the only question nor is it the ultimate question. Racism has been a tool for the oppression of people whether white, black, or whatever. But beyond the question of race lies the economic question. This is one of the things I have learned from our brothers and sisters from Latin America. If we do not take cognizance of the economic question liberation theology will fizzle out and die before we start. We have to make a proper analysis of the realities of power and powerlessness.

The final concern of liberation theology in South Africa is the contribution that African traditional thinking and African traditional religion can make to our contemporary thinking and theology. I believe that both our traditional religion and our traditional thinking have a liberating and humanizing word to say to our situation.

19

A Black American Perspective on the Future of African Theology

James H. Cone (United States)

Because I am a black North American, whose theological consciousness was shaped in the historical context of the civil rights movement of the 1950s[1] and the subsequent rise of Black Power during the 1960s,[2] it is difficult for me to speak about the future of African theology without relating it to the social and political context of black people's struggle for freedom in the United States of America. The effect of this social reality upon my theological perspective could blind me to the uniqueness of the African situation. The concern to accent the distinctiveness of the African context has led many African theologians to separate African theology not only from traditional European theology but also from American black theology. In an article entitled "An African Views American Black Theology," John Mbiti is emphatic on this issue:

The concerns of Black Theology differ considerably from those of African Theology. [African Theology] grows out of our joy in the experience of the Christian faith, whereas Black Theology emerges from the pains of oppression. African Theology is not so restricted in its concerns, nor does it have an ideology to propagate. Black Theology hardly knows the situation of Christian living in Africa, and therefore its direct relevance for Africa is either nonexistent or only accidental.[3]

In order to appreciate the seriousness and depth of Mbiti's concern, it is necessary to point out that his perspective is not based upon a superficial encounter with black theology. On the contrary, Mbiti made these remarks *after* he and I had had many conversations on the subject in the context of our jointly taught year-long course on African and black theologies at Union

Theological Seminary.[4] Nevertheless, it seems to me that he misrepresented black theology.[5] More important, however, was Mbiti's contention that African and black American theologians should have no more than an indirect or accidental interest in each other. This perspective on African theology not only makes substantive dialogue difficult but also excludes black American theologians from a creative participation in the future development of African theology.

John Mbiti is not alone in making a sharp distinction between black theology and African theology. Similar views are found in the writings of Harry Sawyerr,[6] E. W. Fashole-Luke,[7] and (to a lesser extent) Kwesi Dickson.[8] While there are significant exceptions to this perspective among theologians in Southern Africa and also among certain African churchpeople associated with the All Africa Conference of Churches,[9] these exceptions do not remove the risks inherent in any attempt by a North American to speak about the future of African theology. For there is much truth in the widespread belief that the future of African theology belongs to Africans alone.

There is a second difficulty in approaching this topic, in addition to existential and intellectual sensitivities of African theologians. That other problem is the existential conflict inherent in my double identity as American *and* African. This identity conflict is widespread among black Americans, and it is a prominent theme in black literature and theology. This theme is found in Ralph Ellison's *Invisible Man* and in James Baldwin's claim that "Nobody knows my name." In a theological context, Cecil Cone has addressed this problem in his book *The Identity Crisis in Black Theology*.[10] But one of the earliest and most classic statements on this problem is found in the writings of W.E.B. Dubois:

It is a peculiar sensation, this double-consciousness, this sense of always looking at one's self through the eyes of others, of measuring one's soul by the tape of a world that looks on in amused contempt and pity. One ever feels his twoness—an American, a Negro; two souls, two thoughts, two unreconciled strivings; two warring ideals in one dark body, whose dogged strength alone keeps it from being torn asunder.[11]

The significance of the problem of black identity in the context of African theology may be clarified by asking: How can I speak about the future of African theology when my black identity is so inextricably tied to North America? Aside from the technicality of my genetic origin and its relation to the African continent, what right do I have to participate in the future development of African theology? Unless these questions are honestly faced, then the relations between African theology and black theology will remain superficial. The purpose of this essay is to attempt to move our dialogue beyond the phase of theological politeness to a serious encounter of each other's historical options. What is the relation between our different historical contexts and our common faith in God's power to make us all one in Jesus Christ? How do we translate the universal claim of our faith into a common historical practice? These are the issues that define the focus of this paper.

In order to protect against a possible misunderstanding of my concern, an additional word of clarification is necessary. If by African theology we mean an interpretation of the Christian Gospel in the light of the political and cultural situation in Africa, then it is obvious that the future of this enterprise belongs primarily to Africans alone. Persons who have little or no knowledge of Africa or whose theological consciousness was shaped elsewhere should not expect to play a decisive role in the future development of theology on the African continent. This point is applicable not only to white Europeans but to black Americans as well. I want to emphasize this point, because my disagreement with Mbiti and other African theologians who separate radically African theology and black theology does not mean that I believe that black Americans should play a major role in the formulation of the meaning of African theology. My contention is that black and African theologies are not as different as has been suggested and that their common concerns require a dialogue that is important to both. I want to suggest two reasons why we ought to engage in a substantive dialogue, and then use the third section of this paper to say a word about the future of African theology.

A COMMON HISTORICAL OPTION

The history of American blacks cannot be completely separated from the history of Africa. Whatever may be said about the significant distinctions between Africans and black people of the American diaspora, there was once a time when these distinctions did not exist. The significance of this point extends beyond a mere academic interest in historical origins. The recognition of the inter-relation of our histories is also important for assessing our present realities and the shaping of our future hopes and dreams. Whether we live in Africa or the Americas, there is some sense in which the Black World is one, and this oneness lays the foundation and establishes our need for serious dialogue. Marcus Garvey expressed this point in his ill-fated "back to Africa" movement. With a similar philosophical ideal but a radically different political vision, W.E.B. Dubois, George Padmore, and Kwame Nkrumah expressed the unity of the Black World in their development of Pan-Africanism. But we do not need to accept Garveyism or the Pan-African philosophy of Dubois in order to realize that the future of Africa and black people in the Americas is inextricably bound together. International economic and political arrangements require a certain kind of African and black nationalism if we are to liberate ourselves from European and white American domination. This economic and political domination, sharply enhanced and defined by racism, will not cease simply through an appeal to reason or the religious piety of those who hold us in captivity. Oppression ceases only when the victims accumulate enough power to stop it.

The oneness that I refer to is made possible by a common historical option available to both Africans and black Americans in their different social contexts. Each of us can make a choice that establishes our solidarity with the liberation of the Black World from European and American domination. This domination is revealed not only in the particularity of American white racism or European colonialism in Africa, but also in Euro-American imperialism in Asia, Latin America, and the Caribbean. World history has been written by "white hands" (to borrow a graphic expression from Leonardo Boff), and the time has come to recover the memory of the victims of this world. The need to reinterpret history and theology in the light of the hopes and struggles of the oppressed peoples of the world establishes not only a oneness between Africans and black Americans, but also makes possible our common solidarity with the liberation of the poor in Asia and Latin America. This global perspective requires that we enlarge the oneness of the Black World to include our solidarity with the world's poor. It was this assumption that defined the Final Statement of the Ecumenical Dialogue of Third World Theologians that met in Tanzania (August 1976),[12] and it continues to shape our dialogue in Ghana. To be sure, we must recognize that we live in quite different historical and contemporary situations, which will naturally influence certain emphases in our theologies. But we should guard against the tendency of allowing our various particularities to blind us to the significance of our commonality. It is a oneness grounded in a common historical option for the poor and against societal structures that oppress them. This "poor perspective" (to use an apt phrase from Gustavo Gutiérrez) makes us one and establishes the possibility of our mutual sharing in the creation of one humanity.

A COMMON FAITH

The possibility of substantive dialogue between African theology and other Third World theologies is created not only on the basis of our common historical option, but also on the basis of our common faith in Jesus Christ. Because we confess Jesus as Lord, we are required to work out the meaning of that confession in a common historical project. Faith and practice belong together. If we are one in Christ Jesus, then this oneness should be seen in our struggle together to create societal structures that bear witness to our vision of humanity. If our common confession of faith is in no way related to a common historical commitment, how do we know that what we call the universal church is not the figment of our theological imagination? I contend that the unity of the church can be found only in a common historical commitment.

Anyone acquainted with my theological perspective knows that I have placed much emphasis on the social context of theology. And I have no intention of relinquishing this point in this paper. But it is important to recognize the limitation of our particularity so that we will not ignore the universal claims that the Gospel lays upon all of us. Whether Christians live in Africa, Asia, Latin America, or Europe, we have been called by God to bear witness to the Gospel of Jesus to all peoples. Therefore, we must ask not only what does the Gospel mean for me in Africa or North America, but also for Christians in the whole inhabited world. And our explication of the Gospel must be universal enough to include the material conditions in which people are forced to live. There is only one history, one Creator, and one Lord and Savior Jesus Christ. It is the centrality of this faith claim that brings us together and requires us to have dialogue with each other about its meaning in society. Our cultural limitations do not render us silent but open us up to share with others our perspective about the historical possibility for the creation of a new humanity.

What is the universal dimension of the Gospel that transcends culture and thus lays a claim upon all Christians no matter what situation they find themselves in?[13] This is the question that every theology must seek to answer. Because our various theologies are so decidedly determined by our historical option in a given context, different answers have been given to this question. Because dominant European and American theologies have chosen an option that establishes their solidarity with western imperialism and capitalism, they usually define the universality of the Gospel in terms that do not challenge the white western monopoly of the world's resources. There have been many debates in traditional theology about the precise content of the essence of the Gospel, but seldom has the debate included political and economic realities that separate rich nations from the poor ones. This is not an accident, and our meeting together in Ghana means that we recognize the danger of defining the universal aspect of the Gospel in the light of western culture.

We meet here today because we are in search for other theological options than the ones found in traditional theology. I believe that we will find our common vision of the Gospel through a serious encounter with the biblical message as defined by our common historical commitment in our various social contexts. We must be prepared to listen to each other and to learn what it means to be historically involved in the realization of the Gospel. Our dialogue is only beginning, and it is thus too early to expect unanimous agreement on various issues. But if we take seriously our common faith in the crucified Christ, as encountered in the struggle for freedom, then I believe that God's Spirit will break down the barriers that separate us. For Christian unity "only becomes a reality to the extent that we partake of Christ [who] is hidden in those who suffer."[14] It is within this ecumenical context that I will venture to say a word about the future of African theology.

THE FUTURE OF AFRICAN THEOLOGY

The future of African theology is found in its creative interpretation of the Gospel for the African situation and in relation to the theologies of the poor throughout the world. This emphasis does not exclude the legitimacy of African theology's concern with indigenization and selfhood in its attempt to relate the biblical message to the African cultural and religious situation.[15] But selfhood and indigenization should not be limited to cultural changes alone. There is a *political* ingredient in the Gospel that cannot be ignored if one is to remain faithful to biblical revelation. The recognition of this political ingredient in the Gospel is clearly implied in the All Africa Conference of Churches' call for a moratorium and in its continued support of the liberation movements in Southern Africa. It is within this context that we should understand Canon Burgess Carr's highly publicized distinction between the "selective violence employed by the Liberation Movement" and the " 'collective vengeance' perpetrated by the South African, Rhodesian and Portuguese regimes in Africa. Thus, any outright rejection of violence is an untenable alternative for African Christians."[16] These words caused a great deal of unrest. He drew a radical theological conclusion from the liberation struggles of African people, and the churches of Africa and Europe are still trying to assimilate its significance.

If for no other reason, we must give our unequivocal support to the Liberation Movements, because they have helped the Church to rediscover a new and radical appreciation of the cross. In accepting the violence of the cross, God, in Jesus Christ, sanctified violence into a redemptive instrument for bringing into being a fuller human life.[17]

Burgess Carr is not alone among African theologians and church people who define liberation as a common theme in the Gospel. "Liberation," writes Jesse Mugambi, "is the objective task of contemporary African Christian Theology. It is not just one of the issues, but rather, all issues are aimed at liberating Africans from all forces that hinder them from living fully as a human being." According to Mugambi, the idea of liberation is inherent in the concept of salvation. "In the African context, and in the Bible, *salvation* as a theological concept cannot be complete without *liberation* as a social/political concept."[18] A similar point is also made by Eliewaha Mshana: "Africanization must involve liberation from centuries of poverty, humilia-

tion, and exploitation. A truly African Theology cannot escape the require-
ment of helping the indigenous churches to become relevant to the spiritual,
social, and political ills of Africa."[19] Kofi Appiah-Kubi also includes liberation as an important ingredient of African theology. He not only uses
liberation as an important christological theme in Africa,[20] but locates liberation in his definition of African theology. African theology, he contends,
"should be a liberating theology, liberating us from the chains of social,
economic, political and even at times traditional and cultural dominations
and oppressions."[21]

No African theologians, however, have expressed the theme of liberation
more dramatically than South African theologians. Desmond Tutu[22] and
Manas Buthelezi[23] are prominent examples of this new theological perspective emerging from behind the apartheid walls of the Republic of South
Africa. Both have challenged African theologians to take seriously the political ingredient of the Gospel as related to the contemporary problems of
Africa. Desmond Tutu is emphatic:

African theology has failed to produce a sufficiently sharp cutting edge. . . . It has
seemed to advocate disengagement from the hectic business of life because very little
has been offered that is pertinent, say, about the theology of power in the face of the
epidemic of coups and military rule, about development, about poverty and disease
and other equally urgent present day issues. I believe this is where the abrasive Black
Theology may have a few lessons for African Theology. It may help to recall African
Theology to its vocation to be concerned for the poor and the oppressed, about
[people's] need for liberation from all kinds of bondage to enter in an authentic
personhood which is constantly undermined by pathological religiosity and by political authority which has whittled away much personal freedom without too much
opposition from the church.[24]

These are strong words and they remind us all of the prophetic calling of the
church and theology.

Additional examples of this African perspective in theology are found in a
collection of essays entitled *Essays on Black Theology.* This book was banned
by the Republic of South Africa and was later published in Britain under the
title *Black Theology: The South African Voice.*[25] More recently Allan Boesak
has added his contribution to South African black theology with his publication of *Farewell to Innocence.*[26] The central theme among these new theological voices from South Africa is their focus on liberation in relation to politics
and blackness. They insist that blackness is an important ingredient in their
view of African theology.

Unfortunately, John Mbiti and Edward Fashole-Luke have been very
critical of this South African black theology as being too narrowly focused on
blackness, liberation, and politics. Both contend that Christian theology

must transcend race and politics.[27] I believe that their criticisms are misplaced because the theme of liberation, as interpreted by the particularity of the African economic and political situation, provides the most creative direction for the future development of African theology. If God came to us in the human presence of Jesus, then no theology can transcend the material conditions of humanity and still retain its Christian identity. Jesus did not die on the cross in order to transcend human suffering, but rather that it might be overcome. Therefore, any theology whose distinctive perspective is defined by Jesus is required to find its creative expression in the practice of overcoming suffering.

The need for African theology to focus on politics and liberation arises not only out of a christological necessity. It is also a necessity that arises out of the ecumenical context of contemporary theology. By locating the definition of African theology in the context of the political and economic conditions of Africa, African theologians can easily separate their theological enterprise from the prefabricated theologies of Europe and establish their solidarity with other Third World theologies. This point is suggested by Canon Burgess Carr:

The forthrightness of Black Theology and the theology of liberation canvassed today presents a dual challenge to our Christian style of life. In a profound way, it challenges the preoccupation with African Theology to advance beyond academic phenomenological analysis to a deeper appropriation of the ethical sanctions inherent in our traditional religious experience. It also forces Christians to come to grips with the radical character of the gospel of Jesus as an ideological framework for their engagement in the struggle for cultural authenticity, human development, justice and reconciliation.[28]

If black theology's focus on liberation is its challenge to African theology, what then is the challenge of African theology to black theology, Latin American liberation theology, and theology in Asia? Unless the challenge is mutual, then there is no way for substantive dialogue to take place. I believe that African theology's challenge to us is found in its rejection of prefabricated theology, liturgies, and traditions and its focusing of the theological task on the selfhood of the church and the incarnation of Christianity in the life and thought of Africa. African theologians challenge all Christians in the Third World to take seriously popular religion and unestablished expressions of Christianity. Perhaps more than any other Third World theological expression, African theology takes seriously the symbols and beliefs of the people whom all liberation theologians claim to represent. If liberation theology in any form is to represent the hopes and dreams of the poor, must not that representation be found in its creative appropriation of the language and culture of the people? If the poor we claim to represent do not recognize themselves in our theologies, how then will they know that we speak for them? From their earliest attempt to create an African theology, African theologians have agreed that their theology must take seriously three sources: the Bible, African traditional religion, and the African Independent churches. The appropriation of these sources structurally locates the theological task among the poor people of Africa. Until recently Latin American liberation theology has tended to overlook the importance of this cultural ingredient in theology. The same is true to some extent of North American black theology and perhaps, to a lesser degree, of theology in Asia.[29]

The relation between indigenization and liberation does not have to be antagonistic. In fact, we need both emphases. Without the indigenization of theology, liberation theology's claim to be derived from and accountable to oppressed peoples is a farce. Indigenization opens the door for the people's creative participation in the interpretation of the Gospel for their life situation. But indigenization without liberation limits a given theological expression to the particularity of its cultural context. It fails to recognize the universal dimension of the Gospel and the global context of theology. It is simply not enough to indigenize Christianity or to Africanize theology. The people also want to be liberated from racism, sexism, and classism. If theology is to be truly indigenized, its indigenization must include in it a social analysis that takes seriously the human struggles against race, sex, and class oppression. I contend therefore that indigenization and liberation belong together. The future of African theology, and all Third World theologies, is found in the attempt to interpret the Christian Gospel in the historical context of the people's struggle to liberate themselves from all forms of human oppression.

NOTES

1. The beginning of the contemporary Civil Rights movement of American blacks is usually identified with the bus boycott in Montgomery, Alabama, led by Martin Luther King, Jr., in December 1955. For an account of this event, see Martin Luther King, Jr., *Stride Toward Freedom* (New York: Harper, 1958). For more information about the later development of this movement in the 1960s and Martin King's reaction to the rise of Black Power, see his *Why We Can't Wait* (New York: Harper, 1963) and *Where Do We Go From Here: Chaos or Community* (New York: Harper, 1967).

2. For an account of the rise of Black Power, see Stokely Carmichael and Charles Hamilton, *Black Power: The Politics of Black Liberation* (New York: Random House, 1967).

3. John Mbiti, "An African Views American Black Theology," *Worldview*, August 1974, p. 43.

4. John Mbiti was the Harry Emerson Fosdick Visiting Professor at Union Theological Seminary during the academic year of 1972–73.

5. I was especially disturbed by Mbiti's assertion that "Black Theology . . . is full of sorrow, bitterness, anger and hatred." I know of no black American theologian who would accept this description of black theology.

6. See his "What is African Theology?" *Africa Theological Journal,* no. 4, August 1971.

7. See his "The Quest for an African Christian Theology," *The Journal of Religious Thought* 32, no. 2 (Fall–Winter 1975). This issue is devoted to essays presented at the consultation on African and Black Theology, Accra, December 1974. See also an earlier article in which Fashole-Luke questions the possibility of the development of an African theology: "An African Indigenous Theology: Fact or Fiction?" *The Sierra Leone Bulletin of Religion,* 1969.

8. While Kwesi Dickson is not as emphatic about the distinction between black and African theology, as suggested by Mbiti, Sawyerr, and Fashole-Luke, the sharp separation of African theology from black theology is clearly implied in his writings. See his contribution at the Ghana Consultation: "African Theology: Origin, Methodology and Content," *Journal of Religious Thought,* Fall–Winter 1975. See also his "Towards a Theologia Africana," in M. E. Glaswell and E. W. Fashole-Luke, *New Testament Christianity for Africa and the World* (London: SPCK, 1974); "The Old Testament and African Theology," *The Ghana Bulletin of Theology* 4, no. 4 (June 1973); "The African Theological Task," in *The Emergent Gospel,* ed. Sergio Torres and Virginia Fabella (Maryknoll: Orbis Books, 1978).

9. A partial account of these exceptions is treated in the third section of this paper.

10. Nashville: AMEC, 1975.

11. *The Souls of Black Folk* (Greenwich, Conn.: Fawcett, 1961, originally published in 1903), pp. 16–17.

12. See *The Emergent Gospel,* pp. 259ff.

13. This question involves the problem of ideology in theological discourse. I have discussed the implications of this problem in my *God of the Oppressed* (New York: Seabury, 1975).

14. Rubem Alves, "Protestantism in Latin America: Its Ideological Function and Utopian Possibilities," *The Ecumenical Review,* January 1970, p. 15.

15. The themes of selfhood and indigenization are very prominent in African theology. On indigenization, see the important book by Bolaji Idowu, *Towards an Indigenous Church* (London: Oxford University Press, 1965); Kwesi Dickson and Paul Ellingworth, eds., *Biblical Revelation and African Beliefs* (London: Lutterworth Press, 1969, and Maryknoll, N.Y.: Orbis, 1969). On the theme of selfhood, see Kwesi Dickson, "African Theology: Origin, Methodology and Content," *Journal of Religious Thought; The Struggle Continues,* official report, Third Assembly of the All Africa Conference of Churches, Lusaka, May 1974. This theme is also found in the report of the First Assembly of the AACC in Kampala, 1963. See *Drumbeats From Kampala* (London: Lutterworth Press, 1963).

16. "The Engagement of Lusaka," in *The Struggle Continues,* p. 78.

17. Ibid., p. 78.

18. "Liberation and Theology," in WSCF Dossier No. 5, June 1974, pp. 41–42.

19. "The Challenge of Black Theology and African Theology," *Africa Theological Journal,* no. 5, 1972.

20. See his "Jesus Christ—Some Christological Aspects from African Perspectives," in *African and Asian Contributions to Contemporary Theology,* ed. John Mbiti (Celigny: WCC Ecumenical Institute, Bossey, 1977).

21. "Why African Theology?" *AACC Bulletin* 7, no. 4 (July–August 1974): 6.

22. See his contribution at the Ghana Consultation on African and Black Theology, "Black Theology/African Theology: Soul Mates or Antagonists," *Journal of Religious Thought,* Fall–Winter 1975; see also his "Black Theology," *Frontier,* Summer 1974; "African and Black Theologies," an Interview in the *AACC Bulletin* 7, no. 4 (July–August 1974).

23. See his contribution "Toward Indigenous Theology in South Africa," in *The Emergent Gospel;* see also his important essay "An African Theology or a Black Theology," in *Essays on Black Theology,* ed. George Mokgethi Motlhabi (Johannesburg, 1972). Other essays by Buthelezi include "Apartheid in the Church Is Damnable Heresy," *AACC Bulletin* 9, no. 2; "Daring to Live for Christ" in *Mission Trends No. 3: Third World Theologies,* ed. G. H. Anderson and T. F. Stransky (New York: Paulist Press, 1976).

24. "Black Theology/African Theology: Soul Mates or Antagonists?" pp. 32–33.

25. Ed. Basil Moore (London: Hurst, 1973). This book was later published in the United States under the title *The Challenge of Black Theology in South Africa* by John Knox Press. The original book, *Essays on Black Theology*, was edited by Mokgethi Motlhabi.

26. Maryknoll, N.Y.: Orbis Books, 1977.

27. See John Mbiti, "African Theology," *Worldview*, August 1973, pp. 37f.; see also his "Some Current Concerns of African Theology," *The Expository Times*, March 1976, p. 166. See E. W. Fashole-Luke, "The Quest for an African Christian Theology," pp. 87f. Fashole-Luke writes: "In the Republic of South Africa, African Theology is equated with Black Theology and the emphasis on Blackness indicates the ethnic implications of the task; considerable attention is given there to the exposition of the Gospel in terms of liberation from political, social and economic injustice, and the creation of a new sense of dignity and equality in the face of white oppression and discrimination. It is surely at this critical point that African theologians are challenged by the Gospel to raise African Christian theologies above the level of ethnic or racial categories and emphasis, so that Christians everywhere will see that Christianity is greater and richer than any of its cultural manifestations, and that the Gospel of liberation is for the oppressed and oppressor alike" (ibid., pp. 87–88).

28. "The Engagement of Lusaka," p. 78.

29. African theology's concern to use the thought forms of the people is not a slogan. The extensive research that African theologians have done on indigenous African religions and unestablished forms of Christianity does not have its counterpart among Latin American liberation theologians or even among black theologians in the U.S. John Mbiti has been one of the most prolific in this area. His books include *New Testament Eschatology in an African Background* (London: Oxford University Press, 1971); *African Religions and Philosophy* (London: Heinemann, 1969); *Concepts of God in Africa* (New York: Praeger, 1970). Some of his articles that are particularly appropriate in this discussion are "The Growing Respectability of African Traditional Religion," *Lutheran World* (Geneva) 59, no. 236 (October 1970); "The Ways and Means of Communicating the Gospel," in C. G. Baëta, ed., *Christianity in Tropical Africa* (London: Oxford University Press, 1968).

Other African theologians' work in this area includes Harry Sawyerr, *Creative Evangelism: Towards a New Christian Encounter with Africa* (London: Lutterworth Press, 1968); *God: Ancestor or Creator* (London: Longman, 1970); Bolaji Idowu, *Olódùmarè* (New York: Praeger, 1963); *African Traditional Religion: A Definition* (Maryknoll, N.Y.: Orbis, 1973).

EPILOGUE

20

Final Communiqué

Pan African Conference
of Third World Theologians,
December 17–23, 1977, Accra, Ghana

INTRODUCTION

We are African Christians who met in Accra, Ghana, from December 17 to 23, 1977, as part of the Ecumenical Dialogue of Third World Theologians to discuss emerging themes in African theology. We address ourselves and the rest of the Christian community in Africa and in other parts of the world in this statement.

We came together because of our deep concern for faith in Jesus Christ in Africa. It is this faith in the Lord of history that speaks to us concretely today. As we joyfully praise the saving Lord and share our problems, we are aware of the very real presence of the incarnate Jesus who comforts us and gives us hope.

Our meeting here was filled with experiences of a new life. We were able to move beyond denominational barriers and even beyond the usual rules of formal representation. Among us were Protestants, Orthodox, and Roman Catholics who have shared each other's concerns as we moved beyond the limitations of officiality. We have also experienced living together as a community of God's people with our brothers and sisters from the black American world, from Asia, Latin America, the Caribbean, and the Pacific Islands. We have shared the warmth of togetherness as captives in this world full of oppression and injustices that are more than often not of our own making. And above all we have shared the same hope.

The saving World of the Lord which provides freedom to captives has been our guiding stick. This was manifested not only in our daily worship and singing, but also in drama, plenary presentations, and group discussions. We affirm emphatically that it is the message of the Old and the New Testaments which gives boldness and power to our dialogue as African Christians with other Third World theologians.

THE AFRICAN REALITY

The Living Word of the Lord has led us to consider the realities of Africa today.

We thank God for the dynamism and vitality of African Christian communities and churches. The rapid growth of the people of God in Africa, the uniqueness of the African experience in original African liturgy, Bible reading, and Christian community life, are for all of us a matter of hope and confidence.

We realize that African unity is the unity of spirit and soul, an indivisible historical unity that may even transcend geographical differences. Our unity contributes to the total community of God without being blown away in the wind of unspecified universalism. We also realize that there are threats to this unity of our people. We deplore anything that seeks to shake the solidness of our deep-rooted unity, whether economic isolation, power manipulation, or even styles of life.

Colonialism has hampered our unity throughout the history of our relations with the western world. Although we are in a post-colonial era in most of Africa, colonialism continues to be perpetuated in Southern Africa. The white regimes in Zimbabwe, Namibia, and South Africa are nothing but disguised colonial occupations, a white minority's domination of the African majority through military force. In South Africa, the colonial domination is perpetuated through the Bantustans; the minority regime's program of independence for the so-called Homelands is nothing but a fraud aimed at deceiving the world into thinking that the black majority have accepted white domination. The ends of this colonial occupation are served by institutionalized white racism in South Africa, Namibia, and Zimbabwe. Africans deplore the fact that white racists from Zimbabwe and South Africa are now being exported to Latin American countries.

Ethnicity in Africa, as anywhere in the world, must not be confused with racism. Ethnicity is a positive element in any society. It can, however, be misused by outside powers to serve the ends of racism and cause disunity, wars, and human suffering.

We have no intention of underrating the internal misuse of power, but we also realize that often structures of internal oppression are perpetuated by questionable alliances under the disguise of friendship treaties or development aid. We affirm that our history is both sacred and secular. We see God's movement in our hope for a free and just society in Africa. Any destruction of this hope, be it in the misuse of power and authority or in the exploitation of resources by national institutions or by multinational corporations, is a direct and damnable violation of the destiny of God's people. God's demand is that human beings be subordinate to God's will for the total human community, making true Christ's command to love our neighbors as we love ourselves. Love for us signifies a communal act of obedience to God who is eternally with us. In Africa today this love is being destroyed by the ill effects of some national institutions and multinational corporations. Moreover, these ill effects cause great disunity, often perpetuated through militarism. The resultant suffering has led to thousands of deaths, detentions, and painful refugee situations. It is our belief that God's demand of the churches in Africa is that they not only oppose any form of oppression and suffering but also sever any alliances, direct or indirect, with the forces of oppression, e.g., by reviewing their stock portfolios in multinational corporations which facilitate the systematic militarization of governments that suppress human rights and violate human dignity.

THE PRESENCE OF CHRISTIANITY IN AFRICA

The methodology of studying the presence of Christianity in Africa must shift from hagiography of yesterdays to a more critical approach that starts from African worldviews, examines the impact of Christianity, and evaluates the varieties of African responses. Old strategies in mission are no longer relevant. It is not sufficient simply to maintain inherited church structures. Moreover, there is a gap between the rhetoric of church officials, administrators, and theologians and the reality in the villages. This has made the African masses passive. Limited funds to run institutions and the confused concept of stewardship make it impossible to realize self-reliance and moratorium.

The missionary church in Africa has used education as a means of domestication. This has led to misunderstandings with our colleagues in the wider dialogue, as was evident during the Christian-Muslim conference in Chambesy, 1976. This education has also produced an elite class in our countries.

We are therefore impelled to rethink the relevant strategies for the future of God's people in Africa. Efforts are being taken to contextualize the Gospel and to take full responsibility for the maintenance of the church. We proclaim the basis of the church in Africa is the vitality of the African Christian communities. Beyond the missionary structures and power, our Christian communities in poverty, humility, and faith continue to witness to the Gospel of Jesus Christ, creating their own Christian way of life and their own language to express the originality of their Christian experience.

In the traditional setting there was no dichotomy between the sacred and the secular. On the contrary, the sacred was experienced in the context of the secular. This healthy way of understanding our African society must be taken seriously by the church.

THE EMERGENCE OF AFRICAN THEOLOGIES

Context of African Theology

Despite the colonial experience of depersonalization and cultural invasion, the African cultures have kept their vitality. This vitality is expressed in the revival of African language, dances, music, and literature and in Africa's contribution to human sciences and to the human experience. This cultural vitality is the support of the African people in their struggle for complete liberation and for the construction of a human society.

Nevertheless, we must recognize the persistence of the domination that resulted from colonialism. This domination also exists in the churches. The organizational model imported from the West is still proposed and accepted. The life of our churches has been dominated by a theology developed with a methodology, a worldview, and a conception of humanity using western categories.

Present Trends in Theology

African theology has already emerged and is alive. Among the various approaches in African theology are:

1. one which, while admitting the inherent values in the traditional religions, sees in them a preparation for the Gospel;

2. a critical theology which comes from contact with the Bible, openness to African realities, and dialogue with non-African theologies;

3. black theology in South Africa, which takes into consideration the experiences of oppression and the struggle for liberation and gets its inspiration from the biblical faith as expressed in African language and categories as well as from the experience and reflections of black North Americans.

This list of approaches is not exhaustive, but it reveals the dynamism of the theological movement on the continent.

Sources of Theology

1. *The Bible and Christian heritage:* The Bible is the basic source of African theology, because it is the primary witness of God's revelation in Jesus Christ. No theology can retain its Christian identity apart from Scripture. The Bible is not simply a historical book about the people of Israel; through a

re-reading of this Scripture in the social context of our struggle for our humanity, God speaks to us in the midst of our troublesome situation. This divine Word is not an abstract proposition but an event in our lives, empowering us to continue in the fight for our full humanity.

The Christian heritage is also important for African theology. This is the heritage of the life and history of the church since the time of our Lord, with a long tradition of scholarship, liturgies, experiences, etc. African Christianity is a part of worldwide Christianity.

2. *African anthropology:* For Africans there is unity and continuity between the destiny of human persons and the destiny of the cosmos. African anthropology and cosmology are optimistic. The victory of life in the human person is also the victory of life in the cosmos. The salvation of the human person in African theology is the salvation of the universe. In the mystery of incarnation Christ assumes the totality of the human and the totality of the cosmos.

3. *African traditional religions:* The God of history speaks to all peoples in particular ways. In Africa the traditional religions are a major source for the study of the African experience of God. The beliefs and practices of the traditional religions in Africa can enrich Christian theology and spirituality.

4. *African Independent churches:* The Independent churches have developed through their long history a type of worship, organization, and community life rooted in African culture and touching the daily life of the people.

5. *Other African realities:* The experiences of cultural forms of life and arts, extended family, hospitality, and communal life are the expression of deep feelings of love and care. The struggles for the transformation of socio-economic systems, the struggles against racism, sexism, and other forms of economic, political, social, and cultural oppressions, are all to be taken seriously as sources for theology.

PERSPECTIVES FOR THE FUTURE

We believe that African theology must be understood in the context of African life and culture and the creative attempt of African peoples to shape a new future that is different from the colonial past and the neo-colonial present. The African situation requires a new theological methodology that is different from the approaches of the dominant theologies of the West. African theology must reject, therefore, the prefabricated ideas of North Atlantic theology by defining itself according to the struggles of the people in their resistance against the structures of domination. Our task as theologians is to create a theology that arises from and is accountable to African people.

We feel called to proclaim the love of God for all people within the dynamics of a conflictual history. We are committed to the struggles of our people to be free and we believe that the theology that arises from that commitment will have three characteristics.

1. African theology must be *contextual* theology, accountable to the context people live in. In drama, novels, and poetry, Africans demonstrate the importance of contextual expression. Contextualization will mean that theology will deal with the liberation of our people from cultural captivity.

2. Because oppression is found not only in culture but also in political and economic structures and the dominant mass media, African theology must also be *liberation* theology. The focus on liberation in African theology connects it with other Third World theologies. Like black theologians in North America, we cannot ignore racism as a distortion of the human person. Like Latin American and Asian theologians, we see the need to be liberated from socio-economic exploitation. A related but different form of oppression is often found in the roles set aside for women in the churches. There is the oppression of Africans by white colonialism, but there is also the oppression of blacks by blacks. We stand against oppression in any form because the Gospel of Jesus Christ demands our participation in the struggle to free people from all forms of dehumanization. African theology concerns itself with bringing about the solidarity of Africans with black Americans, Asians, and Latin Americans who are also struggling for the realization of human communities in which the men and women of our time become the architects of their own destiny.

3. Throughout this document, we have referred to the need to struggle against *sexism*. If that struggle is to be taken seriously by the church, then our seriousness will be reflected in the way we do theology. We recognize that African women have taken an active role in the church and in the shaping of our history. They have shown themselves to be an integral part of the liberation struggle. But we cannot ignore their exclusion from our past theological endeavors. The future of African theology must take seriously the role of women in the church as equals in the doing of theology.

CONCLUSION

In post-independent Africa and in Southern Africa, theology confronts new challenges, hopes, and opportunities. The vigor of the traditional African religions and cultures and the renewal of the churches, thanks principally to a return to the Scriptures, present us with the resources for our tasks.

Our belief in Jesus Christ Liberator, convinces us that there is a noble future for our countries, if the processes of nation-building are geared to providing the urgent basic needs of all instead of the privileges of a few. We are confident that the creative vitality of our own traditional religions and cultures can provide the inspiration for a free and just form of community organization and national development.

In order to serve the people, the Gospel, and the churches in these tasks we pledge to renew ourselves according to the needs of today discerned by us under the light of the Spirit of God present among us. For this we need an interdisciplinary methodology of social analysis, biblical reflection, and active commitment to be with the peoples in their endeavors to build a better society. Toward this end we have formed today an Ecumenical Association of African Theologians. Conscious of our deficiencies and weaknesses, yet encouraged by the nobility of the task before us, we undertake this journey of service through theology so that all the women, men, and children of our lands may be able "to have life and live abundantly."

21

The Role of Afro-America
in the Rise of Third World Theology:
A Historical Reappraisal

Gayraud S. Wilmore (United States)

It was no arbitrary decision on the part of the leadership of the Ecumenical Association of Third World Theologians that their second conference, in Accra, Ghana, should include an ample representation from the black churches of the United States. This was not the case at the first conference, at Dar es Salaam in 1976; then only two black Americans were invited and only one attended. Until the Accra conference in 1977, doubts were entertained by some—and there is still debate on the question—concerning the appropriateness of black American participation in a meeting designed to clarify and promote theological dialogue in the Third World. Is it not true that black Christians, no less than their white brothers and sisters in America, are citizens of the First World—historically and ideologically identified with the structures of oppression and neocolonialism? Certainly black American churches cannot be absolved from some of the more lamentable features of the foreign missionary movement. Granting this, much more needs to be said. It is too easy to obscure significant differences between the historic relationship of black American churches to the struggle of submerged peoples of the Third World, particularly in Africa and the Caribbean, and that of the predominantly white churches of Europe and North America.

The shameful neglect by western scholarship of black American church history and the bland assumption that theological development in black institutions, from slavery to recent times, is indistinguishable from the ethical

Professor Wilmore's paper was written following the conference.

revivalism and neo-orthodoxy of mainline Protestantism have falsified the true orientation of Afro-American religion.[1] The ghettoization of the black minority and its continuous exploitation by the economic system of the United States give the black underclass the status of a virtual internal colony, including most of the pathologies that Frantz Fanon so ably dissected in French-speaking Africa and C.L.R. James, from a geopolitical and economic perspective, in the Caribbean.[2] The inclusion of a large segment of Afro-America within the ambit of the Third World rests upon solid political, economic, and historical grounds and cannot be gainsaid by the bourgeoisification of certain highly visible black institutions. Moreover, the precarious middle-classism and elitism of some black churches in the United States is little different from that of former mission churches catering to urbanites in metropolitan areas throughout Africa, Asia, and Latin America. If the "Third World" includes the latter, it should include the former. Third World liberation theology is vectored from the submerged and impoverished mass churches of the formerly colonized areas of the southern hemisphere and the line of identification runs directly through the black ghettoes, Hispanic barrios, and Native American reservations of North America.

The purpose of this article is to explore the historical connections between Afro-American and African theological developments almost from the beginning of independent black churches in the eighteenth century, but with special emphasis on events since the end of the 1960s. A more extended treatment would be necessary to do justice to this trans-Atlantic connection. But even a brief inquiry into what it has meant for the struggle against white domination in both Africa and North America should suffice to validate the main contention: that black American religion must be understood in the context of the Third World. Its most exportable product, black Christian theology, has had, and will continue to have, a critical role to play in the development of indigenous theologies in Asia, Africa, Latin America, and the islands of the Pacific.

Wherever black theology has been heard of overseas, through articles, books, lectures, and international conferences, it has occasioned surprise, curiosity, spirited discussion, and appreciation. The crusades of black Americans for freedom and equality have been known and admired by oppressed peoples for many years, but the emergence of a theology of liberation out of the streets and alleys of American ghettoes has had a particular attraction for progressive segments of Third World Christians—mainly among the younger theologians.[3] The seminal black theology of the nineteenth century and the early twentieth century, however, antedates these contemporary influences abroad, and for that it is necessary to go back to the first stirrings of independence in black American Christianity.

THE TRANS-ATLANTIC CONNECTION
IN HISTORICAL PERSPECTIVE

The sea lanes between Africa, the Caribbean Islands, and the North American mainland carried much more than slaves, sugar, and rum. The ships that plied those lanes also carried free black men and women—colonizers, commercial agents, and Christian missionaries. For more than a hundred years, from the outbreak of the American Revolution to the dawn of the twentieth century, black people moved back and forth across the Atlantic and the Caribbean to forge a bond between Africa and the New World that has been overlooked by most historians. An international experience runs through the history of Africa and Afro-America, and while slavery hindered it for 244 years, it could not totally suppress the triangular relationship that evolved between separated brothers and sisters.

It was a desire for freedom, advancement, and the propagation of Christianity that inspired all this moving about, and the black Christian church was at the center of it. We too easily forget that of the four earliest black preachers about whom we know anything—David George and Jesse Peter of Silver Bluff, South Carolina, George Liele, and the man called Brother Amos—three went overseas to establish churches: David George to Nova Scotia and Sierra Leone, George Liele to Jamaica, and Brother Amos to the Bahamas. Even before the first black denomination was founded, two black Christians, John Kizzel, who was born in West Africa and escaped slavery in Charleston, and Paul Cuffee, who was born in Massachusetts and settled in Westport, led black Americans to West Africa to help lay the foundation for Christianity in Sierra Leone and Liberia—Kizzel as early as 1792 and Cuffee in 1811.

Nine years later the man who almost became the first bishop of the African Methodist Episcopal church, Rev. Daniel Coker of Baltimore, went to Africa as an unofficial missionary of his church. We may regard Coker, Lott Carey, and Collin Teague, the latter two having been sent by the black Baptists of Richmond, Virginia, and Scipio Beanes, who was commissioned for Haiti by the A.M.E. bishop Richard Allen, as the first representatives of independent black churches to go into the foreign mission field before the end of the first quarter of the nineteenth century. The pioneer, Daniel Coker, illustrates the zeal of these men, barely out of slavery, to preach the Gospel outside the United States. In one of his letters to the American Colonization Society, Coker wrote back: "Tell my brethren to come; fear not; this land is good; it only wants men to possess it. . . . Tell the colored people to come up to the help of the Lord."[4]

It would be difficult to exaggerate the importance that the first black

Baptists and Methodists attached to the enterprise of foreign missions. For them it was not only the mark of a true church but an emblem of racial pride, and they carried that emblem not only to Africa and the Caribbean but to Asia as well.

Why this enormous interest in leaving families, friends, and the relative security of familiar surroundings to preach in foreign parts? We can better understand it among free white men. But here were poverty-stricken black churches, scarcely able to provide a roof over the heads of their members, fighting off the attempted control of white ministers with one hand while trying to build institutions out of nothing with the other. They were led by untrained, often illiterate preachers, many of them slaves ministering at the behest of their masters—or more often, behind their backs. It was a time when few people knew what it was like to stray more than a few miles from where one was born and when affluent white churches found it burdensome to maintain missionaries in a foreign field. Despised and rejected at home, here were a few struggling Black Baptist Associations and two new Methodist General Conferences trying to launch a missionary enterprise around the world! This is certainly one of the most amazing facts of modern church history. What possessed them?

Somewhere along the way these slaves and recently freed men had heard that the essential meaning of the church is the proclamation to the whole world of the Good News about liberation through Jesus Christ. Against tremendous odds they had formed themselves into churches and they were determined to behave like churches—to "go where the Spirit says go"—into the uttermost parts of the world with the Gospel of freedom. As the A.M.E. bishop Willis Nazery said in 1852:

It has more plainly and fully set before me the duty of the A.M.E. Church to assist in sending out the Gospel to the heathen, who are out of the limits of civilization and Christianity. We have, as an Episcopal Church, as much right to look after perishing Africa, the West India Islands, St. Domingo, and others—and all these who are not Christianized—as any other Christian Church upon the face of the globe.[5]

The presumptuousness and patronizing tone notwithstanding (for that was the way both black and white Christians regarded Africa in those days), this statement by Nazery at the General Convention of 1852 suggests the peculiar concern and motive behind the missionary activity of the early black church. The redemption of Africa and the West Indies was uppermost in their minds and hearts. The major target was Africa, for they were convinced that God wanted them to take back the Gospel and the blessings of western civilization to the ancestral homeland.

Black theology began in those days. The passage in Psalm 68:31, "Princes shall come out of Egypt; Ethiopia shall soon stretch out her hands unto God," which has, incidentally, been emasculated by the translators of the Revised Standard Version, was one of the favorite texts of Afro-American and African preachers in the nineteenth century. It was a prophecy of the coming greatness of the black race. Ethiopia: that was the place where the ancients believed all black people originated. And "shall stretch out her hands unto God" meant that in turning to him, it would take its rightful place beside the great nations of the earth. Black preachers believed that power and majesty would come out of Egypt, the land of the blacks, and Ethiopia—the first black Christian nation—would receive from God due recompense for all that black people had suffered at the hands of their oppressors.

It was on the basis of these convictions that the black church in the United States understood a special vocation to preach the Gospel and take Euro-American learning and technology, such as they had been able to attain, to Africa. Their role was to hasten the day of the fulfillment of the prophecy of Psalm 68:31. Africa must be redeemed. Indeed, both Africa and the Caribbean, the two great centers of black power and pride—symbolized in the former by the kingdom of Ethiopia and in the latter by the Republic of Haiti—had to be restored and liberated through the efforts of the relatively privileged black people of North America. They believed that God himself had given to them this awesome responsibility.

It is not possible to trace here the movement of the black churches from African missions to Pan-Africanism. Suffice it to say that after 1900 Pan-Africanism, the movement that bound together in a single family blacks in the United States, Canada, Africa, and the Caribbean, could not have come into its own without the influence of black American Christians.[6] Black people from all denominations, the predominantly white as well as black, participated in this movement for an independent Africa blessed by Christian schools, colleges, and churches. Alexander Crummell and Bishop James T. Holly were Episcopalians. Lewis G. Jordan and Gregory W. Hayes were of the National Baptists, Inc. Henry M. Turner and R. H. Cain were A.M.E. bishops. Edward W. Blyden and William H. Sheppard were Presbyterians, and Alexander Walters was a bishop of the African Methodist Episcopal Zion church (A.M.E.Z.). All of these men, at one time or another and often in close collaboration, contributed to the development of the movement of Pan-Africanism from a black theological and political perspective, of which Dr. W.E.B. DuBois, a man of profound though unorthodox religious persuasions, was the chief Afro-American representative.[7]

It should be noted here that black American schools and colleges, traditionally imbued with a fervor for human liberation and the elevation of a leadership class, played a crucial role in these developments. The Reconstruction Congresses, white philanthropy, and white educators from the North made an important contribution to the remarkable flowering of black secondary schools and institutions of higher education throughout the South after the Civil War. But it also should never be forgotten that the institutions founded by the black Baptist conventions and the three major black Methodist denominations remained independent of white control and were often seedbeds of racial pride and liberalism in the heartland of Southern prejudice. The main burden for their maintenance fell on the shoulders of struggling black congregations—the chicken dinners and the bake sales.

Virginia Theological Seminary and College was the black Baptist school in Lynchburg where John Chilembwe was tutored for the role he played as the religious leader of the Nyasaland rebellion in 1915.[8] Mbiyu Koinange of Kenya, who was one of the leaders during the Mau Mau resistance, attended Hampton Institute in Virginia, where his Pan-Africanism was shaped in an atmosphere of black Christian education and political activism.[9] Wilberforce, Livingstone College, Howard University, Fisk, and Lincoln University in Pennsylvania all educated several generations of African and Caribbean politicians, journalists, clergymen, and scholars. Among them were such leaders of African independence as Hastings Kamazu Banda, John L. Dube, D. D. Jabavu, James E. E. Aggrey, Nnamdi Azikiwe, Kwame Nkrumah, J. A. Sofala, and others too numerous to mention.[10]

The leadership of both the A.M.E. and the A.M.E.Z. churches began to propagate black liberation in Southern and West Africa late in the nineteenth century. Their bishops participated in the first Pan-African Congresses. Most notable among the early influences upon Ethiopianism, the anti-racist Christian radicalism that broke out in Africa in the 1880s, was the A.M.E. bishop Henry M. Turner, who was an implacable advocate of black nationalism and helped to establish African Methodism in South Africa. St. Clair Drake observes about the planting of revolutionary Christianity in modern Africa by Turner and others during and following the Civil War:

Black people under slavery turned to the Bible to "prove" that a black people, Ethiopians, were powerful and respected when white men in Europe were barbarians; Ethiopia came to symbolize all of Africa, and throughout the nineteenth century, the "redemption of Africa" became one important focus of meaningful activity for leaders among New World Negroes. . . . "Ethiopianism" left an enduring legacy to the people who fight for Black Power in the twentieth century, and some of its development needs to be understood.[11]

Black Christianity in the United States was no less of an anathema to colonial administrators and trading companies following the Emancipation than it was to Southern governors prior to the Civil War. A theology of human rights and liberation underlay the evangelical piety of black preachers in the United States and the Caribbean from the Black Methodist insurrection in South Carolina in 1822 to the Civil Rights movement led by Dr.

Martin Luther King, Jr. The Universal Negro Improvement Association
(U.N.I.A.) of Marcus M. Garvey, which was essentially a black religious
movement, had enormous influence in generating black pride and the spirit
of nationalism throughout colonial Africa in the 1920s. Even though Garvey
had never visited Africa, his name was legendary and his widespread organization carried on a tradition started many years before by black churches,
church-related educational institutions, and the black press.[12] Research remains to be done in this little known area of modern church history if we are
to appreciate the true relationship of black religion in the United States to the
emergence of liberation theology and its role in the struggle against racism
and imperialism everywhere in the world.

RECENT DEVELOPMENTS

Recent history of the connection between American black religion and
Africa begins in the 1960s with the black revolution in the United States and,
more specifically, in the area of religious thought, with the organization of
the National Committee of Negro Churchmen (now the National Conference of Black Churchmen) in 1967. Two years after its founding, NCBC sent
two of its officers as observers to the second Assembly of the All Africa
Conference of Churches in Abidjan, Ivory Coast.[13] Ten years ago the white
churches of America had almost no blacks among the hundreds of missionaries sent to the African continent. Tensions between blacks and whites
at home were high despite the fact that the predominantly white churches
had played a belated but increasingly active role in the Civil Rights movement since 1963. The appearance at Abidjan of two uninvited spokesmen of
the new movement of black Christian activists was not regarded as propitious
by some whites. We were, for the first few days, studiously ignored by both
the Africans and the white patrons of the AACC. The coolness of this
resumed encounter between blacks, long separated by distance, culture, and
the machinations of racist missionaries, must be mentioned here if the
delicacy of the relationship in the presence of whites is to be clearly understood. Not until corridor huddles and protocol had been scrupulously played
out were the Afro-Americans welcomed and given the floor to state their
concerns to the working group on African theology.

The cordiality of the discussions that then ensued completely nullified the
strain of the first days of the Assembly. For many delegates this was the first
acquaintance with black churchmen who spoke positively about Black Power
and the concepts of the new black theology that were just being enunciated in
the United States and the Caribbean. Most of the Africans enthusiastically
endorsed the appeal of NCBC for fraternal bonds and collaboration in
theological work between the National Conference and the All Africa Con-

ference of Churches. Formal action was taken to commence such collaboration and the General Secretariat of the AACC, after the election of Canon Burgess Carr as general secretary, acted to implement the projection of a "Round-Table Discussion on African Theology and Black Theology" with a budget request of $40,000.[14]

Four other important meetings between African and black theologians have taken place since that almost frustrated attempt to overcome the estrangement of many years. The Dar es Salaam consultation in 1971 involved a large delegation from America, including theologian James H. Cone of Union Seminary in New York and L. Maynard Catchings, chairman of the NCBC Africa Commission.[15] The Makerere University (Kampala) consultation on "African Theology and Church Life" met in January 1972. George Thomas, a professor at the Interdenominational Theological Center in Atlanta presented a major paper on black theology and its relationship to African religion at that conference. In 1973 at Union Seminary in New York an exploratory consultation was held between African theologians, led by John S. Mbiti, and members of the Society for the Study of Black Religion, led by C. Shelby Rooks. That meeting was preliminary to a longer meeting that was convened at the Ghana Institute for Management and Public Administration (G.I.M.P.A.) in December 1974. On this occasion the African delegates represented the official theological commission of the AACC.[16]

These dialogues have been increasingly amicable as individuals have come to know one another personally and points of view have become better understood. Books and articles on African theology have appeared in greater number since the publication of John S. Mbiti's *African Religions and Philosophy* in 1969. Interestingly enough, in that same year James H. Cone's *Black Theology and Black Power* set forth the normative position of black theology in the United States. Cone's book was followed by several new publications by black American religious scholars. In this atmosphere of growing excitement and theological maturity agreements and disagreements have been clarified. Neither side has made a deliberate effort to overwhelm the other in a bid for ascendancy, nor has there been any haste to arrive at what most felt would be only a premature consensus. While there have been certain convergences on the issue of racism in western theology, the desirability of bringing an end to domination by white theology, and indigenizing the Gospel in thought-forms and cultures other than European and North American, there has also been dissent about how this is to be effected—with what risk of "throwing out the baby with the bath water"—and about the ineluctable consequences for churches that attempt to address social and political questions.

It is probably true that the Afro-Americans have been the more aggressive partners in this dialogue. No subject people has been more thoroughly attracted to the Christian faith and then developed its own interpretation of that faith in order to survive. And no people understands the white people and their capacity for good and evil better than black Americans. They have, as the old folks in the ghetto used to say, "wintered them and summered them."

This peculiar situation of being Christian and black, rooted in the culture of the West, and yet possessed of a sober apprehension of the foibles and pretensions by which that culture and society have oppressed them for more than 350 years, has made black Americans impatient with certain expressions of ingenuousness on the part of the Africans. It is true that Dr. King taught love and the black people take the hard sayings of Scripture seriously. But they are anything but naive. They are acquainted with racism in all of its forms and look with some curiosity and unbelief on other people of color who have evidently persuaded themselves that Christianity is intrinsically color-blind, and that the greed of a people totally committed to capitalism can be sated by showing them hospitality and good will.

Black theology is hard-headed about the realities of power in the world and the obduracy of sin, black as well as white. It expresses the need for all Christians to have "the wisdom of serpents and the harmlessness of doves," but some black theologians find the African brothers and sisters more dove-like than they have reason to be.

THE 1977 ACCRA CONFERENCE

At the second conference of the Ecumenical Association of Third World Theologians, in Accra, from December 17–23, 1977, it was apparent that the courtship between African and Afro-American theologians would no longer preclude an open confrontation on the issues of blackness as a symbol of radical alienation and struggle and liberation as the defining concept of biblical faith. Although a certain deference was paid to the African hosts, who far outnumbered the other delegates and had written most of the more than twenty papers, there was an undercurrent of latent controversy at this conference. It broke out most decisively between African and Afro-American perspectives on the significance and meaning of black theology. What had happened at other consultations also happened at this one: the South Africans, represented mainly by Allan A. Boesak of the University of the Western Cape, stood squarely with the black Americans. One exception was Gabriel M. Setiloane, presently lecturing in Botswana, who accused the brothers and sisters from the United States of trying to tell Africans how to do theology in Africa. This issue had not been far from the surface since the initial encounter in Abidjan in 1969. What brought it out on this particular occasion?

In 1974 an article by John S. Mbiti appeared in which he sought not only to differentiate between African and Afro-American religious thought, but to separate them once and for all.[17] Mbiti found black theology "full of sorrow, bitterness, anger, and hatred," preoccupied with ideas of liberation, and with little meaning for African Christians. He wrote:

As an African one has an academic interest in Black Theology, just as one is interested in the "water buffalo theology" of Southeast Asia or the theology of hope advocated by Jürgen Moltmann. But to try and push much more than the academic relevance of Black Theology for the African scene is to do injustice to both sides. . . . There is an obvious temptation to make a connection that should not be made.[18]

Many black Americans took this as a subversion of the rapprochement that had begun at Abidjan and, indeed, a repudiation of the whole history of Pan-Africanism. Of course, not all Africans agree with Mbiti. The South Africans were particularly unhappy, as were some blacks in Angola and Zimbabwe. Polarization over the Mbiti article was prevented by a paper read at the Ghana consultation in December of the same year by Desmond Tutu of South Africa.[19] Tutu acknowledged that the two theologies arise out of different contexts, but concluded that they were "soul-mates." He observed that African theology had something to learn from the more abrasive black theology. He feared that "African theology has failed to produce a sufficiently sharp cutting edge," and in response to Mbiti's allegation that the people of Southern Africa "do not need a theology of liberation—they *want* liberation," Tutu rejoined, "Could we not say the same thing about a theology of hope, that what people want is hope—not a theology of hope?"[20]

The issue was taken up at the Accra meeting by James H. Cone, whose paper "A Black American Perspective on the Future of African Theology" (see document 19 in this volume) occasioned the aforementioned clash with Setiloane and, to a lesser degree, with Mbiti. Cone attacked what he considered to be the latent conservatism of an African theology that rejects the relevance of black theology for Africa because it emphasizes blackness and political liberation. He carefully conceded the need for Africans to do theology for themselves and spoke appreciatively of the reciprocal influences that need to be actualized across the Atlantic. But, he said, "indigenization without liberation limits a given theological expression to the particularity of its cultural context. . . . It fails to recognize the universal dimension of the Gospel and the global context of theology."

The obsession of some African theologians with indigenization had already been criticized by Manas Buthelezi, who thought it to be a "pet project" of white missionaries looking for a way to make their continued presence in Africa acceptable. He quotes John V. Taylor to the effect that they were trading on the conservatism of the African clergy.[21] Buthelezi distinguishes between ethnographical and anthropological approaches to the theological task in Africa. It is in the latter that he sees an opening to a "first person," situationally-oriented African theology—a black theology—truly indigenous to the postcolonial period and faithful to the redeeming work of Jesus Christ in the context of the black experience.

CONCLUSION

The purpose of this excursion into one interesting aspect of the dialogue between Africans and black Americans is to indicate the intensity of the interaction that has been stimulated by the initiative of contemporary black theologians who are renewing a tradition that goes back more than two hundred years, when George Liele and David George set sail for Jamaica and West Africa. The conflict, whether occasioned then by the founding of independent black churches outside the United States, or now by the dissemination of liberation theology from black America, is positive and creative. It has the genius of breaking through a silent and alienated consciousness on both sides to bring the powerless together in a search for a common dignity and identity that inevitably stands against the paternalism and oppression of those who would be their masters.

Similar influences of Afro-American religious thought, though less definitive in Latin America and Asia, will doubtlessly be demonstrated by future research. In addition to the almost universal impact of the black revolution upon oppressed peoples all over the world—a revolution fueled by the religious sensibilities of the grandsons and granddaughters of slaves—the black theology movement has triggered imaginations and theological speculation from South America to the islands of the Pacific. The reigning theologies of the North Atlantic community and the systems of oppression and cultural domination that, wittingly or unwittingly, they have upheld can no longer be expected to receive the subordination and deference shown them by the so-called "younger churches" since the beginning of European expansionism. Black theology, explicating the faith that Jesus Christ came to liberate the captive masses of the world, has played a crucial role in unmasking the radical sin of western Christianity—the ideology of white supremacy.

Black Americans, of course, have not been alone in this dethroning of the gods of racism and imperialism. The resistance has been spontaneous. People can never be totally oppressed as long as a spark of humanity remains in them. What Buthelezi calls a "theology of restlessness" has existed everywhere the Gospel has been preached, notwithstanding the most malevolent distortions. But at a time when American capitalists and racists want to persuade black Americans that they now have a seat at the banquet table of the West and thereby should disassociate themselves from the wretched of the earth, at a time when those wretched are mounting an assault upon the bastions of power and privilege, Christians of the Third World need to strengthen their bonds with Afro-American churches. They need to understand the contribution those churches and the theology of black liberation have made to the climate of freedom in the world today—a climate that, though stormy, is full of hope and will invigorate their continuing struggle for selfhood and liberation.

NOTES

1. The highly regarded black sociologist, E. Franklin Frazier, in his book *The Negro Church in America* (New York: Schocken Books, 1964), misdirected scholarly attention to symbiotic and socializing features of institutional Christianity in the black community to the neglect of resistance and protest elements that were more fundamental. Joseph R. Washington's influential *Black Religion: The Negro and Christianity in the United States* (Boston: Beacon Press, 1964), similarly misconstrued the theological content of black faith. Washington tried to correct his earlier impressions but remains ambivalent. See the Introduction to his *Black Sects and Cults* (Garden City, N.Y.: Doubleday & Co., 1972).

2. Frantz Fanon, *The Wretched of the Earth* (New York: Grove Press, 1968), and C.L.R. James, *A History of Pan-African Revolt* (Washington, D.C.: Drum and Spear Press, 1969).

3. The best known among Third World scholars whose work reflects the influence of black theology are Allan A. Boesak (South Africa), Idris Hamid and Joyce Bailey (the Caribbean), Sergio Torres and Gustavo Gutiérrez (Latin America), C. S. Song (Taiwan), Burgess Carr and Kofi Appiah-Kubi (West Africa), and Eulalio P. Baltalzar (the Philippines).

4. Quoted in Daniel A. Payne, *History of the African Methodist Episcopal Church* (New York: The Arno Press and the New York Times, 1969), p. 91.

5. Ibid., p. 293.

6. For a classic study see George Shepperson, "Notes on Negro American Influences on the Emergence of African Nationalism," reprinted in Melvin Drimer, ed., *Black History: A Reappraisal* (Garden City, New York: Doubleday & Co., 1969), pp. 491–511.

7. For a good historical account, including the early history of Liberia, see Rodney Carlisle, *The Roots of Black Nationalism* (Port Washington, N.Y.: Kennikat Press, 1975).

8. George Shepperson and Thomas Price, *The Independent African* (Edinburgh: University of Edinburgh Press, 1958).

9. St. Clair Drake, *The Redemption of Africa and Black Religion* (Chicago: Third World Press, 1970), p. 6.

10. The late Dr. Horace Mann Bond gives an extended analysis of the impact of Lincoln University and the African students who attended there from 1857 to 1954 in his posthumous work, *Education for Freedom: A History of Lincoln University, Pennsylvania* (Princeton: Princeton University Press, 1976), pp. 487–550.

11. Drake, *Redemption of Africa*, p. 11.

12. Pioneering work is being done by Randall K. Burkett of the College of the Holy Cross on Garveyism in this connection. His forthcoming *Garveyism as a Religious Movement* will be published by Temple University Press.

13. Dr. J. Metz Rollins, executive director, now pastor of St. Augustine United Presbyterian Church in the Bronx, and the author, who was a member of the NCBC Executive Committee and chairman of its first Theological Commission.

14. *Profile of the All Africa Conference of Churches, Programme 1972/73*, p. 8.

15. The papers of this consultation have been published: Priscilla Massie, ed., *Black Faith and Black Solidarity: Pan-Africanism and Faith in Christ* (New York: Friendship Press, 1973).

16. The papers of the Accra Consultation appear in the *Journal of Religious Thought* 32, no. 2 (Fall–Winter 1975).

17. John Mbiti, "An African Views American Black Theology," *Worldview*, August 1974.

18. Ibid., p. 43.

19. Desmond M. Tutu, "Black Theology/African Theology—Soul-Mates or Antagonists?" *Journal of Religious Thought* 32, no. 2 (Fall–Winter 1975): 25–33.

20. Ibid., p. 20.

21. Manas Buthelezi, "Toward Indigenous Theology in South Africa," in Sergio Torres and Virginia Fabella, eds., *The Emergent Gospel: Theology from the Underside of History* (Maryknoll, N.Y.: Orbis Books, 1978), pp. 56–75.

List of Participants

Angola

José B. Chipenda, c/o World Council of Churches, 150 Route de Ferney, 1211 Geneva, Switzerland
Andre Conga da Costa, C.P. 235, Cabinda, Angola
Daniel Ntoni-Nzinga, C.P. 1301, Luanda, Angola; 10, Rua de Mouzinho de Albuquerque, Luanda, Angola
Augusto Chipesse, C.P. 109, Lobito, Angola

Botswana

Lopang K. Seloma, P.O. Box 318, Gaborone, Botswana
Gabriel M. Setiloane, University of Botswana & Swaziland, Private Bag 0022, Gaborone, Botswana

Cameroun

Engelbert Mveng, S.J., B.P. 1539, Yaounde, Cameroun
Jacques Ngally Nzie, Faculté de Théologie Protestante, B.P. 4011, Yaounde, Cameroun
Nyansako-ni-Nku, P.O. Box 19, Buea, Cameroun
Rose Zoé-Obianga, B.P. 4011, Yaounde, Cameroun
Marie Therese Essomba Akamse, B.P. 1539, Yaounde, Cameroun

Egypt

George Bebawi, 19 Hussein Ahmad Rashad Dokki, Giza, Egypt

Ghana

Peter Kodjo, World Students Christian Federation, P.O. Box 14782, Nairobi, Kenya
Mercy Amba Oduyoye, P.O. Box 1261, Ibadan, Nigeria
J. H. Kwabena Nketia, University of Ghana, Legon, Accra, Ghana
Mary-Brigid Agbenyo, Our Lady of Fatima Convent, P.O. Box 4263, Accra, Ghana
E. Agyem-Frempong, Tema Industrial Mission, P.O. Box 435, Tema, Ghana
Theophilus Samuel Amos Annobil, Trinity College, P.O. Box 48, Legon, Accra, Ghana
Patrick Akoi, P.O. Box 60, Bekwai, Ashanti, Ghana
Sam Prempeh, Trinity College, P.O. Box 48, Legon, Accra, Ghana
J. R. Leferink, National Catholic Secretariat, Dept. of Ecumenical Affairs, P.O. Box 1989, Accra, Ghana
Clara Akainyah, Department of French, University of Cape Coast, Cape Coast, Ghana
Charles Albert Ansa, Christian Council of Ghana, P.O. Box 919, Accra, Ghana
L.K. Buama, Trinity College, P.O. Box 48, Legon, Accra, Ghana
Francis Kwasi Buor, P.O. Box 802, Kumasi, Ghana
Joshua Narteh Kudadjie, Dept. for the Study of Religions, University of Ghana, Legon, Accra, Ghana
Peter K. Sarpong, Catholic Mission, P.O. Box 99, Kumasi, Ghana

Ivory Coast

Tossou K. Ametonu (see Togo)

Kenya

John Mbiti, Ecumenical Institute, Bossey, CH-1298 Celigny, Switzerland
Peter Kodjo (see Ghana)
Canon Burgess Carr (see Liberia)

Lesotho

Sentle Nthabane, P.O. Box MJ 70, Morija, Lesotho
Desmond Tutu, Bishop's House, P.O. MS87, Maseru, Lesotho

Liberia

Canon Burgess Carr, P.O. Box 9026, Monrovia, Liberia
Mary Antoinette Brown Sherman, c/o University of Liberia, Monrovia, Liberia

Madagascar

Paul Ramino, B.P. 3324, Tananarive, Madagascar

Malawi

P. A. Kalilombe, 2621 Ridge Road, Berkeley, CA 94709, U.S.A.
Simon Andrew Faiti Phiri, Kapeni Theological College, P.O. Box 721, Blantyre, Malawi

Mozambique

Simao Chamango, Ricatla, C.P. 21, Maputo, Mozambique

Nigeria

'Zulu Sofola, University of Ibadan, Ibadan, Nigeria
Ogbu U. Kalu, University of Nigeria, Nsukka, Nigeria
Mercy Amba Oduyoye (see Ghana)

South Africa

Allan Boesak, 6, Hoek Street, Glenhaven, Bellville-South 7530, South Africa
Constance Baratang Thetele, 527 Riverside Drive, New York, NY 10027, U.S.A.
Thomas M. J. Leeuw, Vossendijk 127-6, Nijmegen, The Netherlands

Tanzania

Nat Idarous, Werastrasse 12, 7000 Stuttgart 1, West Germany

Togo

Akue Miwonovi, Foyer Piexii, B.P. 3745, Lome, Togo
Tossou K. Ametonu, I.S.C.R., B.P. 8022, Abidjan-Cocody, Ivory Coast
Fanou Dziedzom, B.P. 511, Lome-Plage, Togo
B. E. Penoukou, CESAC, B.P. 142, Lome, Togo
Noussoukpoe Noussi, 20 Rue du Soldat Nandji, B.P. 2176, Lome, Togo

Uganda

A.B.T. Byaruhanga-Akiiki, Makerere University, P.O. Box 2062, Kampala, Uganda
Kodwo E. Ankrah, P.O. Box 4, Mukono, Uganda
E. Maxine Ankrah, Bishop Tucker Theological College, P.O. Box 4, Mukono, Uganda

Upper Volta

Mme. Nikièma, c/o Mr. Nikièma, In. P. No. 1, B.P. 508, Ouagadougou, Upper Volta

Zaire

Masamba ma Mpolo, P.O. Box 4670, Kinshasa 2, Zaire
Lenoir Nimy, D.P. 14733, Kinshasa 1, Zaire
T. Tshibangu, B.P. 8431, Kinshasa, Zaire
Ngindu Mushete, B.P. 823, Kinshasa XI, Zaire
Mujinga Mbuyi, B.P. 4799, Kinshasa Gombe, Zaire

Zambia

Joel Chisanga, United Church of Zambia, Ministerial Trg. College, P.O. Box 429, Kitwe, Zambia

Zimbabwe

Gwinyai Muzorewa, 527 Riverside Drive, New York, NY 10027, U.S.A.

ASIA

India

Joshua Russell Chandran, United Theological College, 17, Miller's Road, Bangalore 560046, India

Japan

Hiroshi Murakami, 639 Ichinomiya, Tama-Shi, Tokyo, Japan

Korea

Lee Hyo-Chae, Department of Sociology, Ewha Women's University, Seoul, Korea

Sri Lanka

Tissa Balasuriya, Centre for Society & Religion, 281 Deans Road, Colombo 10, Sri Lanka

CARIBBEAN

Guyana

Frederick Hilborn Talbot, 2, Clieveden Avenue, Kingston 6, Jamaica
Sylvia Talbot, 2, Clieveden Avenue, Kingston 6, Jamaica

LATIN AMERICA

Argentina

José Míguez Bonino, Camacua 282, 1406 Buenos Aires, Argentina

Brazil

D. Candido Padin, C. Postal, 550, 17100 Bauru-S.P., Brazil

Cuba

Sergio S. Arce Martínez, Seminario Teológico, Matanzas, Cuba

Mexico

Julia Campos, Peten 197A, Col. Narvarte, Mexico 12, D.F., Mexico
Enrique D. Dussell, Dr. Balmis 199–202, Mexico 7, D.F., Mexico

Peru

Gustavo Gutiérrez, Apartado 3090, Lima 100, Peru

NORTH AMERICA

Canada

Tim Ryan, C–239 Dovercourt Road, Toronto, Ontario, M6 J3 C9, Canada

U.S.A.

Gayraud S. Wilmore, 15 Summit Drive, Rochester, NY 14620, U.S.A.
Barry Hopkins, Bd. of International Ministries, American Baptist Churches, Valley Forge, PA
    19481, U.S.A.
Harry Gibson, 475 Riverside Drive, New York, NY 10027, U.S.A.
Thomas Addo, 825 Gerard Avenue, Apt. 4H, Bronx, NY 10451, U.S.A.
Jacquelyn Grant, 527 Riverside Drive, P.O. Box 88, New York, NY 10027, U.S.A.
George B. Thomas, 3240 Valleydale Dr. SW (H), Atlanta, GA 30311; 671 Beckwith St.,
    Atlanta, GA 30314, U.S.A.
Robert J. Harman, 475 Riverside Drive, New York, NY 10027, U.S.A.
James H. Cone, Union Theological Seminary, 3041 Broadway, New York, NY 10027, U.S.A.
Valerie E. Russell, 297 Park Avenue So., New York, NY 10010, U.S.A.
Yvonne V. Delk, 297 Park Avenue So., New York, NY 10010, U.S.A.
Nora Quiroga Boots, 475 Riverside Drive, Rm. 1519, New York, N.Y. 10027, U.S.A.
Patrick-Augustine Kalilombe (see Malawi)
Constance B. Thetele (see South Africa)
Gwinyai Muzorewa (see Zimbabwe)

THE PACIFIC

Fiji Islands

Lorine Tevi, Pacific Conference of Churches, 4 Thurston Street, P.O. Box 208, Suva, Fiji Islands

EUROPE

Netherlands

Thomas Leeuw (see S. Africa)

Switzerland

José Chipenda (see Angola)
John Mbiti (see Kenya)

West Germany

Dr. Rusch, Walsroderstr. 2, 28 Bremen 1, West Germany
Nat Idarous (see Tanzania)

CONFERENCE STAFF

Kofi Appiah-Kubi (Organizing Secretary), University of Science & Technology, Social Sciences Faculty, Kumasi, Ghana

J. Amoako-Adusei, Catholic Mission, P.O. Box 99, Kumasi, Ghana

Sergio Torres, P.O. Box 1263, Stuyvesant Station, New York, NY 10009, U.S.A.

Kwesi A. Dickson, Dept. for the Study of Religions, University of Ghana, Legon, Accra, Ghana

Rose Taylor, 568 Ntomin Street, P.O. Box 834, Kumasi, Ghana

Virginia Fabella, 475 Riverside Drive, Rm.1268, New York, NY 10027, U.S.A.

Victor J. Asumin, P.O. Box 909, Kumasi, Ghana

A. A. Akrong, Dept. for the Study of Religions, University of Ghana, Legon, Accra, Ghana

Contributors

Kodwo E. ANKRAH: Tutor at the Theological College (Bishop Tucker), Mukono, Uganda.

Kofi APPIAH-KUBI: Lecturer in sociology at the University of Science and Technology, Kumasi, Ghana; organizing secretary of the December 1977 Accra Conference.

Allan BOESAK: Student chaplain; South African theologian; author of *Farewell to Innocence.*

Canon Burgess CARR: African Christian leader from Liberia; former executive secretary of the All Africa Conference of Churches based in Nairobi, Kenya; now on leave in the United States.

José B. CHIPENDA: Born in Angola; presently serves as executive secretary of the Program to Combat Racism of the World Council of Churches, Geneva, Switzerland.

James H. CONE: Professor of Systematic Theology at Union Theological Seminary, New York.

Kwesi A. DICKSON: Professor in the Department for the Study of Religions at the University of Ghana, Legon, Accra.

P. A. KALILOMBE: Catholic bishop from Malawi, East Africa; on leave in the United States.

Ogbu U. KALU: Senior lecturer in church history, Department of Religion, at the University of Nigeria, Nsukka, and secretary general of the West African Association of Theological Institutions.

John MBITI: Kenyan Director of the Ecumenical Institute of the World Council of Churches, Bossey, Switzerland.

Ngindu MUSHETE: Professor of theology and ethics, National University of Kinshasa, Zaire.

Engelbert MVENG: Secretary general of the African Movement of Christian Intellectuals.

Mercy Amba ODUYOYE: Lecturer at the University of Ibadan, Nigeria.

Gabriel M. SETILOANE: Head of Department of Theology at the University of Botswana and Swaziland, Gaborone, Botswana.

'Zulu SOFOLA: Lecturer at the University of Ibadan, Nigeria; dramatist; author of "Wedlock of the Gods."

Constance Baratang THETELE: South African student at Union Theological Seminary, New York.

Sergio TORRES: Executive secretary of the Theology in the Americas program and of the Association of Third World Theologians based in New York.

Bishop T. TSHIBANGU: Catholic bishop; Rector, University of Zaire.

Bishop Desmond TUTU: Anglican Bishop from Lesotho.

Gayraud S. WILMORE: Director of the Program of Black Church Studies, Colgate-Rochester Divinity School.

Rose ZOE-OBIANGA: Lecturer at the University of Yaounde, Cameroun, Faculty of Arts & Social Sciences.